Television's Transformation: The Next 25 Years

Television's Transformation: The Next 25 Years

Stuart M. DeLuca

San Diego • New York
A. S. Barnes & Company, Inc.
In London:
The Tantivy Press

Television's Transformation: The Next 25 Years text copyright © 1980
by Stuart M. DeLuca

A. S. Barnes and Co., Inc.

The Tantivy Press
Magdalen House
136–148 Tooley Street
London, SE1 2TT, England

First Edition
Manufactured in the United States of America
For information write to A. S. Barnes and Company, Inc.,
P.O. Box 3051, San Diego, CA 92038

Library of Congress Cataloging in Publication Data

De Luca, Stuart M.
    Television's transformation: the next 25 years

    Bibliography: p.
    Includes index.
    1. Television broadcasting—United States.
2. Radio broadcasting—United States. I. Title.
HE8700.8.D44   384.54'0973   80–15254
ISBN 0-498-02474-1

1 2 3 4 5 6 7 8 9 84 83 82 81 80

Contents

Dedication

**For David and Patricia, who will know the
tomorrow we so dimly perceive today.**

Acknowledgments

I am a member of the last generation whose homes did not already contain a television set when they were born. I well remember the day (I was about nine years old) when our first 16-inch, black-and-white RCA table model was delivered. We fashioned a makeshift antenna from a wire coathanger and turned on the magic.

Some 25 years later, I was assigned to develop a video production capability for the staff-training program of the governmental agency for which I was a public information writer, and I was introduced to the world of "industrial" (that is, nonbroadcast) video. I soon entered the circle of local noncommercial video producers, a circle that was then very small and confined almost entirely to employees of other governmental agencies; today, there are at least a hundred video production centers in Austin alone, in governmental agencies, large and small businesses, schools, hospitals, and miscellaneous other locations. There is a growing cadre of nonbroadcast commercial producers, producers for the public access cable channel, and individual video hobbyists. They are a prolific, unruly lot.

I mention all this because I must acknowledge the debt I owe to all those who have instilled in me a lasting interest in this most interesting medium.

I am especially grateful to Grant H. Burton, who had more faith in me than the circumstances warranted; to Darrell Gray and Roy Shroyer, who patiently taught me whether I was in a position to buy their wares or not; and to Dan Urban, Frosty Walker, Curtis Dickson, Chuck Carsner, Star Keller and Patrick Gunter, comrades-in-arms.

For their many thoughtful suggestions, ideas and criticisms concerning the content of thas book, I think Jerry Presley, Paul Smolen and, again, Dan Urban. My friend, neighbor and ever-ready technical consultant, Richard Matthews, graciously critiqued the technical portions of the manuscript; Mel

Pennington, operations manager of KTVV-TV, and a steadfast believer in the tattered concept of localism, reviewed the chapters on broadcasting. Both offered good advice.

Many of the photographs in this book were taken by the author, through the courtesy and cooperation of Joe Jerkins, general manager, KVUE-TV; Dan Urban, Texas Education Agency; Bob Merryfield and Allen Bushong, Austin Community Television; Darrell Gray, Gray Electronics Co.; Bill Arhos, KLRU-TV and the University of Texas at Austin Communications Center; Dave Mikol, Seton Medical Center; and Lt. Roger Roundtree, Austin Police Department. I am no less grateful to the several manufacturers and organizations that let me use photographs from their files; Frida Schubert, photo librarian for the RCA Corporation, allowed me to borrow priceless prints from her archives. Credit is given to each source in the caption accompanying each photograph.

Finally, I am thankful that my family and friends have patiently borne the seemingly endless gestation of this book. I promise them that I will never utter the words "communications satellite" in their presence again.

Austin, Texas

Television's Transformation: The Next 25 Years

Introduction: The Way It Is

Twenty-five years from now, television will barely resemble the monolithic communications medium we know today. Indeed, in just ten or fifteen years, the economic, political, social and technological system we have come to know and love (or hate) since 1945 will be largely transformed into something very different—which we also may come to love or hate.

The forces and influences impelling this transformation already exist; they have been at work for much of the past two decades, during the very time that television has reached its peak of popularity, wealth and social influence. There will be new peaks in the future—but they will not be enjoyed by the present princes of the medium, the executives of the three great commercial television networks.

In order to see and understand how these great changes will come about, and why they have already begun, we will have to go back to the very beginnings of the television industry in the United States.

Calvin Coolidge became president of the United States in 1923 after the sudden death of President Harding. The first commercial radio broadcasting station, KDKA in Pittsburgh, was not yet four years old, but already there were more than five hundred radio stations on the air.

Lee DeForest, the eccentric genius who made it possible to transmit voices, music and other sounds over radio waves, demonstrated the first practical sound motion-picture system in 1923. It would be another four years before Al Jolson would speak from the silver screen in *The Jazz Singer* (and then the sound system would be one devised by Bell Laboratories, not by DeForest).

In that same year, 1923, a Russian-born physicist who had emigrated to America, Vladimir Zworykin, applied for patents on his iconoscope camera. Electronic television was born.

Four years later, even while Jolson crooned and Congress passed the Federal Radio Act in a belated effort to bring some measure of order to the broadcasting industry, a complete system for generating, transmitting, receiving and displaying television pictures and sound was demonstrated. The National Broadcasting Company was awarded a license for an experimental television transmitter in 1928, actually began transmitting in 1931, and began regular commercial programming in 1939 with a speech by President Roosevelt opening the New York World's Fair.

It was no accident that television grew out of the great radio network of the 1930s and early 1940s. On the contrary: from the very beginning, the same companies that had brought commercial radio into existence shepherded the development of television.

Our present system of television, consisting of three gigantic commercial networks, one malnourished and muddled "public" network, and (at last count) about 980 local broadcasting stations, is the direct result of decisions that were made or strongly influenced by the great radio networks, particularly the National Broadcasting Company and the Columbia Broadcasting System.

Radio began with the invention by DeForest and later improvements by Reginald Fessenden of the vacuum tube amplifier. Before then, radio waves were used only to carry Marconi's wireless telegraph messages; voices and other sounds could be transmitted only by wire, using Bell's telephone system. The vacuum tube amplifier, which DeForest called the Audion tube, made it possible to convert electrical signals representing sounds into radio waves, and vice versa.

By 1919 there were a dozen and more companies in the U.S. making radio transmitters and receivers. Most of the equipment was used either by amateur operators for their own amusement, or by the Navy and maritime industry for communication with ships at sea. After the *Titanic* disaster in 1912, all U.S.-flag ships were required to have radio communications equipment.

The basic patents for all radio systems were owned by Marconi, who had subsidiary companies in dozens of countries. Equipment manufacturers and users were required to pay substantial license fees and royalties to the Marconi companies. During World War I, the Navy and State Department fretted over the fact that vital international communications were dominated by foreigners—that is, Marconi and his backers. Finally, the Navy persuaded the General Electric Company (which had stayed out of radio altogether rather than pay exorbitant fees to Marconi) to buy out the American Marconi Company, and with it the essential patent rights.

General Electric could not afford to sustain the large investment needed to buy out the Marconi interests, so shares in the newly formed Radio Corporation of America were quickly sold to the Westinghouse Corporation, American Telephone and Telegraph, United Fruit Company and several smaller companies. RCA's initial function was to operate the U.S. end of the trans-atlantic and transpacific radio communications systems that had been established by Marconi. RCA was expected to carry out some research and development functions. In addition, it was to serve as the sales agent for transmitting equipment built by AT&T's Western Electric subsidiary and receiving equipment made by GE, Westinghouse and other companies.

This arrangement lasted only a few years. There were too many conflicting interests among the various partners in RCA, particularly between the "Radio Group" (GE, Westinghouse and the others) and the "Telephone Group" (AT&T). Beginning in 1921 relations between the two "groups" were increasingly strained. At the heart of the quarrel was commercial radio.

David Sarnoff, who had been a telegraph operator and then a manager for American Marconi, quickly rose to the post of general manager of RCA. In 1916 he had written a memo to his Marconi superiors suggesting the development of a "radio music box"—in short, commercial radio entertainment broadcasting. The Marconi executives ignored the suggestion. After the transformation of American Marconi into RCA, Sarnoff raised the suggestion again with his bosses, who now represented GE and AT&T. Again he was rebuffed.

Apparently, no one at Westinghouse (which was a very junior partner in RCA) ever knew of Sarnoff's memoes. The idea of entertainment broadcasting occurred independently to a Westinghouse engineer, Frank Conrad, who experimented as an amateur radio operator from his home near the company's East Pittsburgh plant. Conrad's experiments—which consisted mostly of playing phonograph music over his transmitter—attracted a good deal of attention, and soon a Pittsburgh department store began selling inexpensive wireless receivers to people who wanted to listen to Conrad's broadcasts. Conrad's employer quickly latched onto the idea; a more powerful transmitter was built on the roof of the East Pittsburgh factory, and in a matter of weeks, KDKA went on the air. A few weeks later, the Detroit *Evening News* began broadcasting news bulletins interspersed with music over its transmitter, WWJ. In a matter of months, there were some 400 applications to the federal Department of Commerce (which, at the time, had extremely limited powers to regulate radio broadcasting) for commercial licenses.

Part of the rationale behind Westinghouse's pioneering effort was that people would buy radio receivers if they had something to listen to. The theory proved correct beyond anyone's imagining. Even Sarnoff's most optimistic projection, before 1920, supposed that there might someday be receivers in perhaps a third of all American homes.

By the end of 1920, radio stations were being operated on a commercial basis not only by Westinghouse and the Detroit *Evening News* but by AT&T, RCA, United Wireless Company and at least a dozen metropolitan newspapers. Both RCA and AT&T operated stations in New York, in sometimes heated competition with one another, even though at this point AT&T was still one of the RCA partners.

The first radio network was put together by AT&T in 1921 by transmitting President Harding's Armistice Day speech over telephone wires from Washington to New York and San Francisco. If nothing else, this demonstration clearly suggested that radio broadcasting could be a nationwide industry, not merely a collection of isolated local broadcasting stations. However, it took another two years for AT&T to establish the first permanent network, again using telephone lines, made up of Bell's radio stations in Washington, New York and Providence. By 1925 the AT&T network had grown to 21 stations, some of which participated on a part-time basis.

During this period, RCA's broadcasting efforts were confined to its one New York City station, but Sarnoff could see that the future belonged to the networks; the problem was that his superiors, mostly GE executives, had no such vision. Meanwhile, the relationship between the principal RCA partners, GE and AT&T, grew ever stormier. AT&T began selling off its shares in 1923, but there were more deep-rooted problems than just stock ownership. The heart of the matter, once again, was patent rights. RCA owned the old Marconi patents, plus some patents for improved radio equipment that had been developed in its own laboratories or in GE's. In addition, RCA had the right to use patents for devices that had been developed by Bell, and vice versa. Sorting out all of these rights, and distributing them fairly among the contending parties, would have taxed the wisdom of Solomon and the ingenuity of Jason. Endless negotiations came to nothing; the problem was submitted to an arbitrator, but to no avail (AT&T rejected the arbitrator's presumably binding decision). Finally, it was David Sarnoff who worked out an acceptable compromise. Under Sarnoff's plan, AT&T would abandon all claims against RCA and vice versa; Bell would quit the radio business altogether, except that its Western Electric subsidiary could still make high-powered transmitters. RCA would buy the AT&T flagship station, WEAF in New York, and the other Bell stations would be sold. However, it was agreed that AT&T would provide the telephone lines and connections necessary for intercity radio networks. Thus, as commercial broadcasting grew, AT&T would benefit with virtually no risk.

To carry out the agreement, RCA established the National Broadcasting Company in 1926. Most of the 19 stations that initially made up the NBC network were then owned by AT&T; later, RCA bought some of them and the rest were sold to various parties. So many stations had joined the NBC network by 1928 that it was split into two separate systems: the "Red Network," which served mostly Westinghouse and GE stations, and the "Blue Network," made up mainly of former AT&T stations.

Meanwhile, other entrepreneurs were leaping into broadcasting's crowded and turbulent waters. Arthur Judson and George Coats formed the Judson Radio Program Corporation in 1926; a year later, with additional capital provided by Edward Ervin, the company became United Independent Broadcasters. One of UIB's first advertisers was the Columbia Phonograph Company, an erstwhile competitor of the Victor Talking Machine Company. When Victor was bought up by RCA, Columbia threw in with Judson, Coats and Ervin to form the Columbia Phonograph Broadcasting System. This unwieldy partnership lasted only one month. The fledgling network was bought by a Philadelphia millionaire, Jerome Louchheim, and the name was shortened to Columbia Broadcasting System. Louchheim apparently acted at the behest of his friends, Ike and Leon Levy, who owned WCAU, the Philadelphia affiliate of the would-be network. However, Louchheim's main interest was in contracting, not broadcasting, and he quickly became discouraged by the ever-mounting losses his new business experienced. Finally, in 1929, the Levys found another sucker: Leon's brother-in-law, William S. Paley, who was then a junior executive in his father's Congress Cigar Company (one of the few stalwart CBS advertisers). It was Paley who finally caught the brass ring and made CBS into a colossus of broadcasting.

Throughout the 1930s, RCA, CBS, AT&T and various other interests worked feverishly to develop television. John Logie Baird, a Scottish inventor, had demonstrated a mechanical television system in 1924 but it could not readily be adapted to broadcasting. The essential components of an all-electronic system were developed by Zworykin in 1926 (a primitive camera) and 1927 (an early receiver) and by the American engineer Philo T. Farnsworth (an improved type of camera in 1928). The trick was to put these and a number of other crucial devices together into a working system, one that would be reliable, provide pictures of acceptable quality, and could be built at reasonable cost.

Radio broadcasting blossomed into a cornucopia of social influence, political power and, not least, cash. The passage of the Federal Communications Act in 1934 brought a large measure of order to the industry and, among other things, settled the lingering question of AT&T's role in the new medium. The telephone company was permitted to perform any kind of research and development it wanted and could make and sell transmitting equipment, but could not own stations nor sell consumer equipment. Most important of all, AT&T could lease its telephone lines for the long-distance relay of radio programs.

The competition to establish commercial television broadcasting eventually centered on which of several different transmitting systems should be used. As we will see in Chapter 1, a television signal is made up of several parts, each of which can have a variety of configurations. RCA, CBS, AT&T and all of the other entities and individuals working on the development of television had their own ideas about how the various parts of the signal should be shaped and combined. Each system had its vehement adherents and its equally vociferous detractors. The Federal Communications Commission, established by Congress in 1934, was besieged with proposals, critiques, entreaties and demands for approval to establish one or another television system. Like any good bureaucracy, the FCC responded by doing nothing until the dust began to settle.

Finally, in 1939, RCA was granted permission to begin commercial television broadcasts on a more or less regular basis. No sooner did the first wavering signals pierce the air than the FCC was deluged with applications for broadcasting licenses. As late as 1940, the FCC still couldn't decide how many radio frequencies, or channels, to allocate for television; various proposals ranged from six channels to more than 70.

But then World War II intervened and the whole idea of commercial television was set aside "for the duration". The FCC used this war-imposed interregnum to reconsider, once again, the whole business of television technology. A panel of engineers representing the various manufacturers had been established by the FCC in 1936, with the specific duty of recommending which of the competing systems should be adopted. The National Television System Committee (NTSC) finally settled on the RCA system, with some compromises and modifications, and it was this system that the FCC adopted when the war ended. The FCC in 1945 also set aside a block of radio frequencies for 13 television channels; three years later, channel one was taken away from television and turned over to other users because it was subject to too much interference from mobile radios.

The great radio networks could barely wait for the war to end and the economy to resume its normal growth. By 1945 there were four dominant radio networks: NBC, CBS, the Mutual network, and the American Broadcasting Company, which had been formed in 1943 when the FCC (at the insistence of the Justice Department) required NBC to sell off its "Blue Network." Of the four, only Mutual showed no interest in television—a corporate mistake of astonishing proportions.

The absence of Mutual from the field is even more surprising, considering that although Mutual was considerably smaller than either NBC or CBS, it was a good deal healthier than ABC at the end of the war. Yet there was never any doubt that ABC would enter the television arena, no matter how slim its resources; Edward J. Noble, formerly the president of the Life Savers Candy Company, had made that intention clear when he bought the "Blue Network" from NBC. The relative poverty of ABC, in comparison with NBC and CBS, was to have significant consequences for the evolution of television.

The guns of World War II had not yet fallen silent when commercial television began in earnest. Within a scant three years, almost all of the television broadcasting licenses that could be issued under the 1945 allocation scheme had been awarded and still the demands for channels continued. The FCC's response, once again, was to sit back and think about the problem. For four years beginning in 1948, the issuance of television licenses was frozen. Thus the three major radio networks—NBC, CBS and ABC—gained a virtual strangle-hold on the new industry. Only one other national television network was formed during this early period, the DuMont Television Network.

The DuMont network was started by Allen B. DuMont, an engineer who had worked frantically to develop his own television system ahead of RCA and nearly succeeded. DuMont poured a fortune into his attempt to start a television network, but he had never been involved in radio and thus did not have the access to experienced broadcasters that NBC, CBS and ABC enjoyed. Still, DuMont gave ABC a run for its money; for a while, the DuMont network served about 80 stations full-time and as many as 175 part-time, including several stations owned by Paramount Pictures (which also backed DuMont directly, the only major film studio to make even a tentative commitment to television in those early days). Then in 1951 ABC obtained some $25 million in new capital from United Paramount Theatres (which itself had been split off from Paramount Pictures by order of the Justice Department in 1950); two years later, ABC and United Paramount merged. Although this still left ABC financially shaky, at a time when television was already anticipating the enormous cost of converting from black-and-white to color, the newly formed ABC-Paramount was too much for the cash-starved DuMont. In 1955 the DuMont Television Network turned off the lights.

The licensing freeze ended in 1952, when the FCC allocated another 70 channels to television. These, however, were at much higher frequencies than the original 12. Television receivers built before 1952 were not equipped to receive any of the new channels, which blunted the rush to start stations at the higher frequencies. At the same time, however, the FCC revised its table of allocations for the original 12 channels, allowing stations on the same channel to be located somewhat closer together, thus squeezing in a few more possible assignments; these were quickly gobbled up, and by 1955 there were virtually no channels still available at the lower, VHF (very-high-frequency) band.

The FCC was especially disappointed that the opening up of the UHF (ultra-high-frequency) channels failed to satisfy the relatively small segment of the public that had been clamoring for a noncommercial television service as an alternative to the three commercial networks. Educators and culturemongers had been virtually shut out of radio in the 1930s, partly by the duplicity of commercial broadcasters, partly by their own political naivete, and partly by the indifference of Congress and the early FCC. They were determined to gain a foothold in television, but the freeze of VHF licensing in 1948 caught them off-guard; barely half a dozen VHF channels had ever been given over to noncommercial broadcasters. When the freeze was lifted in 1952, there were not many VHF channels left and the proponents of educational broadcasting were persuaded that they would do just as well with UHF channels. Somehow, what was obvious to many people seems to have escaped the FCC's notice: since very, very few TV receivers were able to tune in the UHF channels in 1952, broadcasting on those channels was largely an exercise in futility. There were nearly 20 million households in the United States with television receivers in 1952 and not many Americans were eager to trade in their two- and three-year-old sets on the promise of being able to receive one more channel, especially if the new channel offered mostly instructional and cultural programs.

(True, a converter could be used to tune the UHF channel and shift its frequency down to the VHF range, but in 1952 these devices were rare, fairly expensive and of doubtful quality.)

The inevitable result was that the rush of UHF licensees soon turned into a rush of abandoned licenses. In 1954 there were about 120 UHF stations in operation out of the 1,400 possible assignments that were authorized in 1952. One by one, those stations went out of business; in 1960 only half of them were still on the air.

The problem was finally settled in 1962, a full decade after the UHF allocation, when Congress gave the FCC the authority to regulate the design of television receivers, and specifically to require all new sets to contain UHF tuners. The UHF channels slowly filled with new stations; as of January 1978 there were 211 commercial UHF stations and 159 noncommercial UHF stations licensed, a total of 370, compared to some 630 VHF stations—despite the fact that there are potentially twice as many UHF assignments as VHF.

The all-channel tuning requirement certainly reversed the tide for UHF in 1962, but to this day there is a stigma of second-class citizenship attached to the upper frequencies. Furthermore, the nature of radio propagation imposes a penalty on UHF broadcasters: it takes about fifty times as much transmitter power to cover the same geographic area with a UHF signal as is needed by the lower VHF channels. Many viewers never bother to use that funny dial with all the numbers from 14 to 83. After all, the really important stations—the local affiliates of the major commercial networks—are almost always found on the familiar VHF dial. In fact, the underuse of the UHF allocation has been so palpable, and the demand for more efficient use of the crowded radio frequency spectrum has been so pressing, that the FCC finally took back channels 70 through 83 and gave them to the land-mobile radio service. In certain large metropolitan areas, the UHF television channels from 14 to 20 may be used for police, fire department, or ambulance service radio systems.

By the mid-fifties, then, the basic structure of television in America had been established. There were three commercial networks, of which ABC was a distant third in resources and in affiliated stations; there also were a small number of local stations devoted to educational and other noncommercial programming. Within the first decade of its existence, the television industry already had become a powerhouse of social, political and economic influence.

We will return to the history of the television networks in Chapter 4 (and, for public television, Chapter 6).

For now, my point is that the television networks grew out of the radio networks because that is the way the broadcasting industry planned it. Television from its inception was regarded as nothing more nor less than radio with pictures. The whole structure of program production, scheduling, the kinds of programs offered for public consumption, the role and uses of advertising, and even the relationship between the networks and the local stations—all of these things were carried over intact from the radio networks to the television networks, then magnified as television became the overwhelmingly dominant medium.

It is not surprising that the public often senses that television does not have to be the way it is. It doesn't.

Nor is it surprising that, when the public complains, the network executives seem genuinely bewildered, defensive and unable to understand why the public is not more appreciative of their efforts. The sheer, unimaginable success of television, at least in material terms, blinds its owners and managers to the possibility that there could be some reasonable alternative.

When public wrath over commercial television's propensity for violence and vulgarity reaches a momentary peak, the moguls of the industry are comforted by "the ratings," those often-quoted but much misunderstood surveys of viewership. The fact is that the ratings purport to tell only that so many television sets were turned on and were tuned to a particular station at a given time. The ratings, even if they are assumed to be reliable, say nothing whatever about whether anyone actually watches the program or cares to watch it again.

Not that the networks are indifferent to the public's taste. On the contrary: the networks spend great bundles of money on all sorts of opinion and attitude surveys. Unfortunately, useful results are terribly elusive. Most of the surveys produce data that are either inconsistent or self-contradictory.

Similarly, the networks try to be responsive to the opinions voiced spontaneously by the public. Because most of the public cannot be bothered to voice an opinion (if, for that matter, most people even *have* an opinion), the networks are left vulnerable to all sorts of pressure groups who represent narrow, self-serving interests.

In the final analysis, then, the networks are as hobbled by the existing system as is the discriminating viewer. All three commercial networks produce much the same sort of "product" year in and year out. As long as there are only three major networks, and as long as each reaches something close to one-third of the total audience at any given time, everyone makes money. A slight shift here or there, a change of emphasis or style, a new star who catches the public's fancy one season and a series that has outlived its popularity the next season— those things determine whether a network makes more or less than its competitors, but the difference is trivial.

For all its faults, the amazing truth is that commercial television has sometimes overcome its mainline banality and has produced a program or series of exceptional value: the coverage of the Apollo space flights, or *The Waltons*, or the Munich Olympics, or *Roots*.

So, to be clear about this from the outset, let me say that this book is not intended as a denunciation of commercial television. It is simply an appraisal of the present state of television in America, which happens to be a state of flux.

One would hardly know, by watching the prime-time fare of NBC, CBS or ABC, that fundamental changes are in the air. Cable television, satellite-borne "instant networks," private television and viewer-controlled television are some of the forces that have just begun to gather momentum. For the past four years, Congress has conducted a series of intensive inquiries into the structure of our television system; eventually, a new Federal Communications Act may replace the antiquated one written in 1934. There could be a substantial restructuring of our communications media—or the present structure could be locked in concrete, ensuring that the networks will be incapable of adapting to new technology and the growing public awareness of television's misspent potential.

Twenty-five years from now, television as a medium for the dissemination of information and entertainment will scarcely resemble the medium of today, the medium whose history began in the back rooms and offices of the burgeoning radio networks. We may discover that there are forms and dimensions of television we never realized.

I hope that this book will help to serve as a sort of guidebook to the starry heavens of television when the networks have been eclipsed. At most, I might inspire you to take part in the far-reaching transformation of television. At worst, I may give you hope that television will not always be limited to its present narrow focus on cheap thrills. Unless, of course, you happen to be a network executive yourself, in which case you may not find this treatise very hopeful at all.

The Technology of Television

Chapter

1

How Television Works

Technological change quite often influences the course of an entire industry, and sometimes of a whole society. In the case of television, technological changes and new developments have had profound effects on the industry's historical evolution, and some of the most interesting developments now are occurring in the way pictures (and associated sounds) are recorded, manipulated, carried from one place to another and re-created.

Essential television equipment that was frightfully expensive only a few years ago has become relatively inexpensive, thus permitting many more people to own and use it. Television devices have grown enormously in sophistication and flexibility, opening new avenues of creative expression and exploration. These developments have built upon the basic technology that was adopted by the FCC in 1945, so in a sense nothing much has changed—so far. Once you understand the fundamental principles of television, it is not hard to comprehend the newer devices. However, in recent years there have been early indications of a major revolution in television technology. This new technology, based on the digital techniques used in computers, could open up an entirely new concept of television in the coming decade.

Before looking at some of these radical developments, first we will examine the more traditional form of television.

The very word *television* means, simply, "seeing at a distance." Any *television system* must consist of three major elements: a device to convert an image (that is, a pattern of reflected light) into some kind of electrical signal; a means of conveying that signal from one place to another; and a device to re-create the light image in an approximation of its original appearance.

As early as 1924, a Scottish engineer and inventor, John Logie Baird, demonstrated a mechanical system for converting images into electrical signals and vice versa. Baird's system worked (although not terribly well), but it was already obsolete: Vladimir Zworykin had come up with a way to accomplish the same thing electronically, without any moving mechanical parts. For several years, both the Baird and Zworykin approaches competed for engineers' approval; many refinements were made before the Zworykin system eventually won. Consequently, when we refer to television, we usually mean an electronic system, although a mechanical system could be built to accomplish the same purpose.

The "converting device" that turns a pattern of light into an electrical signal is, of course, the *camera;* the "re-creating device" is the familiar TV set, more properly called either a *monitor* or a *receiver.* Before getting into the means by which signals are conveyed from one place to another, we should take a closer look at the camera.

The Television Camera

The heart of any television camera is the *image tube* (often called the "pickup tube"), which always can be found directly behind the lens. It is the image tube that converts a pattern of light into a pattern of electrical signals. A *monochromatic* (black-and-white) camera ordinarily has only one image tube, while a color camera may have anywhere from one to three.

The television camera's lens is exactly like any other photographic or telescopic lens. In fact, many television cameras are designed so that their lenses are interchangeable with standard motion picture camera lenses, as a cost-saving convenience to people who use both technologies. The function of the lens in any case is to focus light, reflected from the objects in front of the camera, and to direct the light onto the end of the image tube.

The image tube itself is a metal and glass cylinder with a flat end, the *faceplate,* aimed toward the lens. The inside of the faceplate is coated with a photo-sensitive chemical, usually a compound containing selenium oxide, that reacts to the presence of light by producing a weak electrical current. The coating is evenly distributed over the faceplate so that the particles of the chemical are arranged in more or less a random pattern.

It would be possible to design a television system in which each particle of the light-sensitive material discharged its weak current directly into a wire or some other electrical conductor. The current would have to be amplified and stabilized, and each wire would have to be connected directly to a corresponding point on the image-recreating screen of the TV set. However, a single television image is made up of thousands of such individual points. The bundle of wires from the camera to the receiver would be unwieldy, and attempting to connect a camera to a number of different receivers would be a stupefyingly difficult task. What is needed is a method of sampling the particles of photosensitive material in some orderly pattern. This is accomplished by a *scanning beam* inside the image tube.

The scanning beam is produced by an *electron gun* at the far end of the tube from the faceplate. The electron gun produces a steady stream of electrons and fires them down the length of the tube. Wrapped around the tube are four powerful *electromagnetic coils* which create an electromagnetic field within the tube. As the electron stream passes through the electromagnetic field, the strength of the field is varied by raising and lowering the current to the coils. Thus the magnetic field is made stronger to one side than the other, which causes the electron stream to bend or *deflect*. By varying the magnetic field in a precise pattern, the electron stream can be pulled back and forth in the same pattern.

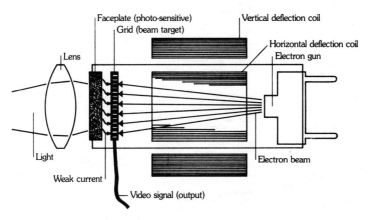

Parts of the Image Tube. The electron gun fires a beam of electrons; the beam is bent by the two pairs of deflection coils, creating a scanning pattern. Meanwhile, light striking the photo-sensitive faceplate causes a weak current to repel the electron beam. The electrons that get past the repelling current are collected on the screen, forming a video signal whose strength (voltage) varies in proportion to the amount of light falling on the faceplate.

As the electrons come near the faceplate, they are repelled by the weak currents generated by the photo-sensitive particles. The more light falling on a particular particle, the stronger its current and thus the more forcefully it repels the on-coming electron beam. Those electrons that get through the repelling field are collected near the faceplate and pass out of the tube.

The electron beam, however, is being pulled back and forth by the electromagnetic coils, thereby producing a scanning action. The scanning pattern begins with the electron beam focused in the uppermost corner of the faceplate (the upper right corner as you face the camera, or the upper left corner if you are looking down the length of the tube from the gun end). The beam sweeps across the faceplate in a horizontal path; then the gun is momentarily shut off, the magnets shift the beam back to the other side and move it down slightly, and the beam is turned on for another horizontal sweep.

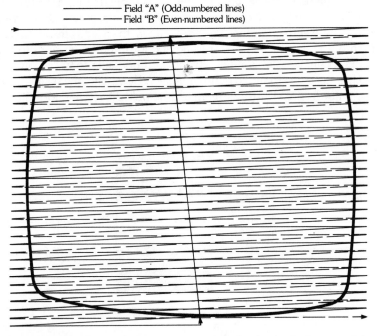

——————— Field "A" (Odd-numbered lines)
— — —— Field "B" (Even-numbered lines)

Scanning. The electron beam traces a pattern that begins in the upper left-hand corner, as you face the screen; it travels in horizontal lines, first scanning the odd-numbered lines to the middle of line 525, then jumping back (the vertical re-trace) to the middle of line 2 and scanning the even-numbered lines. Thus, two fields of 262½ lines form a frame of 525 lines.

Because the electron beam scans the faceplate in this manner, the current flowing out of the collector represents a series of *horizontal lines,* each of them a precise length and each composed of a fluctuating signal that represents the pattern of light falling on the photo-sensitive particles in the corresponding line on the faceplate.

When the electron beam reaches the lowermost corner of the faceplate, a complete image has been recorded. The beam is switched off, the electro-magnetic field is readjusted, and the beam is turned back on at the top of the faceplate to record the next image.

If the image in front of the camera is static, it does not really matter how quickly the scanning beam completes its task of converting an entire image into an electronic signal. However, television is used primarily for moving pictures; even though the images are recorded essentially as a series of still pictures, usually it is desirable to create the illusion of natural motion. Experience with motion picture photography has taught us that the illusion of motion can be maintained if still pictures are presented rapidly in sequence. The standard speed for motion pictures is 24 frames (that is, individual images) per second, but almost any *frame rate* from about 20 frames per second on up will produce a satisfactory illusion. Therefore, to make our television pictures seem to move, each complete image must be recorded and then replaced with a new image at a rate of at least 20 images per second. Furthermore, another factor must be considered: the image will be reproduced by causing phosphorescent materials to glow, and a complete image must be transmitted quickly enough so that the phosphorescent particles at the beginning of the picture will not have stopped glowing by the time the scanning beam reaches the end of the picture. Otherwise, the image will flicker annoyingly.

Since a complete image is defined by the length of time it takes the scanning beam to move from the top of the image area to the bottom (traveling in a series of horizontal lines), the television frame rate is also known as the vertical rate or *vertical frequency.* Similarly, the time required for the scanning beam to complete one horizontal line is the horizontal rate or *horizontal frequency.*

Both the horizontal and vertical frequencies are determined by the current that activates the electromagnetic coils wrapped around the image tube. The current must vary in a precise pattern and it must be timed to work in precise synchronization with the *blanking signals,* which turn the electron gun off at the end of each line and at the end of a completed image. The coil current and blanking signals are produced by a separate signal-generating device within the camera, or, in more sophisticated television systems, by separate devices outside of the camera. These devices, known as *oscillators* because they produce precisely timed fluctuating currents, are the *horizontal* and *vertical synchronizing signal generators*—in verbal shorthand, the *sync generators.*

The time when the electron beam is shut off so that it can be moved back to the beginning of the next line is known as the *horizontal retrace;* the time when the beam is turned off and sent back to the top of the image area to begin the next picture is known as the *vertical retrace* or *vertical interval.*

So far, then, inside the camera there are two main types of electrical signals: the picture signal, which comes from the image tube, and the sync signals, which are produced by the sync generators either in the camera or elsewhere. These two types of signals are combined to make up the *composite video signal*. It is this composite signal that is sent out of the camera, generally by a simple wire, to be amplified, manipulated in various ways and ultimately delivered to the TV set. Every electronic system of television based on the technology developed since 1923 uses a composite video signal containing both the picture signal and sync signals. However, there can be many variations in the way these signals are constructed.

For example, the television image could be made up of any number of horizontal lines. The more lines there are, the more fine details that can be shown; that is, the greater the *resolution*. Many other factors also affect resolution, but the number of horizontal lines is the most basic factor and sets the absolute limit of the system's resolution. For some purposes, one might not need a great deal of resolution, and so a television system using, say, 100 lines might be adequate. On the other hand, if extremely fine resolution were needed, it might be necessary to build a system based on a 1,000-line image.

At the same time, however, it is desirable to change the picture at a rate of no less than 20 frames per second in order to preserve the illusion of motion, and an even higher rate may be necessary to eliminate flicker. If there are too many horizontal lines in each image, the scanning beam will have to flash back and forth at a tremendous rate in order to complete the whole image in one-twentieth of a second or less. In other words, the vertical frequency must be kept within reasonable bounds, and so must the horizontal frequency.

The vertical frequency becomes especially important in a television system that is intended to distribute pictures to a great many TV sets over a large area. Each TV set, in order to reproduce the pictures accurately, must have its own sync signal generators that precisely match the sync generators in the camera (or other picture source). It is extremely convenient for *every* TV set to have some readily available *reference signal* that it can use to regulate its own sync generators. As long as the reference signal is reliably standardized, each TV set can make any minor adjustments to the vertical sync signal that it receives as part of the composite signal, match it to its own internal sync signal, and produce an accurate image.

The handiest reference signal turns out to be the alternating electrical current provided by local utility companies. All American electric companies generate current at a well-controlled 60 cycles per second, or 60 Hertz. The variation from place to place is so slight as to be insignificant. Therefore, for American television broadcasting, the 60 Hertz frequency of ordinary household current is used as the reference signal, regulating the vertical sync signal generators both at the picture source (the camera or studio) and at the receiver (the TV set).

A vertical frequency of 60 Hertz is much faster than needed to maintain the illusion of motion, but it is just about the right speed to eliminate the flicker caused by the rapid decay of light-emitting phosphors (which we will be talking about shortly). However, a 60 Hertz vertical frequency creates another problem. The horizontal frequency is the vertical frequency multiplied by the number of horizontal lines in the image; therefore, an image of a hundred lines with a vertical frequency of 60 Hertz would have a horizontal frequency of 6,000 Hertz, or 6 Kilohertz. But, as we said before, a 100-line image would have poor resolution for most purposes; it would be something like looking at the world through a thick wire screen. A 1,000-line image with a 60 Hertz vertical frequency would require a horizontal frequency of 60,000 Hertz or 60 Kilohertz. That would provide exceptionally good resolution, but there is one problem: in the 1930s, when television systems were being developed, a 60 Kilohertz sync signal generator would have been very expensive and not very reliable. Putting such an oscillator into every television receiver would have been somewhat beyond the state of the art of electronic technology at that time.

Even cutting the number of lines in half, to 500 lines, would have required a 30 Kilohertz oscillator and that was still too high. However, 500 lines produces a reasonably pleasing picture, and any less resolution than that would be unacceptable.

The vertical frequency could have been divided in half, to 30 Hertz. That would put the horizontal frequency for a 500-line image at 15 Kilohertz, a little high but within the range of available technology. Unfortunately, the 30 Hertz vertical rate was simply too slow to eliminate flicker.

The solution to this dilemma turned out to be very simple. The 60 Hertz vertical frequency could be kept as well as the 500-line image—provided the scanning beam only scanned every other line on each vertical pass. In effect, this produced a 250-line image every 1/60th of a second, or a 500-line image every 1/30th of a second; either way you look at it, the horizontal frequency remains at an acceptable 15 Kilohertz and flicker is kept to an acceptable minimum.

Thus, the system adopted by the NTSC and approved by the FCC was based on a frame rate of 30 images per second, but a *field rate* (complete vertical passes) of 60 per second, each field consisting of alternate lines of the image— what is known as *2:1 interlace*. Resolution was set at 500 lines; however, since some lines are unavoidably left dark during the vertical retrace and it is desirable to keep them off the screen entirely, the entire picture area was increased to 525 lines, yielding a horizontal frequency of 15,750 Hertz, or 15.75 Kilohertz.

These standards control the design and manufacture of all television equipment made or sold in the United States. Since our country was the first to adopt a commercially feasible television system and very quickly began exporting equipment to other countries, many other nations also use the NTSC system—but not all. In Europe, electric utilities provide 50 Hertz alternating current, not 60 Hertz. Using the 50 Hertz current as a reference signal, most European countries have adopted the standards set by the International Radio Consultative Committee (CCIR): 625 lines, 2:1 interlace, 50 Hertz vertical frequency, and 15.625 Kilohertz horizontal frequency. During the 1950s, the CCIR adopted a color television system called PAL, developed by German engineers and now used in most European countries. However, the French television industry—mostly for political reasons—developed its own system, SECAM, in cooperation with Russian engineers, and those two countries use the SECAM system. Both PAL and SECAM follow the basic CCIR standards. Most Western European countries, except France, use PAL; most Eastern European countries use SECAM. Outside of Europe and the United States, the system a country adopts depends partly on the frequency of the current provided by electric utilities and partly on whose salesmen get there first with the most convincing sales pitch. Canada, Mexico and most of the Central and South American countries use the NTSC system, as does Japan; all three systems are used in various other parts of the world.

Many Americans visiting in foreign countries find, to their puzzlement, that television "looks different"—aside from the obvious differences in programming styles. Indeed it does look different, and in some ways the PAL and SECAM systems are superior. Our "not-quite-as-good" technology is the price we have paid for being first, and it is certainly much too late to change the system now.

Once the standards for the basic monochromatic television system had been adopted, the commercial television industry turned its attention to the development of a color system. Once again, there were a number of competing systems. Credit for the first workable color television system usually is given to CBS Laboratories, which was virtually the personal domain of the brilliant engineer Peter Goldmark (who later developed long-playing phonograph records, among other things). The Goldmark-CBS color TV system had one or two major flaws, however. First, the system relied on a mechanical spinning disk, somewhat like the electromechanical system invented by Baird two decades earlier; second, because of that spinning disk, the Goldmark system would not be compatible with the television system already adopted by NTSC. In other words, people who already owned a black-and-white TV would not be able to watch programs transmitted by the Goldmark color system, and vice versa.

Meanwhile, RCA and others were determined to find a color system that would be compatible with monochromatic television. The battle between RCA and CBS grew fierce; CBS insisted that its system was perfectly workable and that there was no good reason to delay its adoption since there were relatively few monochromatic receivers in use anyway (in the early 1940s). Twice the FCC approved the CBS system and twice RCA fought back by claiming its compatible system was "almost perfected" and that the FCC could not betray the purchasers of the early monochrome sets by making them obsolete. RCA finally went to court to get approval of the CBS system overturned. After that, the FCC threw up its hands and dumped the problem into the lap of the NTSC, letting the engineers settle the question among themselves. Finally, the NTSC in 1952 adopted standards for color television—using the RCA system, of course—and in 1953 the first color broadcasts began on NBC.

An RCA black-and-white camera in the early 1950s. Each camera had a turret of three to five lenses; to change focal length, the camera operator rotated the turret to bring a different lens into use. There were no "zoom" lenses. (Photo courtesy RCA Corp.)

RCA's first color camera, early 1950s. This monster required a heavy-duty hydraulic pedestal just to keep it from falling on the floor. Note the lens turret; still no "zoom" lens! (Photo courtesy RCA Corp.)

The RCA color system simply took the monochromatic system and tripled it. In color television, the light image focused through the lens is divided by filters into three images: red, blue and green (the primary colors for transmitted light). In the early color cameras, and in the best color cameras today, a separate image tube reacts to each of the three colored light images. (One early model camera had four tubes, the fourth being for the overall light level, but this was found to be unnecessary.)

Each image tube has its own set of deflection coils, but they all run off the same set of sync signal generators. At any given moment, then, three separate images are being produced in the camera. However, they do not leave the camera that way. Instead, they are combined by electronic circuits in the camera to form two signals.

This modern Philips color camera produces pictures far superior to the
early 50s RCA model, even under poor light conditions, and it is easily
carried on one's shoulder. The same camera can be used in the studio,
although most studio color cameras are somewhat larger and more
elaborate. (Photo courtesy Philips Broadcast Equipment Corp.)

One of these is called the *luminance signal*. It is made up of varying portions of the three color signals (mostly green, but with some red and blue as well), and it represents the overall level of brightness at each point in the image. The luminance signal alone is all that a black-and-white TV set needs to create a monochromatic image.

The second signal produced in the compatible color system is the *chrominance signal*; as the name suggests, it contains the color information used by a color TV set to reproduce the image in something close to its original hues. The chrominance signal, too, is composed of a mixture of the red, blue and green signals.

Unfortunately, a single chrominance signal is too crude to provide a satisfactory picture; it must be broken down into sub-signals. One of these, called the *I signal*, contains the general color information for the image: this part is red, this over here is blue and this object is orange. The other sub-signal, called the *Q signal*, conveys the fine details and shadings.

Somehow, the luminance signal and the two components of the chrominance signal, all of which contain the same sync signals, must be transmitted together and yet kept distinct. This is accomplished by a *color subcarrier*, produced by a separate oscillator either in the camera or elsewhere in the television system. The subcarrier is a steady, high-frequency signal (3.58 Megahertz in the American system). The I and Q signals *modulate* the subcarrier; that is, the chrominance components make the subcarrier vary slightly in frequency from moment to moment. These variations in frequency are detected by the color TV set and converted back into the I and Q signals' information. The color subcarrier also contains a brief, moderately intense pulse of current at the beginning of each line; this *color burst* serves as a "cue" to the color TV set that chrominance information is coming in, and it helps to keep all of the different signals aligned. A monochromatic TV set, of course, ignores the subcarrier and the color burst altogether.

Before we examine some of the most recent developments in camera technology, a closer look at how the picture is re-created in the television set is needed.

The Television Monitor and Receiver

Converting the television signal back into a pattern of light really amounts to reversing the process by which the signal was created.

Just as the image tube is the heart of a television camera, the *cathode ray tube* (CRT, or what people often call the "picture tube") is the heart of the TV set. The CRT has an electron gun at one end that produces a steady stream of electrons. These electrons are deflected by a set of four electromagnetic coils, wrapped around the neck of the tube, thus forming a scanning beam. The scanning beam is aimed at the faceplate of the tube. Instead of having a layer of light-sensitive material on the inside of the faceplate, the TV set has a coating of *phosphorescent* material: chemical substances that glow briefly when struck by an electrical current.

The TV set has its own oscillators to serve as horizontal, vertical and blanking sync signal generators, all of which control the two pairs of electromagnetic coils and the electron gun. The sync signals in the composite video signal—actually just brief pulses at the end of each horizontal line and each vertical field—regulate the set's oscillators, keeping the set working in unison with the camera (or whatever the source of the picture might be).

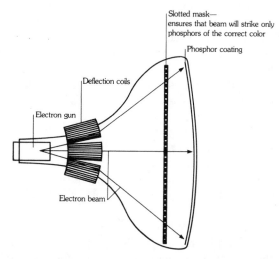

Slotted mask— ensures that beam will strike only phosphors of the correct color

Phosphor coating

Deflection coils

Electron gun

Electron beam

The video receiver. The electron gun fires an electron beam whose intensity varies according to the video signal it is receiving; the deflection coils cause the beam to scan over the phosphor-coated faceplate. The slotted mask (only in color tubes) ensures that the electron beam for red strikes only the red phosphors, the green beam hits only green phosphors, and the blue beam only blue phosphors. The mask itself is black, which increases contrast and makes the colors seem more vivid.

In a color TV set, there are three separate coatings of phosphors, one of which glows red, one blue and one green. The phosphor particles are applied to the inside of the faceplate in triangular groups, or "triads," of round or rectangular dots. The dots are surrounded by a black mask that makes them seem brighter than they really are, thus improving the apparent detail and contrast in the color image.

Some early color TV sets had three separate electron guns, one for each color, but modern sets usually have only one gun with three separate electron-emitting elements. The electronic circuits of the TV set decode the information in the luminance, I and Q signals; this information is then used to vary the intensity of the electron beam as it strikes the phosphor dots. The result is that the dots glow with different levels of brightness and the human eye blends them together into a pattern of colored light. (You can see the individual phosphor dots by studying a television screen with the aid of a strong magnifying glass.)

That is really all there is to the TV set, other than a complex assortment of circuits to amplify, stabilize and regulate the picture signal, a separate set of circuits for the sound signal (which is essentially just like any other voice radio signal), and the circuitry necessary to detect and receive broadcast signals—that is, if the set is a receiver.

There are two general types of TV sets, the *receiver* and the *monitor*. The receiver, as its name implies, is intended to receive television signals that are transmitted through the air. A receiver must have electronic devices to detect the broadcast signal, select the particular frequency desired and separate the composite video signal from the carrier wave. A monitor is a TV set that is intended to use only the composite video signal, directly from the camera or other picture source. There are also *monitor-receivers*, hybrid sets that can be used for either purpose.

What most of us have in our living rooms (assuming that we are among the 99 percent of American families that have a TV set) is a receiver. Monitors are found mainly in television studios and control rooms. The hybrid monitor-receivers are often found in school classrooms, industrial training centers and other places where small videotape recorders are used in addition to broadcast programs.

Television receiver technology has improved steadily since the first TV sets were manufactured in the late 1930s. Most of these improvements have been merely refinements or extensions of the existing technology; the basic structure of the CRT, the receiving and tuning devices, and the amplifying circuitry have not changed. However, in recent years there have been some major new developments in the way people watch television, and more significant changes are looming. Some of these changes involve fundamental new approaches to the creation and transmission of television pictures and the associated sound signals. We will look at some of the new receiver technology toward the end of this chapter, but first let us see how the signal gets from the camera to the monitor—or receiver—or both.

Transmitting the Signal

The composite video signal, as it comes from the camera, is pretty weak. Even though the original signal from the image tube is amplified several times within the camera, it is still too weak to travel very far through wires. External amplifiers can be used to strengthen the signal, but every time an amplifier is used, "noise"—undesirable signals, something like static—is introduced as well. If the signal is amplified too many times, soon the "noise" is strong enough to interfere with the desired information.

As a rule, a video signal coming from the camera can be carried about a hundred feet by wire before it must be amplified at least once. Some cameras produce signals strong enough to travel five hundred or even a thousand feet before amplification, but that is true only for the more expensive broadcast cameras. Obviously it would not be possible to distribute these weak signals directly by wire to the hundreds or thousands of homes in a community.

A modern television transmitter: everything you need to broadcast a video signal, except the signal itself (which comes from the camera) and the antenna. (Photo courtesy RCA Corp.)

The problem is solved by using a high-frequency *carrier*, in much the same way that the color subcarrier is used to transmit the chrominance signal. The video carrier is a steady, closely regulated signal produced by an oscillator at a given frequency. The composite video signal is used to modulate the carrier—not by varying the carrier's frequency, as with the color subcarrier, but by varying the carrier's amplitude, or voltage. The bright portions of the picture signal cause the carrier's voltage to increase, while the darker portions of the picture signal cause the carrier voltage to decrease. (This is known as amplitude modulation, and it is the same technique used for AM radio; varying a carrier's frequency is called frequency modulation, or FM. Frequency modulation is used not only for the color subcarrier but also for the audio portion of a television broadcast.)

The high-frequency carrier can be made just about as strong as one wishes at the original point of transmission, and it can be amplified many times before "noise" becomes a serious problem. Cable television systems often distribute signals through a network of wires twenty or more miles from the origination point to the farthest subscribers' homes, with amplifiers strung along the line every few hundred feet. If the system is properly designed and carefully maintained, the most distant subscriber should be able to receive a picture that is as clear and free from noise as it would be coming directly from the studio.

However, there is another, equally important reason for transmitting television signals by high-frequency carrier. Virtually any number of signals can be transmitted simultaneously as long as they are on different carrier frequencies. This is possible because the receivers' tuners act as a sort of "gate," admitting only one signal at a time.

Furthermore, the television signal on its high-frequency carrier can be broadcast through the air. The signal is pumped into an antenna, which causes a strong electromagnetic field to radiate in all directions. Anywhere within that field, as much as 50 or 100 miles from the transmitting antenna, another antenna can be placed. When a weak electromagnetic field envelopes a receiving antenna, a current is produced inside it; this current can be fed to the television receiver, where it is accepted just as if it were brought by a wire. Thus we are able to receive television signals from broadcasting stations that are many miles away.

There is only one problem in using high-frequency carriers for television broadcasting: their relatively large *bandwidth*.

A simple telegraph signal, consisting only of dots, dashes and the pauses in between, requires nothing more than a carrier current a few Hertz wide—perhaps 10 Hertz. Radio signals intended to carry only human voices can use carriers about 5 Kilohertz wide; that is the bandwidth of each of the forty Citizen's Band channels. However, if the radio signal is intended to carry subtler sounds, such as music, more bandwidth is required: the channels for FM radio are 200 Kilohertz wide.

A broadcasting antenna tower in San Francisco. Each vertical mast radiates the signal of a different radio or television station. Because desirable locations for broadcasting antennas are so scarce, especially in urban areas, it's not unusual for an antenna tower to support four or five separate stations' antennas. (Photo courtesy RCA Corp.)

A single television channel requires 6 Megahertz of bandwidth—6,000,000 Hertz, or the equivalent of 1,200 CB radio channels. Actually, only 4.5 Megahertz of the television channel is used for the composite video signal; the rest is taken up by the audio signal and by "guard bands," or empty spaces that keep one channel separated from the next.

It is because of the enormous bandwidth required for each television channel that there are so few channels available for broadcasting. Originally, the FCC set aside frequencies for 13 channels, but then cut the number to 12, later increased it to 82, and most recently cut back again to 68. The electromagnetic spectrum is a very precious and scarce resource. It must accommodate every sort of device from CB, stereo FM radio and television to airport radar, astronomers' radio telescopes and even the kitchen microwave oven. Learning how to manage this resource wisely is one of the most difficult tasks undertaken by the world's political institutions.

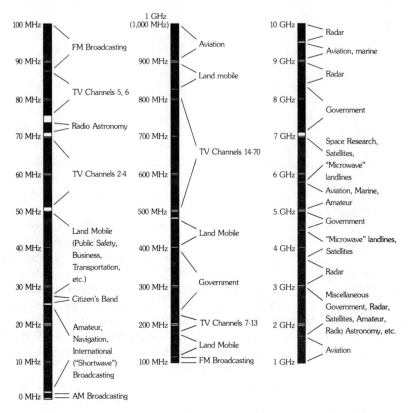

The radio frequency spectrum. Nearly every possible frequency is used for something, and some frequency bands are used for a variety of purposes. Notice that *all* of the left-hand column would fit at the bottom of the middle column, and that all of the middle column would fit at the bottom of the right-hand column. (The allocations shown here are based on FCC allocations as of January 1977; some minor changes have been made since then. Some of the bands are also available, on a secondary basis, for purposes other than those shown here.)

It might seem that 68 television channels would be plenty, since there is not a city in the world that has anywhere near that many. Only a few of the largest cities in the United States have more than four or five channels. The 68-channel ceiling will permit only four or five channels per city because two stations operating on the same channel must be a considerable distance apart to avoid interfering with each other. Whenever possible, two stations in the same city should not transmit on adjacent channels. In the late 1950s, the FCC used some very sophisticated computer analyses to determine the optimum distribution of television channels across the entire country. Each reasonably large city was assigned a certain number of television stations on certain frequencies, and only those frequencies are available for those cities. Who gets to use those frequencies is another question, one that is settled in the licensing process described in Chapter 4.

The restrictions imposed on broadcasting generally do not apply to cable transmission systems. There are only 68 broadcasting channels because that is as many as the FCC has decided to devote to television, but a cable television system has no such limitation. In theory, a cable system could carry any imaginable number of television signals. The lowest frequency available for a television carrier would be about 7 Megahertz, allowing for a cushion at the bottom of the spectrum, and the highest carrier frequency would be at whatever frequency an oscillator could generate. Current technology reaches that limit at about 300 Gigahertz, or 300 billion Hertz. If that entire spectrum were used only for television, there could be 50,000 channels. That would be absurd, of course, and incredibly expensive and difficult to accomplish with present technology. However, cable television systems routinely provide their subscribers with 20, 30 and even more channels of programming; some cable systems offer 84 channels.

Recently there has been much interest in the use of optical-frequency carriers for television and other types of communication. An optical-frequency carrier is merely a beam of light, usually generated by a laser because laser light consists of a pure beam at a regulated frequency. Light is electromagnetic energy just like radio waves, but at much higher frequencies. How much higher? Well, the lowest optical frequencies are in the general range of seven quadrillion Hertz. An optical-frequency carrier system used only for television might be able to carry—oh, say about a billion channels.

The world probably does not need a billion channels of *Mork and Mindy*. However, an optical-frequency system might permit every single person in the world to have a unique channel, for person-to-person, sight-and-sound communication.

New Developments in Television Technology

During television's 30-year-plus history, the basic technology has been continuously refined but there have been no fundamental changes since the RCA compatible color system was adopted in 1952. However, that might not hold true ten years from now.

The kind of television signal we have described is properly known as an *analog signal;* that is, the signal itself is a direct representation or analog of the information it is derived from (the pattern of light in an image). The same is true for radio (sound) signals and the signals in audio tape recordings, phonograph records and most other electronic communications devices.

Analog signals are inherently stupid. When the signal is converted back into an approximation of the original image or sound, the re-conversion device cannot tell whether the signal is defective in some way. If part of the signal is missing, the television receiver, radio or other playback device simply leaves a blank space. If noise has gotten mixed into the signal, the playback device plays the noise right along with the signal. There are some ways to filter out part of the noise, if it is sufficiently different in frequency or volume from the desired signal, but some noise inevitably distorts the desired signal.

The problem is most familiar to stereo hobbyists who go to enormous trouble and expense to eliminate noise and distortion from their music reproduction systems. Alas, as they know all too well, it is a hopeless task. No matter what they do, there is an irreducible minimum of hiss, wow and flutter in any analog system.

The constant search for "perfect sound" has led audio engineers to develop an entirely different system of recording and reproducing sound: *a digital system.* In a digital system, the signal is not a direct representation of the original sound "image," but, rather, it is a numerical representation. In other words, instead of recording and transmitting a signal that fluctuates in frequency and volume according to the original sound patterns, a digital system records a series of numbers that represent the frequencies and volumes, from moment to moment, of the original sounds. The reproducing device then produces sounds according to the "instructions" in the digital signal.

Digital audio equipment is still being developed; as of this writing, only a few digital audio devices have come onto the market, and those primarily for professional use in recording studios. However, many audio experts believe that "digitalization" is the wave of the future (no pun intended) and that even the most sophisticated conventional stereo system will be hopelessly obsolete in a few years.

A prototype of an experimental digital video tape recorder. (Photo courtesy Ampex Corp.)

The great advantage in digitalization is that the "instructions" in a digital signal can be manipulated in any number of ways, simply by changing the numerical values that the signal represents. Extraneous noise and distortion can be completely eliminated. Random electrical noise, present in any electrical system, has no effect on the digital signal. Furthermore, the reproducing device can compare one instruction with the next, and can be "programmed" to ignore any instructions that do not make sense. Thus, the digital signal is "intelligent," not stupid, and that intelligence can be built into the entire recording, transmitting and reproducing system.

What is good for audio is even better for television, and digitalization is likely to have a tremendous impact on television technology. There are already a number of fully digital television signal processing devices; their function is to amplify the signal, remove some of the accumulated noise and restore the sync signals to their proper values and relationships. These devices take the analog signal and convert it into a digital replica, manipulate the digital signal, then reconvert it to an analog signal.

Complete digitalization of the television system will require not just digital signal processing and amplification, but digital cameras and receivers. The problem, again, is that all of the existing cameras and receivers would have to be replaced—or else a compatible analog-digital system will have to be used at least for a while, and so far no one has come up with a workable compatible system.

Digitalization will represent a major break with the technological history of television. A digital camera might not require a scanning beam, magnetic deflection coils or separate sync signals. A digital receiver might look entirely different from a conventional television set, yet it would display a picture that ought to be a perfect replica of the original scene.

It is impossible to estimate how long the digitalization of the television system will take, but almost certainly it will not be accomplished within the current decade; a likelier time frame would be the middle to late 1990s.

One current technological development should hasten the change to a digital system. New kinds of cameras and television sets, based on *charge-coupled devices* (CCDs), are already moving out of the engineers' laboratories.

A CCD is a solid-state device that can replace either the image tube or the CRT in a camera or receiver. Without getting involved in the complexities of solid-state electronics, let us just say that the CCD is capable of converting a light image into an analog signal, or vice versa, without using a scanning beam, deflection coils and all the rest. The analog signal produced by a CCD-based camera is identical to a conventional composite video signal; when such a signal is fed into a CCD-based receiver (or monitor), the original light image is faithfully re-created.

The difference between conventional technology and the CCD-based devices is that the CCDs are considerably smaller than ordinary image tubes or CRTs. Furthermore, a CCD is flat; there is no bulky glass envelope, since it is not necessary for a scanning beam to pass through an electromagnetic field.

Similarly, a CCD-based television set can consist of a flat screen attached to a box containing the necessary electronic circuits. Several companies already have begun to manufacture and sell CCD-based receivers, although at present they are available only with very small screens and are quite expensive.

Eventually, as CCD technology continues to evolve, it should be possible to make flat television screens that can be hung on the wall, in whatever size one wishes. For that matter, the entire wall could be the TV screen; all the necessary electronics can be stuck in a small box out of the way. Best of all, once this radically new technology moves from the laboratories to the production lines, it is expected that CCD-based cameras and receivers will be much less expensive than their conventional counterparts—and there will be no more worry about worn-out image tubes and picture tubes.

Meanwhile, one interesting new development is already in the market-place, and has been for several years. Unfortunately, it has been largely overlooked by television consumers.

A prototype of an experimental color camera based on charge-coupled
devices in place of the image tube. This camera presumably would produce
a video signal comparable in quality to the Philips camera shown above, but
it could be mass-produced for perhaps $400. (Photo courtesy RCA Corp.)

One problem with color television has always been the fact that the colors
recorded in the studio may not reach the home TV set intact. What the camera
sees and what is seen in the living room often are not the same at all. Technicians
in the control room may adjust the colors to suit their own taste; the signal is
then transmitted from the network to a local television station, where another
technician may adjust the colors a little differently. The signal is then broadcast
to home viewers who have adjusted the colors again. This would be bad enough
if, once all these adjustments had been made, everything remained stable.
However, television programs can originate from a variety of sources: some are
broadcast directly from the local TV station's studio, live or on videotape or film;
others are sent out by the networks from live studios, remote locations (such as
sports events), or from videotapes or films. Each source has its own peculiar
color characteristics, and technicians at each source may adjust the colors a
little differently.

Unfortunately, the television set has no way of knowing what color things are supposed to be. (Here again, the inherent stupidity of the analog signal shows up; if the signal consisted of digital instructions, the TV set would have no problem.) Since the mid-1960s, manufacturers have built automatic color controls into most TV sets in an effort to keep the range of color variation within tolerable limits. Since television pictures consist mostly of human faces, and since human flesh tones are the most important colors in terms of satisfying the viewers' visual taste (who has not gagged at the sudden sight of a purplish-green anchorman reading the news?), the automatic controls attempted to adjust the colors so that the dominant color in any picture would be pinkish-brown. That did not work too well when the picture consisted of a landscape or a non-Caucasian face.

Then someone got a really bright idea. Remember that there are a number of blank lines at the end of each vertical frame in the television picture so that the scanning beam can be turned off and sent back to the top of the next field; this is the vertical interval. Most of these blank lines are tucked out of the way, just beyond the top and bottom edges of the mask around the picture on a TV set. It occurred to someone that a reference signal could be put into the vertical interval, telling the receiver how to reproduce the colors in the associated picture.

The *vertical interval reference* (VIR) signal is simply a standard pattern of colors; the TV set merely adjusts itself until the standard pattern matches a built-in standard. If this is done properly, the colors in the associated picture should be faithfully reproduced.

If you have a color TV set, adjust the vertical hold control until the picture "rolls" a little. The VIR signal should be visible just below the bottom of the picture, whenever the local TV station is transmitting it. It looks like a color spectrum squashed into a narrow line.

Unfortunately, the VIR signal will not do any good unless the TV set has the necessary circuitry to use it. And having such a TV set will not do the viewer any good unless the local TV station broadcasts the signal. It would seem, since the VIR system virtually ends the problem of color matching, that every station would broadcast it and every manufacturer would build in the necessary circuits. However, that is not the case. General Electric developed the VIR system and persuaded the FCC to approve its use—but only on an optional basis. Not all television stations broadcast the signal, and some use it only for network programs. Only GE builds the VIR circuitry into most of its color receivers; other manufacturers include the circuits only in a few selected models.

Why has the VIR system failed to achieve universal adoption? Partly because the FCC does not require it, partly because other manufacturers invested a lot of money in their own automatic color controls and want to recoup their investment, and, most of all, because the general public has not demanded VIR-equipped sets. Apparently, most people are content to leap up two or three times every evening to fiddle with the color controls—or, if they are as lazy as I am, they just shut their eyes when the anchorman turns green.

Eventually, unless digitalization progresses rapidly enough to make it simply unnecessary, the VIR system may come to be standard equipment in all broadcast stations and TV sets. However, whatever happens, it has served one very useful purpose: it has made television's engineers aware that the blank lines of the vertical interval need not go to waste. In the next chapter, we will discover that some very interesting things can be stuck into those blank spaces.

Chapter

2

Manipulating the TV Signal

Television would be unbearably dull if the receiver could be connected only to one camera or other picture source. By the time television had become a practical reality, audiences had become accustomed to the visual conventions of the motion picture, and they would not have accepted anything less sophisticated from the new visual medium.

Motion pictures are produced by shooting a great number of short lengths of film from different angles and perspectives; these are then physically spliced together or, for duplication, a master negative is made photographically from the separate bits and pieces. When a new master is made, sophisticated editing effects can be introduced; not only can there be "cuts," or instantaneous changes from one image to an entirely different one, but also such elaborate effects as "dissolves" (one image slowly appearing in place of another), "wipes" (one image being visually wiped off the screen while a second image appears in its place), and so forth. Two images can be combined on the screen through "superimpositions" (one image appearing over the other), "split screens" (two or more images appearing in different parts of the screen), and "mattes" (one image replacing a portion of another image). All of these effects are produced by physically manipulating the film while the new master negative is being exposed; simple cuts, of course, are produced by placing two lengths of film end to end.

Notice that all of these effects are produced *after* the image has been recorded on film. During the actual recording, very little can be done other than to move the camera itself—which must be done with great care in order to maintain sharp focus, proper exposure and overall composition.

When television broadcasting began, there simply was no practical method to preserve the television image; *all* television was "live." What one saw on one's receiver at home was actually being recorded by a camera somewhere, most often in a studio, at that very moment. There was not any way to "edit" the image after it had been recorded, because as soon as it passed out of the camera and reached the receiver, it ceased to exist. Yet, somehow, the television engineers had to devise a way to produce visual effects comparable to what people were used to seeing in movies.

The first step was to connect two cameras to a single stream of signals. This permitted switching from one camera to the other, while maintaining a continuous picture signal. The camera that was not "on" at a given moment could be repositioned to a different angle, its lens could be changed to give a different perspective on the scene, and so forth. Both cameras could be used to record a single scene, or they could be any distance apart—perhaps one in the studio and one at an entirely different location.

We will study this situation a little more closely because it is not quite as simple as it seems. An ordinary electrical switch could be used to change from one camera to another, but the results would not be very satisfactory. The problem is that the actual act of switching takes too long. In a simple toggle switch, there may be a tenth of a second when the switch is midway between two contacts, and current is flowing from neither source or from both. Since a television picture changes sixty times every second, a tenth-of-a-second interruption is very disruptive indeed. Furthermore, with an ordinary electrical switch, there is no way to tell precisely when the change from one contact to the other will take place. It might be while one camera's scanning beam is in the middle of an image. If the switch occurs at that point, part of the synchronizing signal will be lost for a split second—again, long enough to disrupt the picture. Another problem is that the scanning beams in the two cameras might not be at corresponding points in their scanning patterns; the beam in camera A might be halfway down the screen, while the beam in camera B is just starting at the top of the screen. Again, if the switch occurs at that point, the synchronizing signal will be disrupted. All of these problems have the same result: when the picture reaches a receiver, the disrupted signal confuses the receiver and produces a "tear" or "glitch"—a momentarily scrambled picture—until the sync signal is restored and the receiver gets everything lined up again. This sort of visual disruption would be intolerably distracting if it happened very often.

The solution is to devise an electronic switch that keeps track of the sync signals in the incoming picture signals. When someone presses a button, ordering a switch from camera A to camera B, the switch does not occur at once. The device waits until it senses the vertical sync pulse from camera A, then cuts off that signal; the device then waits until it senses the vertical sync pulse for camera B, and immediately turns that signal on. Since each camera completes an image and produces a vertical sync pulse once every one-sixtieth of a second, that is the longest time that the electronic switch will be completely shut off— and that is too short to be detectable by the viewer.

The only problem is that the interval when the switch is completely shut off (waiting for camera B's sync pulse) may vary from nearly zero up to a sixtieth of a second. During that period, no signal at all is being transmitted. A very sensitive receiver may be thrown into a tizzy by this interruption, and may go hunting for a sync signal; this, too, can produce a glitch when the signal finally comes back. Fortunately, most home television receivers are deliberately made to be rather insensitive and sluggish. However, the entire process of producing and transmitting television signals is so tenuous that engineers work hard to eliminate every possible source of disruption. The solution in this case is fairly simple: all of the cameras, and the switching device itself, must operate from a common source of sync signals. The *system sync generator* may be in the switching device itself or in a separate electronic component, or, in a few instances, the sync generators in one camera may be used to supply sync to all the other components. However it is arranged, everything must be synchronized to the same source.

Anyway, we now have a device that switches signals from one camera to another only during the vertical interval. By using an electronic switch instead of a mechanical one (such as an ordinary electric toggle), the time required for the switch to take place can be reduced to a minimum. It is now possible to make a smooth, "glitch-free" cut from one camera to another.

If you look into a television studio's control room, no doubt you will be impressed by the control console—usually built into a desk or counter—with its rows of pushbuttons. Most of the buttons are nothing more than electronic switches as just described. A typical video *switcher,* or control console, has at least four rows of buttons. Two of the rows represent incoming signals from various sources: cameras, video recorders, or other studios, for example. The other two rows of buttons enable the operator to connect an incoming signal directly to any of several possible outputs; one output usually is a monitor, enabling the operator to preview the picture before it is sent anywhere else; another output may be a recorder, or the cable to a transmitter, or merely the wire to a receiver somewhere.

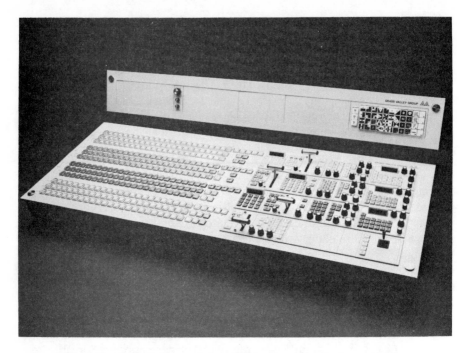

A television studio's video switcher. The banks of pushbuttons at left represent sources of signals (cameras, recorders, etc.); the controls at right determine where the selected signal goes and add electronic special effects. (Photo courtesy Grass Valley Group, Inc.)

Why are there *two* rows of buttons for incoming sources? Because the operator might want to do more than just switch, or cut, from one source to another. Most studio switchers also contain *special effects generators,* or SEGS, that produce visual effects comparable to—and in some cases much superior to—the effects that can be obtained while editing film. Signals from two or more sources may be combined, so the operator may need to switch at least two different signal sources on at the same time. Meanwhile, the operator may be looking at a signal from a third source on the preview monitor, while a signal from the fourth source is actually being transmitted through the output, or *program,* line. (You can always tell the person in a control room who operates the switcher-SEG; he or she usually has a slightly dazed expression from having to watch four rows of pushbuttons, two banks of camera monitors and output monitors, and a script, all at once.)

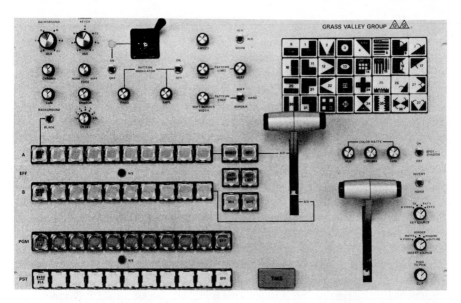

A video switcher and special effects generator. At upper right are pushbuttons to select any of 32 "wipe" patterns. The black lever at top, left of center, positions the "wipe" pattern in the picture. The split lever just to the right of center controls the "wipe" between signal sources selected by the pushbuttons in rows A and B. The controls in the lower right corner, including the second split lever, operate the chromakey effect (along with the controls on the upper left corner). The pushbuttons in row PGM determine where the signal is sent from the switcher (for example, to one of several video tape recorders); row PST is used to preset an effect while it is viewed on a monitor. (Photo courtesy Grass Valley Group, Inc.)

Special Effects Generators

There is almost no limit to the number of special effects that can be produced by the more elaborate and sophisticated SEGs. The most basic of all effects is the simple *fade;* a lever control permits the operator to reduce the video signal's voltage from the maximum (one volt in most television systems) to zero, without interfering with the sync pulses. If one picture is faded out while another picture is simultaneously faded in, the total effect is that of a *dissolve.* (On nearly all switcher-SEG control panels, there are two fader levers side by side, arranged so that they can be controlled together, fading out the signal from camera A and fading in the signal from camera B, or vice versa.)

Or two images can be combined on the screen at one time by bringing both fader levers to the halfway point; this produces a *superimposition.*

Wipes and *split screens* are a little more complicated, but even the least expensive nonbroadcast switcher-SEGS contain a couple of wipe patterns. The wipe is controlled by a separate electronic circuit that, in effect, "instructs" the SEG to accept the signal from source A for one part of the screen, then switch to source B for the rest of the screen. The switches can be made in the middle of any line, or at any vertical point in each field. Again, lever controls are usually used to control the wipe pattern. If a horizontal wipe pattern is used, as the wipe lever is operated the picture from source A seems to be wiped off the screen and replaced with the picture from source B (or vice versa) by a moving horizontal line.

A vertical wipe pattern produces a comparable effect, except that the picture changes from source A to source B somewhere along each horizontal line. If a vertical wipe and a horizontal wipe are combined, the wipe takes the shape of a box, moving from one corner of the screen diagonally to the opposite corner; this is known as a corner wipe.

The split-screen effect also is produced by wipe patterns, simply by stopping the movement of the wipe lever at some point. If the horizontal wipe lever is stopped midway, the screen is split horizontally: one picture appears in the upper half of the screen, the other picture in the lower half. A vertical wipe held at the midway point puts the two pictures side by side. A corner wipe can be used to insert the picture from one source into one corner of the picture from the other source.

Horizontal and vertical wipes only begin the possibilities. The wipe pattern can be made in almost any shape—round, triangular, star-shaped, oval—and circuits can be designed so that the wipe begins in the middle of the screen instead of at the edges. Bar patterns divide the screen into a series of vertical or horizontal bars, each of which "wipes" individually, creating a sort of venetian-blind effect. Furthermore, the edge of the wipe pattern, which ordinarily is a sharp line, can be "softened" into a blurred line. Or a colored border can be introduced along the edge of the wipe, in a color system. Or the edge can be made to scintillate. Or the border can be made to wiggle and pulsate. Or . . . As I said, the possibilities are almost endless.

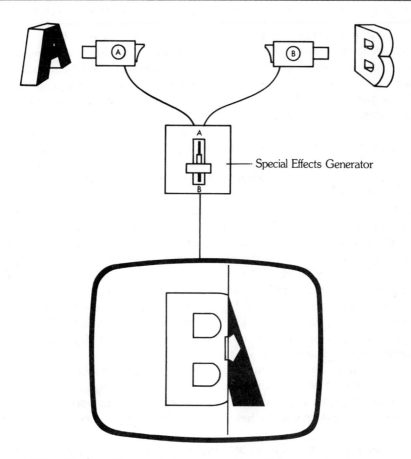

A "Wipe" Pattern. The signals from camera A and B are mixed in the special effects generator so that, as the lever is moved from the A position to the B position, signal B replaces signal A on the screen. This would be a simple horizontal wipe; if the wipe stops, the effect is called a "split screen."

These effects are not seen very often, since they are almost never used in dramatic programs (most of which are filmed in the first place, anyway) or newscasts. However, special visual effects, produced by SEGS, are frequently used in musical variety programs, commercials and sports programs. As dazzling as they are, they are produced by merely pressing a button or moving a lever on the SEG console.

Special circuits similar to wipe patterns also can be used to create something comparable to the *matte* effect in motion pictures. However, another and more interesting effect can be produced only in a television system: the *key*.

In a monochromatic system, there is not much difference between matting and keying, except that the matte pattern is produced entirely within the SEG, but the key pattern is produced by a separate camera. Briefly, it works this way: one camera provides the "basic," or A picture. A second camera is focused on something that contains a fairly simple, high-contrast pattern; usually a title card containing lettering or a graphic design is used. The second camera is the key camera. The edges of the pattern in its picture provide the key pattern. A third camera then supplies the B picture, which is inserted into the key pattern.

If a third camera isn't available, the B camera can be used for both the key pattern and the B picture—if the SEG is capable of "self-keying." This produces an effect similar in appearance to a matte, except that the pattern can be whatever shape the B camera is focused on.

Keying is even more interesting in a color television system, thanks to an effect known as *chromakey*. In monochromatic keying, the key pattern is determined by the contrast between the light and dark portions of the key image. In chromakeying, the key pattern is determined by color. It works this way:

Camera A is aimed at a scene that contains an area of a particular color, blue perhaps. The chromakeyer is "told" to ignore anything in picture A that is blue, and to replace it with the picture from camera B. It does not matter whether there is something blue in picture B, since the keying takes place only in picture A.

Chromakeying is so simple that it is used almost universally whenever two pictures are to be combined into a single image. During a baseball game, the batter's name, position, batting average and other facts appear at the bottom of the screen in colored letters; often, the lettering is actually done on a light blue title card (or on a large board) and the image of the batter is chromakeyed behind the lettering. On almost every television news program, there is a large, light-blue "screen" behind the announcer, on which slides or on-the-scene action appear. The slides or action scenes are chromakeyed into the picture of the anchorperson. In a commercial, a Lilliputian model clambers over a giant-sized sofa, pointing out the details of construction that make the sofa a bargain. Actually, the model performed in front of a light-blue drapery, onto which a close-up of the sofa has been chromakeyed.

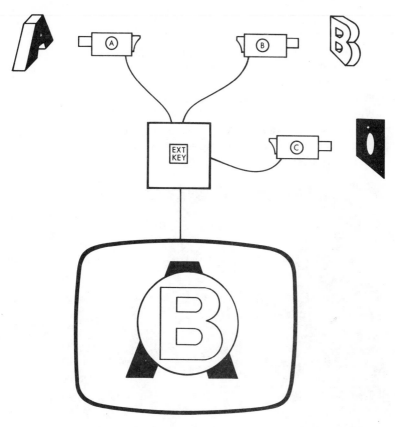

Keying. The signal from camera C determines the shape of the key pattern, which is then "cut out of" the image from camera A and the image from camera B is inserted in its place. Some SEGs are capable of "internal keying," which means that, for example, the image from camera B could be used to establish the shape of the pattern for the "cut out" in image A. A chromakeyer simplifies everything: it simply ignores anything of a given color (usually blue) in image A and replaces it with image B.

An actor wearing blue coveralls can be made to appear bodiless, or an actor wearing ordinary clothes but with a blue hood over his face can be made to appear headless—or someone else's head can be substituted for his own.

A hula dancer invites you to join her on the beaches of Waikiki (with the help of an airline). Actually, the dancer never left the studio; the beach scene is chromakeyed into the blue background behind her.

These are just a few very simple examples of the visual magic that can be achieved with chromakeying. When this effect is combined with some of the more elaborate wipes, or when multiple chromakeys are used in a single image, the creative possibilities are mind-boggling.

A character generator. This device electronically creates the images of letters, numbers, and sometimes other shapes, and arranges them into a video signal. Most character generators are used simply for titles, but more elaborate uses are possible. (Photo by the author, courtesy KVUE-TV.)

There is one limitation to the chromakey effect, however. Since the two images actually have no physical connection, moving the camera—either camera—during a chromakey can produce a jarring sense of dislocation. For example, a typical sequence during a news program begins with camera A on the anchorperson, who introduces a story. Videotaped footage of the action appears, chromakeyed, in the panel behind the announcer. The announcer then disappears (camera A was cut off) and the videotaped scene fills the screen. While you are watching the taped action, camera A is being repositioned to a different angle; when the taped story is over, a simple cut is made back to camera A. However, once in a while a careless technical director (the person who operates the switcher-SEG) may forget to cut off camera A before ordering the camera operator to reposition it. You will then see the anchorperson suddenly flying about the set in front of the on-the-scene action—a most bizarre effect!

Similarly, in the airline commercial, the hula dancer must remain in front of a stationary camera; if she walks down the beach, the camera cannot pan (move horizontally) to follow her, since the beach setting will not move.

A British company has found a solution to this problem that could open up new frontiers of creativity. The company has developed a computerized system that connects two cameras together, so that any movement of one camera will be faithfully duplicated by the other camera. The master camera can be aimed at actors cavorting on a bare stage in front of a blue background while the slave camera is aimed at a miniature setting. When the slave camera's picture is chromakeyed into the master picture, the actors seem to be in the setting. Since any movement of the master camera (including "zooming" the lens in or out) will be reproduced proportionally by the slave camera, the action can be extremely realistic. For little more than the cost of building the miniature sets, the action can seem to take place almost anywhere: in a huge castle, a cavernous dragon's lair, outer space or some totally imaginary locale.

The best place to see examples of some imaginative use of video special effects is a Saturday morning children's show (many of which are rerun on weekday afternoons). These programs are produced on comparatively minuscule budgets, and they must be turned out rapidly by as few technicians, actors and artists as possible. With few exceptions, they are produced on videotape rather than film; thus, the full panoply of video special effects can be used to create visual interest. Sid and Marty Krofft, perhaps best known for their traveling puppet shows, produce several children's shows that make extensive, and very effective, use of chromakeying with miniature sets, animation and a variety of other special effects.

The effects described all involve replacing part of one picture with part of another picture; generally, the two pictures must originate with cameras somewhere. The next step in manipulating the video image is to create images where none existed before—without a camera.

Character Generators

From the beginning, television has needed to transmit not only pictures of people and actual places, but also pictures of words and drawings. In fact, the first image Zworykin transmitted with his experimental television system was a drawing of Felix the Cat.

It is no great trouble to prepare graphic material for television; all that is required is a sheet of stiff posterboard, or any similar material, on which the lettering or drawing is rendered. This *title card* is placed on an easel in front of the camera. What could be simpler?

The problem arises when a great quantity of graphic material must be prepared, or when the information to be presented is subject to rapid change. Television programs are made through the combined efforts of dozens of actors, artists and technicians, all of whom want their names shown in the credits at the beginning or end of the show (a desire that is reinforced in their contracts). All these names cannot be squashed into a single title card. Engineers devised a large drum, called a *crawl,* that could contain dozens of lines of graphic material. The crawl is placed in front of the camera and slowly turned, creating the effect of a continuous flow of information that appears at the bottom of the screen and rolls upward, disappearing off the top (or vice versa). This was a good solution—provided the information could be prepared some time in advance, and that it was not likely to change.

For more ephemeral information, the slotted crawl was invented. The crawl itself was made with a black, velvety surface divided by slots half an inch apart. White plastic letters could be attached to the crawl by sticking tabs into the slots. This system was the mainstay of local news and weather shows for many years. Unfortunately, the little plastic letters had a nasty habit of getting lost or broken, or of falling out of the slots; also, putting up a long list of titles was a tedious chore for some lowly technician.

While television engineers sought a new way to create graphics directly on the television screen, computer designers wrestled with a similar problem. They needed a way to display information being fed into and coming out of the computer. Conventional, typewriter-like printers were simply too slow. What they came up with was a device that permitted "typing" from a keyboard directly onto a CRT screen—a pretty neat trick.

Remember that the scanning beam in a CRT travels continuously, 15,750 lines every second; it creates an image on the screen by changing the beam's voltage, raising it to produce light areas on the screen and dropping it to create dark areas. Producing graphic material on the screen—letters or drawings—simply requires telling the scanning beam *when* to change voltage. If the instruction is, "Raise voltage on the 7,374th cycle and drop it on the 7,376th cycle," a white dot will appear in the middle of the screen. In essence, that is how a computer display generator works: when a key on the keyboard is pressed, coded instructions are given to the scanning beam, raising and lowering its voltage at the appropriate times to cause the desired image to appear on the screen. The computer itself can "write" on the screen by translating its data output into the same kind of coded instructions. Thus, the computer operator and the computer can "speak" to each other.

This sophisticated character generator can produce an elaborate display of letters, numbers and symbols in various colors, can store them in its own memory, and can mix them with a standard video picture. (Photo courtesy of 3M Company.)

What worked for the computer required very little adaptation to serve equally well for television. By the early 1970s, a number of companies had begun to produce television *character generators:* computerized keyboards that create letter shapes by manipulating the video scanning beam. Usually the character generator is a separate device with its own CRT screen; the lettering is created by operating the keyboard, then stored in a magnetic memory within the device or on magnetic tape, and later fed into the composite video signal. However, some character generators are perfectly capable of feeding directly into the video signal. As far as the television system is concerned, the character generator is just another picture source, not unlike a camera.

Most character generators are able to produce only letters and a few standard symbols. However, there are also generators that can "draw" on a CRT screen. A computer can then treat the "drawing" as a stream of information and can manipulate it according to the operator's instructions. The drawings can be made larger or smaller, or rotated on an imaginary axis.

The creative potential of character generation has only begun to be realized. Nearly all television stations have thrown out their old title card easels and crawls, replacing them with character generators that can insert lettering into the picture signal at any time. The devices are used to identify the talking head on the TV screen—the newsperson, witness, miscreant or whatever. They are also used to present weather data, sports scores and the like. More elaborate generators are used by network news and sports programs to present continuously updated voting results, stock market quotations, sports scores and various other kinds of information, often with colored lettering and various special effects.

However, no one has yet taken the obvious next step. A character generator creates video images that have never existed in reality outside of the electronic circuits. There is no reason that this capability could not be used to create images of places, settings for dramatic action, that exist only in the video artist's imagination. And if settings can be created in this way, so can the images of actors.

Controlling the creation of images such as these would require some very elaborate computer programming, especially if the "actors" are to move within the "settings," as we would expect. However, there is nothing to prevent such computer programs from being written, and once that is accomplished, the same program could be used to create any sort of image. Television would be totally free of the need to hire actors, directors, camera operators and most of the other technicians required to produce even the simplest program. One person operating a computerized signal-generating console could create whole worlds of video images.

Animator and filmmaker Ralph Bakshi used such techniques in somewhat primitive form to create *The Lord of the Rings*. Live actors were photographed performing the actions required by the script; the actors' images were then used to control a computer that produced animated drawings, based on the artists' designs. The resulting combination of realistic action and imaginary images is utterly haunting. But it is barely a taste of what could be done with a fully computerized video system.

At present, the most elaborate and sophisticated signal-generating devices are known as *video synthesizers*. Synthesizers are one-of-a-kind, handcrafted assemblages of equipment, usually built up of some standard components such as character generators and color-pattern generators hooked to small computers. Usually they require a camera signal as a source of "raw material," although some synthesizers operate solely from character generators. In either case, the original image can be manipulated by operating the synthesizer's controls to alter colors, to increase or reduce contrast (creating "posterized" effects, for instance), to distort shapes and to combine two or more images in a single picture. Most synthesizers are hand-operated, with rows of pushbuttons, dials and levers, although a computer may be used for some effects. So far, synthesizers have been used primarily for experimental purposes, to produce exotic visual effects and to try out aesthetic ideas: in short, to "paint" electronically. However, the video synthesizer is not far short of the total image-generating system of the future.

Something for the Vertical Interval

Meanwhile, back in the present, more practical uses have been made of the character generator's image-creating capabilities.

In Chapter 1, we talked about the "wasted lines" of the vertical interval, those blank lines that unavoidably result when the scanning beam is turned off at the end of each field. The vertical interval reference (VIR) signal can be neatly tucked away in one of those "wasted lines." However, there are still a number of other lines in the vertical interval, and there ought to be some good use for them.

In the early 1970s, it occurred to someone that deaf people could not derive much pleasure from television because they could not enjoy the dialogue. Even those comparatively few deaf people who are adept at lipreading would miss anything that is said off-screen or by a character whose back is to the camera.

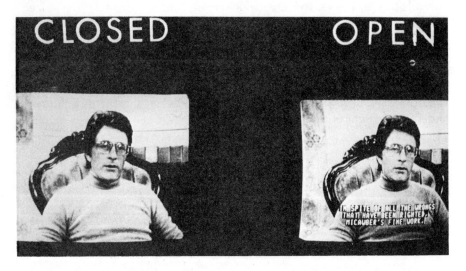

The PBS closed captioning system (used also by ABC and NBC) allows the ordinary viewer to watch an ordinary picture, at left, while a hearing-impaired viewer uses a special decoder to see a captioned picture (at right). (Photo courtesy of Public Broadcasting Service.)

The Public Broadcasting System, responding to requests from organizations for the deaf, experimented with captioned programs. This involved merely preparing an abbreviated version of the dialogue on a character generator and inserting the captions, or subtitles, into the picture. The results were better than had been expected; captioning turned out to be perfectly feasible, and very much appreciated by the deaf and hearing-impaired in the TV audience whose needs had been overlooked for so long. With the generous cooperation of the American Broadcasting Company in 1974, PBS began preparing a captioned version of the ABC evening newscast, which most PBS stations carried in the late evening (usually at 10:30 or 11:30).

The only drawback to captioning was that the captions were very distracting to viewers whose hearing was unimpaired. Since the captions represent a highly condensed version of the dialogue, sometimes what the viewer hears and what appears in lettering on the screen would not quite correspond; furthermore, the mere presence of the lettering was an annoyance to many viewers. Engineers quickly found a solution: the captions could be put into the vertical interval, and adapters could be installed on deaf viewers' TV sets to recapture the information and insert it into the visible picture.

This technique, known as *closed captioning*, was developed largely by PBS, and the public system lobbied long and hard to get the Federal Communications Commission to accept it. Finally, in 1979, the FCC authorized all television broadcasters to use closed captioning whenever they like, and approved the technical design of the captioning equipment and adapters. PBS announced that it would begin captioning as many of its programs as possible. The commercial networks took diverse positions on closed captioning; ABC quickly agreed to begin captioning its programs—if someone else would pay for the preparation of the captions. NBC also agreed, rather reluctantly, to caption some of its shows. However, CBS, which had lobbied against the closed captioning system, turned its back on the whole idea. In fairness, it should be said that CBS was not insensitive to the needs of the deaf; the network simply felt that closed captioning was much too expensive and that some other solution should be found. Besides, CBS was interested in using the vertical interval for something else: teletext.

For many years, visionaries have predicted that someday newspapers and magazines will be transmitted directly to people's homes by television, instead of being printed on paper and either mailed or hand-delivered. The development of character generators eliminated one obstacle, the cost and difficulty of preparing graphic material for television, but one other impediment remained. People do not read newspapers and magazines the way they watch television.

When you watch television, you turn to a particular channel and watch whatever information is presented, in whatever sequence someone else chooses to present it. You may choose to change channels, or you may ignore what is on the screen at a given moment, or you may go to the refrigerator during a commercial, but you have no control whatsoever over the stream of information.

When you read a newspaper or magazine, however, you have a great deal of control over the stream of information. You can skip articles or whole pages that do not interest you; you can skim over pages to see whether there is anything worthy of your attention; or you can stay on one page for as long as you like, reading every detail; or you can go back to a previous page, to pick up something you overlooked or to read something you previously skipped. You can read the sports pages first, then the comics and then the political news in the front section—or, if you are like my wife, you can read a magazine backwards, starting with the back cover and working toward the front.

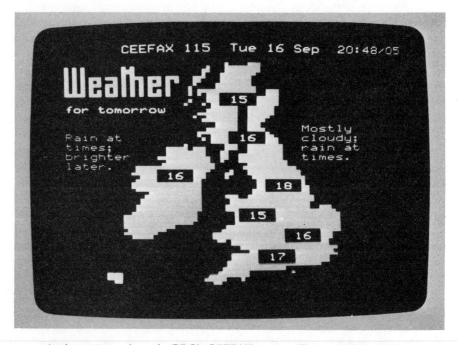

A teletext image from the BBC's CEEFAX system. The image is created electronically and compressed to fit into the lines between picture fields. Special circuitry must be added to the television set to retrieve the teletext image and present it on the screen. Some U.S. stations are experimenting with teletext systems now. (Photo courtesy Texas Instruments, Inc.)

Giving the viewer comparable control over a television "magazine," using conventional technology, would be virtually impossible. One way would be to transmit each "story" on a separate channel, but that would be absurdly expensive—and even then the "pages" within a "story" would have to be transmitted in sequence, changing automatically at predetermined intervals. Both slow and fast readers would find this annoying.

British television engineers found a better way to do it—and, once again, they found the solution in the vertical interval's "wasted lines." Their solution, now known as teletext, was formally adopted by the BBC; the British commercial television system, IBA; and the British government in 1974.

In the British teletext system, a full "page" of information can be condensed into not more than 24 horizontal video lines (less, in most cases, since portions of the screen image—such as between the rows of letters—are intentionally left blank). These 24 lines are inserted, two at a time, into the vertical interval—which, of course, changes 50 times per second in the British television system, or 60 times per second in our system. One page after another is transmitted in this manner; a hundred pages can be transmitted about every 24 seconds.

Of course, not many people can read 100 pages in 24 seconds. The teletext adapter, which must be installed on the TV set in order to receive the information, simply collects whatever pages you wish to read and displays them for as long as you like. One page is always used for an index; you press a button to see it, then select the stories you wish to read and call them up by using a calculator-like keypad.

The BBC began broadcasting its teletext service, called CEEFAX, in September, 1974. Since then, the service has been gradually expanded, bringing more areas of Britain into the system and expanding the number of pages of information offered by CEEFAX. By 1978, the service provided 800 pages of information at a time, all continuously updated by a staff of editors and technicians. A typical CEEFAX index lists "stories" such as headlines, home news, foreign news, farm news, consumer news, a weather map, sports and gardening. There are even games for children to play. No comics, alas.

The independent (that is, commercial) television system, IBA, also has a teletext service; it is called ORACLE, which is supposed to stand for "Optical Reception of Announcements by Coded Line Electronics"—surely one of the more ingenious acronyms in recent years. Anyway, ORACLE provides much the same sort of information service as CEEFAX.

The British Post Office also offers a teletext service, but one that is considerably different from the two networks' offerings. The BPO system, VIEW-DATA, is more of an electronic library, designed to provide basic reference material. Instead of separate magazine-type articles, VIEWDATA has files of information arranged in increasing levels of comprehensiveness. For example, you might select from the main index the file on "health." A subindex would then appear on your screen, listing the various aspects of health for which information is available; you would then choose the subtopic that interests you and call it up. The first article to appear under the heading "heart disease" might be a brief summary of the major classes of heart diseases, statistics on their incidence, and typical symptoms. You might then be directed to call up a subentry for additional information on, say, "heart attack." Keying in the index number would bring to your screen a more complete discussion of heart attacks, their symptoms, treatment and so forth, and additional cross-references would give index numbers for "prevention," "cardiopulmonary resuscitation (CPR)" or "national statistics."

Obviously, developing material for VIEWDATA is a much more complex task than it is for the magazine-type services. On the other hand, the VIEW-DATA articles are not continuously updated, nor do they need to be. The VIEW-DATA system also includes some "interactive" features, such as quizzes and games; when you respond by pressing a button on the control box, the system may tell you not only whether you answered correctly, but why—and where you can get more information.

CEEFAX, ORACLE and VIEWDATA are still regarded as experimental systems more than five years after their introduction. Public acceptance has not been as rapid nor as enthusiastic as some people had hoped. However, there appear to be two good reasons for the public to respond rather slowly. First of all, the present teletext system does not provide information in a visually appealing form. The images are made up entirely of small, rectangular dots; all letters are five dots wide and seven dots high, and all "drawings" or designs also must be made up from the rectangular dots. The result is visually very crude.

However, a more serious obstacle to ORACLE and its cousins is cost. The adapter needed to pick up the teletext signal and make it visible, including the control box, is exorbitantly expensive. At last report, a TV set with the teletext equipment built in was priced at just under $2,000. Separate adapters could be attached to ordinary sets, but the adapters still cost several hundred dollars.

However, these costs were expected to drop drastically as the equipment designs became more refined and as the teletext service became available throughout Britain, thus creating a mass market. As more people come to use teletext, presumably the teletext producers would be encouraged to improve the service, which in turn would attract more users. Meanwhile, government-run television networks in Germany, Belgium, France, Sweden and several other European countries either have begun experimental teletext services or have indicated a strong interest in doing so.

Across the wide Atlantic, U.S. television viewers heard almost nothing about teletext until late in 1978 when a few newspaper and magazine articles began to appear, describing this technological triumph of the English. That seems strange, considering that one of the first companies to manufacture teletext equipment was Texas Instruments, Ltd., the British subsidiary of one of the largest U.S. electronics companies. Could it be that the whole British teletext program was merely a pilot project for the introduction of teletext in the United States?

Could be.

In any case, by 1979, interest in teletext had begun to blossom in the western hemisphere. CBS was one of the first major advocates of teletext, and quickly began putting money into the system, with experimental teletext systems in Denver and St. Louis (operated by CBS affiliates). Interest also was expressed by a number of cable system operators and satellite networks—a segment of the television industry we will meet later in Chapters 7, 8 and 9.

The big question with teletext is, *Who will pay for it?* In Britain, both CEEFAX and VIEWDATA are basically government-supported through the BBC and the British Post Office; ORACLE is supported by IBA mainly to keep up with the competition. A government-funded teletext system is not likely to develop in the United States, which leaves two possibilities: an advertiser-supported system or a subscriber-supported system. The former seems to be a fairly good bet, if the public accepts a teletext system in sufficient numbers to be attractive to advertisers, but it is not at all clear how advertising can fit into the teletext format, especially in its present visually primitive stage of development. A subscriber-supported system would eliminate those problems, but no one is sure whether the public would be very interested in an "electronic magazine" if it represented a direct cash outlay. For that matter, it is not certain what the system would cost, or how many people would be interested even if it were free.

It will take a number of years to begin to resolve all these uncertainties, although the CBS pilot projects will answer some questions rather quickly. If teletext catches on, and if the economic questions can be settled to everyone's satisfaction, the whole concept of television will change radically in just a few years. Meanwhile, a mass market for teletext would encourage the engineers to develop a more sophisticated technology, capable of providing more attractive visuals. If that does not happen rather quickly, teletext is likely to limp along as a supplemental information source for people with particular interests and needs (stock market quotations for business executives, for instance).

Chapter
3

Video Recording: TV's Liberation

Television initially was strictly a "live" medium; there was no method for preserving the images generated by the camera. Not that anyone wanted it this way. Live television was an unavoidable necessity with few redeeming virtues. The best that can be said for it is that there were almost no reruns.

Veterans of the television industry often wax nostalgic over those early days, between 1945 and 1955, when the new medium was open to all sorts of experimentation. News and sports programs were comparatively rare because of the great logistical difficulties in providing live pictures of the events and the cost of obtaining filmed coverage. Instead, the evening hours were given over to variety shows, comedies and dramas, all of which had to be produced live in the studio. Nearly all of the dramatic programs were anthologies, with different actors portraying different characters each week. It took several weeks to build the sets and rehearse the actors for each program, which had to be performed flawlessly at the appointed hour.

Television's "Golden Age" in the early 1950s certainly was an exciting period, at least for the participants if not for the relatively small TV audience. Much of the excitement, however, can be attributed to the pioneering spirit that infected the medium, rather than to any imaginary virtues of live performance. In fact, live television imposed tremendous restrictions on creative expression, and additional limitations were imposed by the rather primitive state of television technology. Dramatic action had to be staged indoors, in the studio; the cumbersome cameras inhibited the actors' movements. Most of those fabled "Golden Age" dramas would bore an audience if they were somehow retrieved and shown again today. Only a handful of creative geniuses, such as Ernie Kovacs, rose above the technological limits and found whole new forms of creative expression in the medium.

From the very beginning, the television industry saw the need for some means of preserving the video image. John Logie Baird, the indefatigable Scot, had developed a television recording system based on the phonograph in 1927, but the results were so poor that he gave up.

By the time the television industry got rolling in the late 1940s, the most advanced image-recording technology available was that of motion pictures. Television engineers devised a system, called *kinescope recording*, that involved nothing more elaborate than aiming a movie camera at the screen of a television monitor. This system was used heavily by the networks from around 1948 until the middle 1950s, and only occasionally thereafter, to permit live programs produced on the East Coast to be shown during the evening hours on the West Coast—a day late. Before that, a program transmitted at 8 p.m. in New York had to be broadcast in Los Angeles at 5 o'clock in the afternoon. By using kinescopes, the program could be filmed while it was being transmitted live, and the film could be rushed by air to the West Coast for broadcast the following evening.

Unfortunately, kinescope recording produces dismal results. The film faithfully records the video image as an assemblage of horizontal lines, but the movie camera is not as "forgiving" as the human eye, and films at that time were not as sensitive and tolerant as they are now. The result was a grainy, blurry, streaked film image. When this image was then transferred back to video (by projecting the movie into a television camera's lens), technological limitations further degraded the image. Kinescope is still used today, once in a great while, when a television image (usually one that has been recorded on videotape) simply must be transferred to film; in spite of some improvements in the technology, the results are still very poor.

For many years kinescope recording was the *only* method of preserving the television image. Furthermore, it had the side effect of bringing film into the television control room.

In its earliest days, the television industry had no interest in film. Television was an electronic medium, an offspring of radio, and somehow using it to transmit movies seemed immoral. Besides, the Hollywood film industry had made its position on television abundantly clear: the major movie studios declared that any actor, director, writer or technician who worked in the new medium would be unwelcome on the studio lots thereafter. (Actually, this boycott, which was instigated more by the theater owners than by the studios, was never consistently enforced; more than anything, it merely served to engender bitterness in some segments of the television industry.)

When television began, the only medium for storing images was film. This is an early RCA "film chain." The film reels were loaded onto the two projectors at right and left; the picture was projected into a mirror (atop the column at center), which reflected it into a camera at rear. Similar equipment—though not so bulky!—is still commonplace in both network and local station control rooms, since 16 mm film is still used for most commercials and old movies; at the network level, 35 mm film is used for prime-time series. (Photo courtesy RCA Corp.)

However, television simply could not do without film, especially after the networks came into operation. *Something* had to go out over the telephone wires every minute, and it was physically impossible for all of it to be produced live in the New York studios. Additional studios were built in Chicago and Los Angeles, but the fundamental problem was only partially relieved. Furthermore, live television imposed terrible restrictions on what could be produced and seriously hampered news and sports programming.

From the very beginning, a few old movies came into the hands of the TV programmers. In 1948 Republic Studios sold a package of old *Hopalong Cassidy* and other western films to individual broadcasting stations; these moth-eaten "oaters" proved spectacularly popular. Other minor-league studios and independent movie producers also sold their wares to television, mostly because these low-budget films had long since exhausted their theater market potential.

The old movies and kinescopes brought film into television, but it was television news that came to depend most heavily on film technology during the early days. In 1948, CBS started the first television news program, *Douglas Edwards and the News*. Initially the program delivered no more than its title promised: Douglas Edwards reading the news. Once in a while, a blown-up photograph or a chart might be brought onto the set to add visual interest. However, that obviously was not good enough, so CBS contracted with a newsreel company, News of the Day (jointly owned by MGM and the Hearst newspaper syndicate), to supply film of news events. NBC went a step further and took over a newsreel outfit formerly owned by its parent, RCA, to supply footage for *The Camel News Caravan with John Cameron Swayze*. ABC's John Daly just kept on reading for quite a while.

The newsreel producers and camera operators found themselves in a bewildering new world. Where formerly they had been expected to put together half a dozen stories once a week, now they had to produce at least that many stories every day. Suddenly they were no longer making movies; they had to learn how to use film to accomplish the same functions as newsprint. Much of the credit for developing both the form and the spirit of television journalism is given to Edward R. Murrow and his chief behind-the-scenes producer, Fred Friendly.

Film became increasingly important in television after 1950. In Chapter 5 we will see how prime-time TV was all but taken over by the Hollywood movie studios. But we are getting a little away from the subject of this chapter, which is how the television image itself can be preserved. Until 1956, it couldn't be, except in the crude form of kinescope recordings.

Videotape

Meanwhile, the technology of magnetic tape recording was being developed rapidly—not for television, but for the audio industry.

Both the producers and the consumers of phonograph records longed for something that would provide better sound fidelity. As long as recordings were made on wax discs, the inherent inefficiencies of the system made higher fidelity unobtainable. There had to be a better way—and there was.

Magnetic recording eliminated a large part of the noise and distortion that was inherent in the phonograph recording system, by the simple expedient of eliminating mechanical contact between the recording instrument and the recording medium.

In any magnetic recording system, tiny particles of magnetizable metal (that is, some compound containing iron) are held in a binder, which in turn is applied as a coating to some sort of carrier: tape, disc, flat sheet or a drum. When a fairly powerful electromagnet is held close to the magnetic particles, the particles "copy" the magnet's *polarity* (its positive or negative charge.) If the electromagnet's field fluctuates according to changes in the current flowing to it, these fluctuations are reproduced by the magnetic particles. The particles themselves give off a very weak electromagnetic field; if an electromagnet is brought into this field, it will pick up the particles' charge and reproduce it as a weak electrical current. Thus, the particles not only record the original pattern of magnetic charges, but they can cause the pattern to be reproduced.

During World War II, magnetic recorders were developed using spools of metal wire as the particle-carrying medium. Wire recorders were widely used by the military and were adopted by radio journalists, but they proved unsatisfactory for several reasons—not the least of which was the tendency of the stiff wire to tangle and break. Meanwhile, the plastics industry had developed suitable materials that could be used to make a reasonably strong but very flexible tape. Soon the technology was developed to apply a coating of magnetizable particles to an acetate carrier, and magnetic recording tape was born. By 1950 magnetic tape was rapidly becoming the principal means of making sound recordings (which could be later transferred to phonograph records).

The similarities between audio and video signals, both of which are analog signals, strongly suggested that magnetic tape could be used to record video as well. There certainly was no theoretical barrier, but there were plenty of practical problems.

In audio recording, the tape simply runs past a fixed electromagnet, or "head," at a fixed speed; the audio signal is recorded as one long, continuous stream of information. The speed at which the tape moves is important because it determines the rate at which fluctuations in the magnetic field can be recorded, and thus the range of frequencies that can be reproduced. The greater that range, the more information that can be recorded. In audio recording, a tape speed as low as 1⅛ inches per second is adequate to record and reproduce the somewhat limited frequency range of the human voice; higher tape speeds, as high as 16 inches per second, are commonly used for very high fidelity reproduction of music.

The first big problem with magnetic video recording was that television signals require an enormous frequency range. In order to reproduce the television signal accurately, using the same technique as for audio recording—that is, *longitudinal recording* (recording down the length of the tape)—the tape must travel at a tremendous speed.

One of the first engineering laboratories to develop a "practical" videotape recorder was Bing Crosby Laboratories. In 1951 the Crosby lab demonstrated a longitudinal recorder that ran at 100 inches per second. A reel of half-inch-wide tape three feet in diameter could hold a little more than fifteen minutes of video. Even at that tape speed, the picture resolution was only about half as good as a standard television picture, and there were other technical problems—mostly because of the mechanical difficulty in maintaining a steady tape speed. It just was not practical.

Of course, there were a lot of other people working hard on the same problems. RCA demonstrated a longitudinal recording system in 1953 that could even accommodate a color signal, but it was not much better than the Crosby system. The engineers at the Ampex Corporation, a hitherto undistinguished electronics outfit in California, finally gave up on longitudinal recording altogether—and hit on the perfect solution.

Instead of keeping the recording head stationary while the tape moved past, the Ampex engineers decided to put the head into motion, too. By recording the video signal as a series of short passes across a fairly wide strip of tape, they could achieve the necessary recording speed while keeping the actual traveling speed of the tape within reason. Their system is called, logically enough, *transverse recording*—recording across the tape.

The Ampex engineers found, however, that if they had only one rotating head passing the tape, there would be large gaps between the strips of information being recorded. Therefore, they added first a second head, then two more. This resulted in what is known as *quadruplex transverse recording*, or, as it is universally known to television engineers today, "quad."

The first network broadcast from a two-inch quadruplex video tape recorder. The program was CBS's *Douglas Edwards and the News*, on November 30, 1956. (Photo courtesy Ampex Corp.)

The first Ampex quad video recorders were offered to the television industry in 1956. They used tape two inches wide; a reel about two feet in diameter could hold a half-hour program. Later improvements brought the tape speed down drastically, so that ninety minutes of program could be recorded on a reel about 15 inches in diameter, and for nonbroadcast use a not-quite-as-sharp picture could be recorded for three hours on the same reel at seven and a half inches per second.

The response of the television industry was immediate; Ampex literally couldn't make the machines fast enough and soon licensed RCA to help serve the market. In 1958 the two manufacturers jointly announced a color recorder. These machines have been the workhorses of the television industry ever since. Every broadcasting station has at least two or three quad recorders, and major production centers have bank after bank of them.

A quad recorder is not something you would want in your living room. The basic models used in broadcasting are about as large as a refrigerator-freezer; they cost anywhere from $50,000 to $250,000, depending on optional accessories. In the early 1960s, Ampex tried to develop a suitcase-sized portable quad recorder for use by news units and for on-the-spot recording of sports and other events, but it was not very successful.

Meanwhile, Japanese television engineers were experimenting with a somewhat different recording technique. They, like the folks at Ampex, recognized that the key to a practical video recorder involved recording across the tape rather than along it. However, Ampex's transverse system has some problems. With the heads spinning at a 90 degree angle to the tape path, the wear on the heads from friction is tremendous; keeping exactly the right tension on the tape, to maintain a perfectly steady speed without unnecessarily damaging the heads, is extremely difficult. The Japanese came up with a sensible compromise: *helical scan recording.*

In helical recording, the heads also spin as the tape rolls past, but the angle between the heads and the tape path is relatively shallow. This results in a long, diagonal stripe of information being laid across the tape. The early models of helical scan recorders required the tape to be wrapped completely around the drum containing a single head; the tape path thus was a helix, or spiral, and thus the name. Later it was found that the tape merely had to be wrapped about two-thirds of the way around the drum, which greatly simplified the mechanical arrangement. Helical scan recorders also now use two heads, so I suppose they could be called "duplex," but I have never heard that term applied to them.

The standard video tape recorder for broadcasting since its introduction in 1973, this two-inch quad machine (Ampex's AVR-2) now faces stiff competition from the new one-inch helical scan equipment. (Photo courtesy Ampex Corp.)

The first practical helical scan recorders were produced by the Sony Corporation and by a California firm, International Video Corporation, or IVC. Both systems used one-inch wide tape; a half-hour program could be recorded on a reel about seven inches in diameter. These machines first came into use in the middle 1960s, strictly for nonbroadcast use since they were not capable of producing a picture signal of the quality required for broadcasting.

By 1970, Sony, IVC, Ampex and a number of other companies in Japan, the United States and Europe had begun to market helical scan recorders using half-inch-wide tape. These machines were even lighter, less cumbersome and considerably less expensive than the one-inch machines, which were in turn a great improvement over the two-inch quad recorders. For the first time, it began to seem that television would become a practical medium for all sorts of nonbroadcast applications; again, however, the half-inch machines were definitely not suitable for broadcasting. In fact, the half-inch machines barely worked at all, and besides, each manufacturer had developed its own unique recording system and format (the precise way the signal is recorded). Tapes made on a Sony recorder could not be played on a Panasonic, Ampex, RCA or recorder made by any other company. In fact, a tape made on one Ampex model would not necessarily be playable on a different Ampex model.

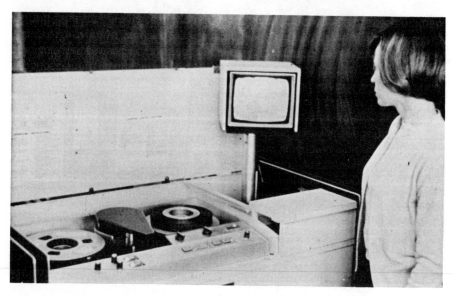

An early one-inch helical scan recorder. This machine was not much less bulky, costly and intimidating than the early quad recorders. Today's new generation of one-inch recorders are much smaller, easier to operate and more reliable; they also produce far better pictures. (Photo courtesy National Audio-Visual Association)

The lack of interchangeability and the generally poor reliability of all the small helical-scan recorders seriously discouraged many potential users. However, in 1971 the Electronics Industry Association of Japan (EIAJ) formed a committee of engineers to develop a standardized format for the half-inch equipment; these standards were adopted in 1972 as EIAJ Technical Standard No. 1, or just EIAJ-1. The standards covered the basic recording format for half-inch helical scan video recording and incorporated the American (NTSC) standards for color television. Almost overnight, both Japanese and American manufacturers began producing new half-inch recorders to the EIAJ-1 standard.

An early one-half-inch helical scan recorder, Sony's first color "porta-pak" model. (Photo by the author, courtesy Austin Community Television)

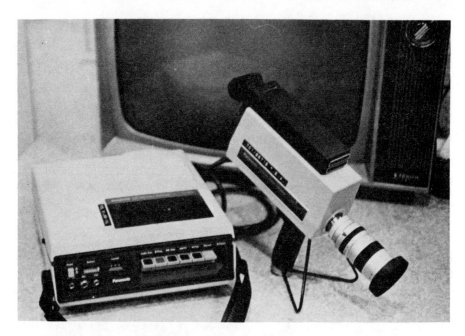

A mid-1970s black-and-white portable one-half-inch recorder and its camera. This equipment paved the way for thousands of video hobbyists, amateurs and enthusiasts to begin producing their own programs; one result was the demand for public-access channels on cable television systems (See Chapter 7). Another result was the gradual introduction of portable recorders and "mini-cams" into broadcasting, eliminating the traditional 16-mm film equipment. (Photo by the author, courtesy Texas Education Agency)

One of the first of the new machines was the Sony "Port-a-pak," a video recorder that weighed less than ten pounds and came with a rechargeable battery and a shoulder strap. Sony also developed a black-and-white camera that was, for its time, a marvel of electronic miniaturization; it was only slightly larger than an 8 mm movie camera, came with a pistol grip and a built-in microphone, and operated off the Port-a-pak recorder's battery. The Port-a-pak, which was quickly copied by Panasonic and other Japanese companies, had a sensational effect on the growth of video as an independent medium for creative expression, as well as countless workaday applications. Television no longer meant an enormous investment in a well-lighted studio full of costly electronics; anyone who could come up with a couple of thousand dollars for a Port-a-pak could become a video producer.

And there were more wonders yet to come.

Cartridges and Cassettes

Ever since videotape recording was first introduced, television visionaries dreamed of the day when everyone could have a videotape recorder in their living room. The idea was that the home video recorder would free viewers from their total reliance on broadcasting, and in particular on the dominant commercial networks with their monotonous mass-taste programming. While a network could not consider programming for a prospective audience of, say, 100,000 people nationwide, a producer of prerecorded video tapes could reap a bonanza from a single program that sold 100,000 copies.

There were two technological problems that had to be solved first, however. According to the marketing people in the electronics industry, a home video recorder had to be designed so that the user would be relieved of the task of threading the tape from one reel to another. Actually, threading a half-inch helical scan recorder is no harder than threading an 8 mm movie projector, and much simpler than threading a 16 mm projector, but the marketing people were convinced that the average consumer would not be willing to perform this chore. Secondly, the cost of a home recorder must be no more than $400, which, at the time, the electronics industry considered the "magic number" below which almost any new gadget could be sold to a mass market. In 1972, the least expensive black-and-white recorders were selling for about $1,100 (without a camera), so there was a long way to go.

The EIAJ-1 standards acknowledged the interest in developing a home recorder, and included standards for a cartridge system based on the half-inch standard format. In 1972, Panasonic, Sony, Japan Victor Company (JVC) and Hitachi all began to produce an EIAJ-1 cartridge system. The machines themselves were fairly bulky, about the size of a large toaster-oven but considerably heavier. A cartridge containing a 30-minute supply of half-inch tape was simply inserted in a slot in the front of the recorder, in much the same manner as an eight-track stereo cartridge. The tape was automatically pulled out of the cartridge, wrapped around the video head drum and wound onto an internal take-up reel. Some cartridge recorders included television tuners so that broadcast programs could be recorded off-the-air.

The cartridge machines worked quite well, as did most of the EIAJ-1 equipment. However, they had a couple of major drawbacks. One was the 30-minute playing time, which was a limitation imposed by the amount of tape that could be packed into the cartridge. Another drawback was the cost; the least expensive machines were priced at around $1,000, out of the range of the mass market. Some cartridge machines were used in schools, industry and other nonbroadcast applications, but their bulk compared to the more popular portable recorders limited their acceptance here, too.

Perhaps a more important factor in the destiny of the EIAJ cartridge machine was the development by Sony of the three-quarter-inch videocassette, which was announced almost at the same time the EIAJ standards were promulgated.

The three-quarter inch cassette system was not intended to be a home recorder system, although Sony made some halfhearted attempts to market it as such. More important, it gave Sony and the rest of the industry a chance to recover part of the enormous investment that had already been made in the effort to develop a practical automatic-threading recorder. Secondly, it established once and for all the cassette as the preferred format over the cartridge. The difference between a cartridge and a cassette is very simple: a cartridge contains one reel, from which the tape must be removed and wound onto a take-up reel inside the machine; a cassette contains two reels, so that the tape only has to be pulled part-way out of the case to be wrapped around the video head drum.

The fact that the three-quarter inch cassette was Sony's own design, for which other manufacturers would have to pay a licensing fee, and that it thoroughly undermined the arduously achieved EIAJ standards, was, of course, purely fortuitous.

The three-quarter inch videocassette had a number of immediate and long-lasting effects on the video industry. First, it wiped out the market for one-inch equipment. By 1975 only Sony and IVC still manufactured one-inch recorders, but IVC was in bankruptcy and Sony barely produced enough machines to provide replacements for those already in use. The three-quarter inch machines represented a superior technology, and they took over the industrial and educational video markets. Anyone could operate a three-quarter inch recorder or player; it was something that could be entrusted to mechanically inept classroom teachers or showroom salesmen. The three-quarter inch system also drove the EIAJ half-inch system into an early grave, with the half-inch cartridge system stillborn and the established open-reel system prematurely obsolete.

More importantly, the three-quarter inch system produced a video signal that was almost adequate for broadcasting. The chief barrier for all helical scan recorders had been the fact that the head path across the tape, or *track*, was so long that the slightest variation in the rotating speed of the head or in the speed of the tape would introduce some instability into the composite video signal. As long as the recorder was connected directly to a monitor, the instability could be minimized and the effects usually were not too damaging. However, even this minimal instability was too great to allow the signal to be transmitted through the air, which unavoidably introduces plenty of problems by itself.

Half-inch videocassette equipment, designed for professional use: this
Panasonic VHS recorder, along with its mate at right, is capable of the
same sophisticated editing and high-quality picture as more expensive
three-quarter-inch recorders. When VHS was first introduced, Panasonic
claimed that it was "strictly for consumers." Sony made the same claim for
its Betamax equipment—which is also available now in "professional"
models. (Photo by the author, courtesy Gray Electronics, Inc.)

Because the three-quarter inch system provided for the tape to be wrapped around the head drum by an automatic mechanism, and because of other refinements in the helical scan technology, a more stable signal could be produced dependably. Also, by 1975 several companies had begun to manufacture *time base correctors,* electronic "black boxes" that remove the instability by replacing the horizontal and vertical sync signal. Time base correctors, or TBCs, had been developed several years earlier for quad recorders and had become standard fixtures in broadcasting, but the development of smaller, much less expensive TBCs specifically for use with helical scan recorders—and particularly for three-quarter inch recorders— meant that the helical scan signal could be brought up to broadcast standards.

By 1976, there were portable three-quarter inch recorders not much larger than the original half-inch Port-a-pak. There were also, by that time, portable color cameras that could produce a picture comparable to a broadcast studio camera. These "minicameras" and three-quarter inch portable cassette recorders soon made their way into the news departments of television broadcasters, where they replaced the 16 mm film equipment that had been the industry standard since the early 1950s. Between 1975 and 1978 a virtual revolution in television journalism took place as the film technology was tossed into the back closet and replaced with *electronic news gathering,* or ENG: color minicameras and portable three-quarter inch machines.

The three-quarter inch videocassette still did not satisfy the need for a home video recorder; for one thing, it was still too expensive—well over $1,000 for the cheapest model. But it pointed the way toward the half-inch videocassette systems introduced by Sony and Panasonic (among others) in 1976. Moreover, the three-quarter inch system taught broadcasters that helical scan recording had a place in their studios.

Meanwhile, back in the laboratories, the television engineers were busily cooking up another generation of fancy new gadgets: the video disc machines.

Video Discs

Apparently the first attempt to design a video disc system was Baird's abortive effort in 1927. Baird seems to have had an uncanny knack for being far ahead of the available technology; not until the development of magnetic recording would any kind of video disc system be practical.

The first video disc system was developed by Ampex to serve a rather special need of the broadcasters. While transmitting live events, especially sports events, the broadcasters wanted a means of replaying a brief recorded sequence. This could be done with video tape, but stopping the tape, rewinding it to the correct point, and starting it again was time-consuming and awkward. If the information could be recorded on a disc, it would be much simpler to move the video head to the correct point on the disc for playback; in fact, it would be simple enough that it could be done automatically by pressing the right switches.

Ampex's engineers created the first "instant replay" machine specifically for television sports programs, and the "instant replay" has since become an indispensable part of every sports telecast. The disc recorder operates in fundamentally the same manner as any other magnetic recorder, the only difference being that the signal is recorded magnetically on a metal disc rather than on a strip of plastic tape. The head moves across the surface of the spinning disc in much the same way that the pickup arm of a phonograph moves across the spinning record. However, the signal on a phonograph consists of a spiral groove that starts near the outer edge and winds in toward the middle. In most video disc systems, the signal is recorded as a series of individual tracks in concentric rings; usually, each track consists of one video field. Thus, the same field can be repeated over and over, "freezing" the action by merely holding the pickup head over one track. Or the head can be moved slowly from track to track, creating a "slow-motion" effect. The head can even be moved backward, reversing the action.

All of these effects were quickly added to Ampex's broadcast disc system, which in turn added a new dimension to television sports coverage. For the first time, the fan watching the game at home could see something that no fan in the stadium could ever see: the slow-motion instant replay, isolating crucial action and revealing the most subtle details.

A video magnetic disc recorder. This kind of equipment is used in broadcasting, especially for sports (the "instant replay"). The recording disc is at the top; below it are the various electronic components (which are not necessarily arranged in a stack). At lower left is the controller. Every thirty seconds, whatever is already on the disc is erased and new images are recorded. (Photo courtesy Ampex Corp.)

The Ampex magnetic disc was never intended for anything other than the broadcasting industry, but the similarity between the disc and a phonograph record set some people's imaginations humming. Why not develop a home video disc system? Making copies of programs on discs probably would be cheaper than copying magnetic tape (which is a tedious, and therefore expensive, business). Cheaper copies would mean a larger potential market. If video discs could be reproduced for about the same cost as phonograph records (about 10 cents apiece, once the master has been produced), the market would be virtually inexhaustible!

Thus began one of the greatest technological horse races of the twentieth century, as different inventors, corporate engineering laboratories and even different divisions of the same company all sought to crack the home video market with either a tape cassette system or a disc system.

We will see how the race turned out in Chapter 12, when we continue our discussion of home video systems. Actually, as this is written, the race is not yet over—but a lot of horses have fallen by the wayside.

For now, let's get back to broadcast technology.

Videotape Editing

The instant-replay video disc serves its special purpose admirably just as it is; Ampex has added a few refinements since it was first introduced in the early 1960s, and a couple of other companies have brought out their own models, but there have been no significant changes in the basic concept.

Videotape technology, on the other hand, has never stopped evolving. One aspect of this evolution has been the growing sophistication of helical scan recording, coupled with the trend toward videocassettes. Another and equally important tendency has been the development of increasingly sophisticated tape editing systems.

Audio recording tape can be edited very simply, either by physically cutting sections of tape apart and splicing them together or by electronically switching signals from one tape to another. Since the signals are continuous, a carefully made edit can be almost undetectable. The same is not true, however, for video tape. It is nearly impossible to cut and splice sections of video tape without slicing across the signal track, which immediately disrupts the signal. (Also, video tape travels at such high speeds that a physical cut and splice is likely to knock the video head out of whack.) Therefore, the only way to edit video tape is by electronic switching.

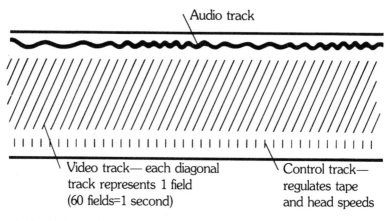

Audio track

Video track— each diagonal track represents 1 field (60 fields=1 second)

Control track— regulates tape and head speeds

Audio, Video and Control Tracks on Video Tape. This arrangement represents the EIAJ-1 format, adopted by the Electronic Industries Association of Japan for half-inch video tape in 1972. (The drawing is not to any particular scale; in reality, the video track is recorded at a much more nearly horizontal angle.)

It is possible to feed the signal from one or two videotape recorders into a switcher-SEG and use its electronics to switch from one tape signal to another, perhaps even inserting special visual effects such as dissolves and wipes. However, such an arrangement is rather clumsy; each recorder must be separately started, stopped, rewound, played forward and so forth, and all of the recorders plus the switcher must be hooked up to the system sync generators. Furthermore, most video switchers are not capable of routing the audio signal that is usually recorded along with the video signal on tape, so through-the-switcher editing requires a separate signal path for the audio.

A simpler and more direct system takes advantage of one of the unique characteristics of all videotape systems: the control track.

Every videotape format, from quad to videocassette, involves recording multiple signals on the tape. In addition to the composite video signal, recorded as a series of individual tracks across the tape (either transversely or helically), there is at least one audio track and sometimes two or three, plus the control track. The control track consists of nothing more than a series of precisely timed pulses, one pulse for each video track. These pulses are recorded along with the video and audio signals; when the tape is played back, the recorder detects the control track pulses and uses them to adjust the speed of the tape and of the video head(s) to correspond to the timing of the original recording.

The existence of the control track makes editing video tape a relatively simple and precise matter, since electronic switching can be timed to correspond to particular points in the control track.

Suppose, for example, you have recorded a number of individual scenes on two separate tapes. Now you want to transfer them to a new master tape, changing the sequence of scenes and eliminating the portions that didn't turn out well. Let's say that you have scenes one, two and four on tape A and scenes three and five on tape B; they are to be edited onto tape M.

How you proceed will depend in part on what kind of editing equipment you have. Some editing controllers are able to accept only one "source" signal; other controllers can be connected directly to two or more "source" recorders. We will assume that you have this more flexible type of controller, so you put tape A on recorder A, tape B on recorder B, and a blank reel of tape on recorder M—the master recorder. Recorders A and B are connected to the "source" inputs of the controller, and the output, of course, will be to recorder M.

The first step is to locate the point on tape A where scene 1 begins; the editing controller's buttons or switches will operate recorder A by remote control to do this. You then set recorder M to record. Next, you press a button marked "cue" or "pre-roll." This causes each recorder to back up a predetermined distance, usually equivalent to six seconds—the length of time it takes for most recorders to reach the optimum operating speed. Now all you have to do is hit the "edit" button on the controller. It will start both recorders playing forward; at the same time, it will detect the control track on tape A and lock recorder M to its pulses. At the point you have selected for scene one to begin, the controller electronically switches the signal from tape A to tape M. Whenever scene one is over, you just touch a button to stop both recorders.

A professional-quality video tape editing controller. This device "reads" the control track on the tape and translates it into playing time, in hours, minutes, seconds and frames; the playing time for each edit then can be selected, down to the exact frame when the edit is to be made, and "programmed" into the controller. Video editing has become so sophisticated that many Hollywood motion pictures are now "pre-edited" on a video tape made from the original footage, and the "pre-edited" tape is used to control the final editing of the film. (Photo courtesy Ampex Corp.)

Now to add scene 2. First, of course, you would play back tape M to make sure the first scene was properly recorded; this time, you would stop the tape at the precise point where you want scene one to end. Then you locate the point on tape A where you want scene two to begin. Next, pre-roll both recorders, and hit "edit." The recorders will roll forward; the controller will automatically lock recorder M to the control track pulses from tape A; at the point you have selected, the controller routes the signal from tape A to tape M and simultaneously puts recorder M into the "record" mode. When scene two is over, you stop the two machines.

Adding scene three (which, remember, is on tape B) is easy with a multiple-source editing controller; you just use another set of buttons to control the second source. If your controller does not have this capability, no matter; you would simply have to remove tape A from the source recorder and replace it with tape B. Of course, this will get pretty tedious if you have a large number of scenes recorded on two or more separate tapes, but tedium may cost less than a fancier controller. Another alternative would be to put each tape on a separate recorder, but switch the input plugs when you have to go from tape to tape; at least this avoids the time-consuming business of changing tapes.

Anyway, now you have, on tape M, scenes one, two and three. If you like, you can add scene five next, instead of scene four. But what if, having done that, you decide to substitute a brief portion of scene four in place of a portion of scene five? That is still no problem.

First, you find the point in scene five (which is now on tape M) at which you want to insert part of scene four. Next, you find the beginning of the section in scene four that you want to insert. However, before you pre-roll, you roll both recorders forward until you find the point in scene four where you want to switch back to scene five, and you indicate this point by pressing the "end edit" button. Now you go back to the starting point and pre-roll, hit the "edit" button, and the controller does the rest: it rolls both recorders forward to the edit point, switches recorder M to record, and sends along the signal from the source recorder. The only difference is that this time the source recorder is locked to the control track that has already been recorded on tape M. When the "end edit" point is reached, the controller switches off the signal from the source recorder and puts recorder M back into playback. You have now inserted part of scene four into scene five. The same effect could be produced by the assembly technique, which you used to put together scenes one, two, three, and five; you would simply add scene four at whatever point you like in scene five, then add the remainder of scene five to whatever point you like in scene four. The insert editing technique is used most often when there are scenes of equal length, shot by two cameras at the same event, and the editor simply wishes to switch back and forth between them at will, or when a brief section of new material must be added to an existing tape.

Notice, however, that the editing controller is only capable of switching from one video signal to another; it does not have the ability to add special visual effects comparable to those of a switcher—SEG. However, that is changing, and new *editing switcher-SEGS* are now coming onto the market that combine an editing controller with a switcher.

Manually operated editing systems were first available for Ampex quad recorders in the mid-sixties. A few half-inch helical scan recorders in the early 1970s had limited editing capabilities, but editing helical scan recordings really came into its own with the introduction of improved three-quarter inch cassette machines and separate editing controllers about 1975. Since then, there has been continual expansion in the equipment's capabilities.

Editing video tape, as I hope you can see from the forgoing description, is not especially difficult but it is time-consuming and it can become complicated. Fortunately for those who do that sort of thing for a living, there are automated editing systems that take much of the tedium out of the job.

Video editing with nonbroadcast-type three-quarter-inch videocassette equipment. The original material is put into the player at left; the recorder at right edits the scenes together, in sequence, starting and stopping according to the instructions given by the operator. (Photo by the author, courtesy Austin Community Television)

The automated systems rely on time coding. Some time-code systems use the control track that is already in the source tape, or a control track is recorded by itself on the master tape before any editing is done. Most time-code systems require a new track to be recorded on all of the tapes; this new track contains digitally-coded time signals. Once the tapes have been prepared, the editor previews the original footage and selects the edit points where each scene is to begin and end, compiling a list of the time-code references for each edit point. This list is then fed into a computer; the tapes are put on the appropriate recorders and the editing controller takes over. It simply follows the computer's directions, according to the time-code reference list prepared in advance. If everything works right and the instructions have been prepared properly, an hour's worth of tape can be edited automatically in minutes.

The time-code editing system was devised by a committee of the Society of Motion Picture and Television Engineers (SMPTE), but only a few manufacturers—those who cater to the broadcast market—have adopted the SMPTE system. Manual editing systems have improved so rapidly that the complexity and expense of the SMPTE system is hard to justify except in major production centers where hundreds or even thousands of hours of tape must be edited each week.

However, the SMPTE editing system has had one peculiar and very unexpected result. In recent years, the motion picture industry has begun to abandon conventional film editing techniques—techniques that can be traced back to the days of D. W. Griffith—in favor of videotape editing. Original motion picture footage is transferred to video tape, the video tape is edited electronically, and the master tape is then used to control the creation of a new optical master film. Hours of tedious cutting, splicing and marking raw film are eliminated—not to mention the considerable expense of producing crude "work prints" to be cut up, spliced and marked upon.

And that brings us full circle, in a sense, from those early days when the only way to preserve the video image was to put it on film. Now, producing a film often involves transferring it first to video tape.

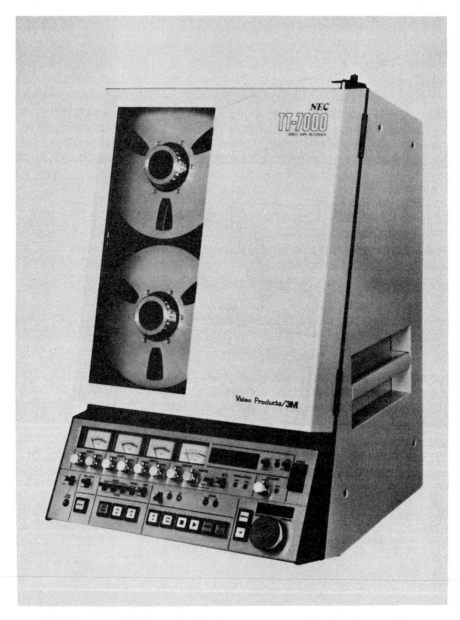

The "new breed" of one-inch helical scan recorders offer broadcast quality in a compact, relatively inexpensive package. This recorder is made by Nippon Electric Co. (NEC) and sold in the U.S. by 3M. (Photo courtesy of 3M Co.)

New Video Recording Technology

Aside from the continuing effort to create a home video recorder of one sort or another, there are several interesting developments currently underway in video recording technology.

One of them, as mentioned in Chapter 1, is the radical shift from the conventional video signal to some kind of digital encoding. Ampex demonstrated a prototype digital video recorder at the 1979 SMPTE convention, but does not expect to have a production model until the mid-80s at the earliest.

A more current trend is the revival of interest in one-inch helical scan recorders. Half a decade ago, one-inch systems seemed to be dead, but they have risen from the grave. Ampex, Bosch Fernseh (one of Europe's major suppliers of broadcast equipment), IVC (which has done its own return-from-the–grave act), Philips and Sony, among others, all have brought out new one-inch recorders in the past two or three years. These are not just refurbished models from the early 70s, either; they employ entirely new recording formats. Unfortunately, there are in fact *two* new formats (plus the old one), and tapes made in one format cannot be played on machines that require a different format —the old interchangeability problem again! Ampex, Philips and Sony all seem to be committed to the eventual replacement of quad with the new one-inch systems, all of which cost far less than quad equipment but provide comparable results.

The average television viewer probably is not very concerned with what kind of videotape equipment his local TV station uses. However, that choice does influence the kinds of programs a broadcaster can offer; the three-quarter inch videocassette and the minicamera, for example, opened the era of electronic news gathering which has had substantial effects on local news coverage. The new one-inch formats appear to offer most of the portability of three-quarter inch equipment, only slightly higher cost, but considerably better quality. Broadcasters might be tempted to put this new equipment to new uses.

But, then, local broadcasters are not known to be a very adventurous lot. In the next three chapters, we will see why.

Part
II

Broadcast Television

Chapter
4

The Local TV Station

Governments, like individuals, are often prone to wishful thinking.

Between 1920, when the first commercial radio station went on the air in Pittsburgh, and 1934, when Congress finally passed the Federal Communications Act to provide for permanent regulation of broadcasting (and other modes of communication), there were two major issues in the running debate over commercial radio: first, should advertising be permitted over "the public's airwaves"; second, should there be a single, national commercial radio system, or should commercial radio be primarily a local service?

Herbert Hoover, who was Secretary of Commerce when KDKA went on the air in 1920 and was President during the period 1928-1932 when the debate over commercial broadcasting was running hottest, was an implacable foe of commercialization. As Commerce secretary, he had very limited authority to regulate all forms of radio communication; among other things, he issued the licenses that were required under the Wireless Ship Act of 1912.

In 1923 AT&T proposed what was called "toll broadcasting": anyone could have the use of AT&T's transmitters to communicate any sort of message for a reasonable fee, in much the same way that people use the telephone system. Hoover adamantly opposed the "toll broadcasting" scheme because he was convinced that it would be used solely by commercial interests to advertise their wares, something he vigorously opposed. He insisted that broadcasters could not operate as "common carriers," offering time on their stations to anyone willing to pay for it the way telephone and telegraph companies did. Hoover believed that a commercial radio license, since it gave the operator access to a "natural resource" (the electromagnetic spectrum), conferred an obligation on the operator to serve the public's interests. Acting as a common carrier, in Hoover's opinion, would amount to abandoning this obligation.

Hoover's legal powers as regulator of the airwaves were undermined by a series of court decisions throughout the 1920s, but his political power and personal stature lent his opinions a good deal of weight. AT&T finally abandoned the "toll broadcasting" idea, but only with the understanding that a broadcasting station did have the right to accept fees from "sponsors" of individual programs.

The problem, of course, was that someone had to pay for the production and transmission of the programs. That someone would have to be either the operator of the station or the listeners, perhaps through subscriptions (which David Sarnoff of RCA favored) or, as in Britain, through a tax on receivers (which Martin Rice of General Electric favored). It was soon apparent to all sides that neither option would be practical. Radio station licensees could not continue indefinitely to pay for their own operations as a goodwill gesture or merely to induce people to buy receivers (as Westinghouse had done in 1920). Relying on public subscriptions or taxes would simply mean the perpetual impoverishment of radio; probably no more than one station in each community could be supported by public subscription, and any sort of taxation scheme raised the specter of governmental involvement in broadcasting—something the American public of the 1920s would not countenance.

The only other alternative seemed to be commercial sponsorship of radio programs. The objection was primarily on grounds of taste: who would want to listen to advertisements on the radio? (Bear in mind that advertising in the 1920s was a good deal less subtle and sophisticated than it is today, and there were very few laws or regulations to inhibit blatantly deceptive and objectionable ads.) On the other hand, America in the 1920s believed in free enterprise and unrestrained commerce with an almost religious fervor. Commercial sponsorship of radio, in the opinion of many, would be merely an extension of the principles of competition and entrepreneurship that had made the nation fabulously wealthy.

It would be interesting, but certainly fruitless, to speculate on the outcome of this debate if it had occurred a decade later, during the depths of the Depression. During the late 1920s and early 1930s, the outcome was never really in doubt: the advocates of commercial sponsorship gradually took over broadcasting. By the time Congress addressed the issue squarely in 1933, there was nothing left to debate; broadcasting was a commercial advertising medium, and the omelet could not be turned back into an egg.

That still left the question of localism versus a national radio system. The advocates of a national system were, as might be expected, AT&T (which by the late 1920s no longer owned broadcasting stations but did supply the indispensable telephone lines that connected stations into networks), RCA and other big business interests. The advocates of localism were mostly local politicians who did not want their local radio stations to be owned by distant, faceless—and unmanipulatable—corporations. The great majority of the 750 or so radio stations in operation in the late 1920s were, in fact, owned by local entrepreneurs and small companies, and of course they embraced localism.

The Federal Radio Act of 1927 did nothing to resolve the issue, since it merely gave the secretary of commerce more or less the same limited regulatory powers that Hoover had tried to exercise until they were stripped away by the courts.

The 1934 Communications Act also failed to address the question directly. President Roosevelt wanted a law to replace the weak 1927 Act (which had to be renewed each year or it would self-destruct), and he was convinced that no law would ever be passed if Congress had to settle so many controversial issues first. Instead, he proposed to leave the controversies up to a Federal Communications Commission that would be established under the new law. And that, in essence, is what the Congress did. The law authorized the FCC to regulate radio stations as it saw fit, the only standard being "the public interest, convenience and necessity."

The FCC approached the question of localism in a spirit of compromise. There were already a number of "clear-channel stations," metropolitan radio stations that had been given the exclusive, 24-hour-a-day use of their frequencies. The FCC simply decided to allow those stations to continue to operate as a kind of quasi-national service. Meanwhile, the remaining channels available in the AM radio band were divided into three classes: full-time, high-power stations that could serve a relatively large geographic area; full-time, medium-power stations that would serve only a single metropolitan area; and daytime-only, low-power stations that would serve a single, small community. In establishing these classes, the FCC made it clear that it expected every radio station to serve primarily the community in which it was licensed. In short, the commission endorsed and adopted, with minor reservations, the concept of localism.

Later, when the FCC began licensing television stations, this concept prevailed; the commission's explicit goal was to provide for the maximum possible number of stations so that there could be at least one station in every community of sufficient size. In 1952 after the four-year "freeze" on television licenses, the FCC issued a table of channel assignments that provided for a little more than 2,000 stations in about 1,300 cities. However, more than two-thirds of these channel assignments are for UHF channels and no one has ever applied for the right to use most of them. Consequently, in 1976 the commission took back channels 70-83 and reassigned the frequencies to other uses.

(Later in this chapter, we will discuss the licensing process and the significance of channel assignments; for now, the point is that no one can apply for a license to operate a television station—or radio station, either—in a given community unless the FCC has previously assigned a channel to that community.)

A local television station. The tower on the roof holds three microwave antennas: one to receive the network signal from the telephone company, one to send signals from the studio to the transmitter (on a mountaintop several miles away) and one to receive signals from a mobile production unit. (Photo by the author, courtesy KVUE-TV)

Localism is much more than just a matter of where the stations are located, however. The heart of the issue is that, under the philosophy that has guided the FCC for more than 45 years and is reflected in countless regulations and policy decisions, every broadcasting station is obligated to give first consideration to the needs and interests of the community that station is licensed to serve.

Ideally, the local broadcaster is supposed to be a small business operator, an entrepreneur whose commercial interest is inextricably tied to the interests of the community, and who therefore must be acutely sensitive to local needs and interests.

There is not a single word in the Federal Communications Act concerning broadcast networks, and therefore the FCC has no power to regulate the networks—except by the indirect and clumsy method of regulating the relationship of individual broadcast stations to a network. At times, this amounts to a game of regulatory "let's pretend" in which rules are drafted as if the networks did not even exist.

The philosophy of localism also is reflected in the FCC's rules concerning media concentration. This is an issue that, in itself, goes well beyond the question of localism. But the spirit of localism is evident in the rule that no one person or entity may own more than seven television stations, not more than five of which may be VHF. Again, this rule is supposed to discourage the formation of a monopoly over broadcasting, thus ensuring that the station owners will be responsive to their audiences.

Actually, the great majority of commercial television stations are owned by large corporations; nearly all of the stations in the 100 largest "markets" are members of multistation "groups." The three major networks themselves own five stations apiece, and, not surprisingly, all 15 of those stations are in the 10 largest television markets. Most of the other stations in the largest markets are licensed to groups whose interests also include radio stations, cable television systems, newspapers, magazines, book publishers and miscellaneous other communications media. Several of the major television groups produce programs for *syndication* (the sale or rental of programs to individual stations).

Furthermore, the overwhelming majority of commercial television stations are affiliated with one of the three major networks. Of roughly 725 commercial TV stations, only about 100 are "independent"—that is, not affiliated with a major network. Actually, some of these independent stations are affiliated with one or another of the minor networks, such as the Christian Broadcasting Network (CBN) or the Spanish International Network (SIN—and that does not mean, in Spanish, what you think it means!), that have sprung up since the advent of satellite transmission; but we will discuss that subject in Chapter 9.

Nearly all "local" broadcasters rely on a national network to provide anywhere from 60 to 90 percent of their programs. Even when the network is not feeding new programs down the telephone lines, the local station most often is running *old* network shows that have been bought from syndicators.

How can the FCC ignore this flagrant abandonment of the broadcasters' responsibility to their communities? Well, in the first place, the broadcasters claim that their audiences really prefer to see the slick, well-produced network shows. Secondly, the FCC recognizes that the economics of broadcasting have made networks inevitable and essential. Even the unaffiliated, independent stations rely heavily on syndicated "off-network" shows (that is, programs that originally appeared on the networks) for the bulk of their schedule. Since the early 1950s, localism in television has been little more than a fond theory.

It is hard to fault the FCC. Lord knows, it has done just about all it could, short of prohibiting network affiliation altogether, to remind broadcasters of their local obligations. For example, the FCC requires every station to *ascertain* its community's "communications needs" each year. Since 1970, the commission also has required the networks to give up broadcasting for at least half an hour out of each evening's prime time—the hours when television attracts the largest (and thus most lucrative) audiences.

The concept behind ascertainment is fairly simple. Since each broadcaster is expected to serve local needs, it stands to reason that the broadcaster should know what those needs are. In 1960, the FCC formally adopted a policy that every broadcast licensee would be expected to determine the needs of the community each year, and would be required to develop an explicit plan for serving those needs. Failure to do so would jeopardize the broadcaster's chances of having the station's license renewed, which must be done every three years.

For 10 years, broadcasters agonized over how to meet the ascertainment requirement with the least possible effort and with the least possible effect on their actual programming practices. These were years of great doubt and uncertainty. Finally in 1969, the FCC issued a document cleverly called *A Primer on Ascertainment of Community Needs*. While the primer did not constitute official rules, it did serve as a set of guidelines that indicated what the FCC considered to be the minimum acceptable ascertainment procedure. Two years later, the primer was amended and clarified (which means it was made less troublesome to the broadcasters); otherwise, it is still in effect today.

The broadcaster may use any of several strategies to "ascertain community needs." A formal survey may be taken of a random sample of people who live in the community, for example. That, of course, could get expensive.

Most broadcasters settle for a "survey" of "community leaders." The community leaders may be local politicos, business kingpins, socially prominent individuals, or the heads of influential organizations such as major churches, colleges or charitable agencies. In any case, each community leader is asked to define the "community needs" that might be served or alleviated by the television station. The broadcaster then devises a plan to serve those needs during the coming year. Usually the plan amounts to a promise to address each "need" in the station's ordinary news programs. Those stations that have a regular public affairs program (such as a Saturday afternoon interview show) will make it a central feature of their plan. Another step in the ascertainment procedure is an evaluation of the station's fulfillment of the previous year's plan —in other words, a list of the programs that have been shown (or minutes of news time) on the subjects that were identified as "community needs" last year.

This necessarily brief account of ascertainment may seem positively ridiculous. Within reason, the station is free to ask whomever it likes to identify community needs and it can translate those needs into a plan that in no way alters what the station probably would have done anyway. But to the owners of those precious broadcasting licenses, the ascertainment process is a solemn ritual. Of course, some take it more seriously than others, and the more conscientious broadcasters make a sincere effort to use the ascertainment process in a meaningful way. However, when all is said and done, ascertainment is probably good for the soul, harmless at worst, but it almost certainly does not change anyone's behavior in the real world.

The other direct effort of the FCC to make localism manifest is the prime-time access rule. It is an unmitigated fiasco.

The idea behind the prime-time access rule is that local stations are unable to present timely, locally meaningful programs at the most desirable hours— that is, during prime time—if the networks greedily fill those hours with entertainment shows. But if the networks are forced to give up part of prime time, the local stations will be able to schedule documentaries, interviews, cultural events and other worthy offerings at an hour when they can hope to attract an audience large enough to pay the bills.

Donald H. McGannon is most often credited with thinking up the prime-time access rule. McGannon has been the head of Westinghouse Broadcasting Company, better known as "Group W," since 1955; before that, he was an executive of the defunct DuMont Network. Group W consists of five VHF stations in Pittsburgh (the direct descendant of that first radio station started in 1920), Philadelphia, Boston, Baltimore and San Francisco—all of which are very large television markets. Under McGannon's guidance, Group W has become something of a maverick in the TV industry. For instance, even though all five stations are network affiliates, Group W insists on producing many of its own programs. After the programs have played on the group's stations, they are syndicated to other stations around the country. Some of those programs are *The John Davidson Show, The Merv Griffin Show,* the *David Frost Show,* and, at one time, the *Steve Allen Show.* They all have made a great deal of money for Group W.

Perhaps it occurred to McGannon that, if every station had an hour each evening that had to be filled, some stations might fill that hour with programs produced by Group W. But that is not exactly what he suggested to the FCC. He and the other advocates of the prime-time access rule insisted that it would mean the flowering of creativity throughout the land.

Most of all, it would mean that the stations would have no excuse for burying their public service programs in the weekend afternoon ghettoes. The FCC liked that idea.

However, the FCC was not quite prepared to put an entire hour into the prime-time access rule, so it compromised: half an hour. The networks previously had scheduled everything from 7:30 to 11 p.m. (Eastern time) on weekdays. Under the rule adopted in 1970, they could schedule only three hours during that period—any three hours. There were also a few exceptions: news, children's programs, cultural events and a few other kinds of programs would not count if they were scheduled in the access period. Otherwise, the access period was to be left to the local stations.

(Strictly speaking, of course, the prime-time access rule does not tell the networks what they can or cannot do; it merely tells the local stations when they can and cannot run network programs.)

Ten years after the prime-time access rule was adopted, on nearly every commercial TV station in the land, the so-called access period is filled with off-network reruns (*I Dream of Jeanie, My Three Sons,* and *Adam-12* are among the more popular offerings), game shows (*The Dating Game* is one of the biggies), and such locally significant fare as *Hee-Haw.* A very few stations, mostly in the major metropolitan areas—and including some of the Group W stations—have simply expanded their local news programs, which previously had filled the half hour preceding the "access period."

When McGannon first proposed the access rule, his colleagues in broadcasting were outraged. When the FCC adopted the rule, prophesies of doom were heard across the land. Now, most station owners would not give up the access rule if their marriages depended on it. Why? Because it has turned out to be a bonanza. The stations can make considerably more money by running cheap off-network reruns and sleazy game shows, charging local advertisers for "prime-time" exposure, than they could ever get in station compensation from the networks. As for the syndicators—well, you can imagine.

Of course, if very much in the way of significant programming that addresses community needs has appeared in the access period, it must have been either by accident or out of a desire to beef up the stations' public service record at license renewal time.

I do not mean to seem cynical about the access rule, or about ascertainment, or about the concept of localism. There are a lot of good, earnest, talented people in local television stations. Many of them sincerely wish they could produce more hard-hitting documentaries, stimulating cultural programs and the like. The cards are stacked against them.

By and large, local TV stations do a pretty good job of covering local news events, for the simple reason that it is profitable to do so: local news shows, if handled properly, usually make money. Local documentaries, cultural programs, public service programs and so forth generally do not make money. Television stations make money by selling time to advertisers, who pay according to the number of people who are presumably watching. When a minute of commercial time has elapsed, the station can never recover it and sell it again; it must make as much as possible the first time. It really is as simple as that.

Economics is not the only threat to the concept of localism; there are other dangers that could undermine the entire system of locally operated (if not locally owned) broadcasting stations. One such threat is cable television, and the other is direct satellite-to-home broadcasting.

Broadcasters and the networks have been whining and complaining about the threat of cable since the early 1960s, and in a few instances have mounted hugely expensive campaigns to outlaw cable altogether. Many of their complaints are utterly groundless—but not all. We will try to sort them out in Chapter 8, when we discuss the relationships between cable and the rest of the television industry.

Direct satellite-to-home broadcasting is an even more potent threat to local stations because they would have no place at all in such a scheme. Cable TV systems at least carry the local stations' signals to their subscribers. With satellite-to-home transmission, anyone who leases a satellite channel automatically gains direct access to the home audience, and the local station becomes superfluous. Whether that is good or bad depends on how you regard the value of localism.

Clearly, the philosophy of localism has not been implemented by the present television system to the extent envisioned by the forefathers of broadcasting. Again, the reasons are primarily economic, as we can see by examining more closely the economics of local broadcasting.

How Local TV Stations Make Money

Lord Thompson, one of the founders of British commercial television, once observed, "A television license is a license to print money." While that may be true, it does take a certain amount of cranking to get the presses rolling, and occasionally they break down altogether.

Suppose you wanted to start a TV station in your town. What would you have to do, and what would it cost?

First and foremost, of course, you would have to get a license from the FCC. Let us set that topic aside for the moment and assume that you have successfully run that gauntlet and have a license in hand.

A local television station's studio. A broadcaster may have a quarter of a million dollars' worth of equipment—most of which is likely to be obsolete in five to seven years. The real pity is that this costly, sophisticated equipment is used for little more than two hours of programming each day (plus the production of local commercials). (Photo by the author, courtesy KVUE-TV)

Next, you will have to build a transmitter and transmitting antenna. They will need to be on the highest ground in the area, since mountains and tall buildings absorb and reflect television signals. The higher you can put your antenna, the farther your signal will reach (all else being equal). Depending on where you put the transmitter, whether your license is for a VHF or UHF channel, and how powerful your transmitter is to be, you might spend anywhere from half a million to two million dollars on these items.

You will have to construct a building to house your studio and offices, unless you are lucky enough to find an empty building that can be remodeled into a decent studio. Figure on another half-million to one million dollars for the building, more if you are in one of the major metropolitan areas where land and construction costs are high.

You will need offices for at least 25 people for a small station; assume that office furniture and equipment will cost, on average, around $500 per person. That's $12,500.

The control room of a local television station. (Photo by the author, courtesy KVUE-TV)

Studio and control room equipment will add another $600,000 to one million dollars. Put in another $50,000 for equipment for the news department.

The total, so far, comes to almost two million and possibly as much as four and a half million dollars. This is, very roughly estimated, the capital investment required to start a TV station. It can be done for somewhat less, or considerably more can be spent.

Now you are ready to begin operating, which means you will begin to incur operating costs. These costs can be divided into three main categories: personnel, overhead and programs.

The number of personnel you have is a critical factor, of course. You can get by with as few as 25 people, but 50 would be more reasonable for all but the tiniest operations. Salaries in local television are not very high, so figure on an average of $12,000 annually per employee; with 50 people, that comes to $600,000 a year. Add another 15 percent, or $90,000, for employer taxes and fringe benefits.

Overhead for a TV station consists mostly of utility costs—especially electricity and telephone. These two items can easily run about $20,000 a month, or $240,000 annually. Other overhead expenses—office supplies, travel, advertising, building and equipment maintenance, and so forth—should run no more than $5,000 a month, or $60,000 a year.

That leaves programs. Programs produced by the station are not terribly expensive if the station's own staff is used, if the production takes place entirely in the studio, and if no elaborate sets, costumes and such are needed. The direct costs of producing a half-hour news show, for example, may be around $500 (since the on-camera and off-camera personnel are salaried employees and the same set is used continuously for several years). A more elaborate program, such as a high school quiz show, might run around $1,000 per half hour.

Syndicated movies, off-network reruns, game shows and the like cost anywhere from $50 to $50,000 per program. The cheapest programs are old movies, usually purchased in "packages" of 50 to 100 titles, each of which can be shown at least twice during a two-year period. The price for an off-network rerun depends on two factors: how popular the show is in other markets, and how big the station's own market is. The early episodes of *Laverne and Shirley* were sold recently to a Los Angeles station for $61,500 per program. However, very few local stations will pay anything close to that amount for routine syndicated programs.

Some syndicated shows cost the local station nothing; they are "bartered" by the show's producers. These deals, which were once much more common than they are now, involve programs that already have a national sponsor whose commercials are inserted by the producer. Additional commercial "breaks" in each program (from one to three per half-hour show) are left vacant for the local station to fill with local advertising.

Network programs are not only free, but the station actually gets paid to run them. On the average, the network supplies about 65 percent of an affiliate's programming. In a typical 20-hour broadcast day (from 6 a.m. until 2 a.m. the following day), that means the station must fill about seven hours. Typically, one and a half to two hours are taken up by local news programs; the rest is filled with syndicated programs—off-network reruns, game shows, talk shows (Merv, Mike, Phil and Dinah), and the like. On the weekends, much more time is left for the local stations to fill; this time is usually taken up with old movies. As a rough estimate, a local station in a medium-sized market might have to come up with about 60 hours of programs per week.

Using the cost estimates I gave earlier, we can take $750 per half-hour program, or $1,500 per hour, as a very rough guide to the program costs for a station in a medium-sized market. This means that programming costs $90,000 per week, or $4,680,000 a year. And that's for all those "cheap" shows we have been talking about!

Adding in personnel and overhead costs, we come up with total operating costs of about $5.7 million. Paying off the capital investment goes on top of that, and then taxes. A station operating budget of $7 to $10 million a year would not be at all unreasonable.

How does a local TV station earn all that money back, plus a profit? Essentially from two sources: the sale of commercial time, and the payments a station receives from the network.

A local station has between 125 and 150 commercial minutes each day that it can sell to local businesses and to national advertisers who buy "spots" in the particular markets that interest them. That comes to roughly 900 minutes per week, or almost 47,000 minutes per year. Television advertisers expect to pay anywhere from three to seven dollars per half-minute commercial for every thousand viewers. At five dollars per thousand viewers, a station must *average* 25,000 viewers in order to make money. (Five dollars times 25,000 is $125 per half-minute spot, multiplied by 94,000 spots a year is $11,750,000. Actually, of course, few stations sell all of the commercial time they have available; most stations are doing well if they sell 80 percent of their time, which would bring the revenue down to $9.4 million—still enough for a healthy profit if one watches the budget.)

The other major revenue source is the network's station compensation. Again, there are many variables that affect the amount a network pays a given station to carry the network's programs: the station's market size and its general competitiveness are just two such factors. Overall, the station compensation for a typical medium-sized station might run about $150 per hour. If the network supplies 80 hours of programming per week, that is $12,000 weekly or $624,000 a year. Nothing to sneeze at, but it seems paltry compared to the station's direct earnings from advertising. However, bear in mind that those network programs attract viewers, and viewers attract the advertisers who pay for the locally sold spots between the network shows.

To summarize: what Lord Thompson said about a television license is true, provided the licensee works hard enough to keep the presses rolling—and provided the licensee has a network affiliation, which nearly guarantees a substantial audience during the most profitable prime-time hours and for much of every television day. Independent stations do not get station compensation, nor do they get the audiences that a network attracts. But they do get to sell every available commercial minute locally, and if they can keep their program costs low enough (mainly by running a lot of cheap syndicated shows and old movies), they, too, can make a whole lot of money.

Just to round out our discussion of broadcasting economics, let us consider the station's asset value. Here we will not be able to come up with even very rough estimates since the number of factors that can influence asset value and the possible range of values are too great.

Obviously, any well-run, profitable business is worth a good deal of money. If you should decide to sell your station, you would first consider the value of your physical facilities: the studio, equipment, transmitter and such. These things depreciate very quickly, however, because of the rapidly changing technology of television; anything more than ten years old is almost worthless. Still, even an empty building is worth something.

Next, you would include the value of any program rights you might have. When a station buys a movie package or a syndicated series, it is actually buying the right to show the programs within a given period of time. That right has a market value in itself. You might also own some programs that your own station has produced and that are still usable, although that would be fairly rare.

Third, you would add to your "asking price" the intangible value of your station as an on-going business. You probably would have contracts with advertisers, specifying that an advertiser plans to run a given number of commercials during a certain period of time. Your business's "good will" and reputation in the community also would be worth something.

All of these assets together are mere frosting on the cake, though. The real value of your station depends more than anything on your network affiliation and your license.

As a rule of thumb, a network affiliation doubles the value of any television license.

How much is a license worth? Well, in 1976, a New York City license was transferred for $100 million. And that was a *nonnetwork* station. (The networks themselves each own a station in New York, and they are very unlikely to sell those stations, so we may never know how much a network-affiliated station in that market is really worth.) A network-affiliated station in a medium-sized market could probably sell for anywhere from 25 to 50 million dollars.

Of course, strictly speaking, you cannot sell your license. According to the Federal Communications Act of 1934, you have no ownership interest in or right to your license, and you cannot sell what you do not own (unless you like to have numbers stenciled across your shirt). However, you can be paid to transfer your license to another person, as long as the FCC approves the transfer—which it almost always does.

Sometimes the FCC seems more concerned with protecting the asset value of a license than with serving the public interest, convenience and necessity.

The Broadcast License

A broadcasting license, according to the Communications Act of 1934, merely confers a privilege to use a specified portion of the electromagnetic spectrum under the terms and conditions imposed by the Federal Communications Commission. No licensee has any ownership right or interest in the license or in the licensed part of the spectrum. In fact, since the spectrum is a "natural resource" that belongs to the public, the licensee is expected to act as a public trustee.

All of which sounds fine, but what does it really mean? Getting a television license is not easy; once the license has been obtained, the licensee must make a substantial investment in the facilities to broadcast. A television license can produce large profits if the licensee is reasonably diligent. Under our free-enterprise system, people who make substantial investments and work diligently are supposedly entitled to large profits. Besides, the theory that guides the FCC in its decisions holds that large profits are not only a fair reward, they are necessary in order to induce the licensee to serve the public interest. It therefore follows that the FCC encourages licensees to serve the public interest by helping to protect their large profits. Taking away licenses, or even just threatening to do so, would discourage licensees from making substantial investments and working diligently, it would deprive them of their large profits, and, ergo, it would not serve the public interest.

The FCC rarely takes away licenses or even threatens to do so.

It is not even possible to apply for a television license unless a channel has already been assigned to the community in which you wish to operate. The channel assignments were made in the 1950s; they have been amended from time to time since then, but by far the most important change is the elimination of all UHF assignments for channels 70 through 83, which took place in 1976.

If there is a channel assigned to your city (and you can find out simply by asking the Broadcast Bureau of the FCC in Washington), and if no one else is already using it, you are free to apply anytime you like. Anyone can apply for a license; the minimum requirements are that you be a U.S. citizen over 18 years of age. A corporation or partnership may apply if its officers or principal partners meet the same qualifications. Again, the Broadcast Bureau will be happy to supply forms and guidelines for the application.

A television broadcast station license. This unimpressive piece of paper may be worth millions of dollars and may be the subject of fierce battles before the Federal Communications Commission or the courts. (Photo by the author, courtesy KVUE-TV)

Be prepared for a bit of work. A typical application may be several hundred pages. The applicant must describe in detail exactly what equipment will be used to produce and transmit the carrier signal and programs, who will be hired to operate the station, and what services (that is, programs) will be provided to the public. The applicant's financial status, experience in broadcasting and moral character all must be disclosed. The application must explain why the station is needed in the community, and there must be environmental impact statements showing how the transmitter, antenna and other facilities will affect the ecology. Engineers must prepare detailed specifications and maps showing exactly what geographic area will be covered by the station's signal and what other radio signals might be affected by the proposed station.

If you are the only applicant for a given channel at the time, your application will be considered on its own merits. However, if someone else applies for the same channel before your application is approved, you will have to show why you are better qualified to serve the community than the other applicant. Also, anyone may challenge your application and attempt to persuade the FCC that you should not be granted a license, for whatever reason.

If you survive all of these dangers, you still would not have a full license; you will be granted a *construction permit*. This allows you to build your transmitter and other facilities, and you must do so within a specified time or your application will be automatically denied (unless there are extenuating circumstances such as a siege of bad weather).

Once the station is built and ready to operate, it must be thoroughly inspected by FCC engineers; if it passes inspection, unless there has been a challenge or a competing application in the meantime, ordinarily you will be granted an operating license.

The standard license term is three years. At one time, all television licenses throughout the nation expired at the same time; this produced a very hectic period for the FCC, since all renewal applications had to be considered simultaneously. Now, the workload has been spread out by setting all of the licenses in each state to expire simultaneously, and no more than two states have the same expiration date.

Your initial license term, however, is almost certain to be less than three years, unless you happen to be granted a license during your state's expiration month. If the initial term is less than a year and a half, you had better get started on your renewal application right away; it takes at least that long to prepare the application, file it and have it considered.

Meanwhile, you must go through the ascertainment process every year, and you must file annual financial and operating reports with the FCC. You must keep a log of everything you transmit, from sign-on to sign-off, and either transcripts or tapes of every program you actually produce. Your employment contracts, contracts with advertisers and program suppliers, day-by-day schedules, published advertising rates and records of any maintenance you perform on your transmitting equipment all are subject to FCC inspection at any time.

Anyone who feels you are operating improperly or violating any of the hundreds of FCC rules and regulations may file a complaint at any time. If the commission staff feels that the complaint might have merit, you must defend yourself. This usually means hiring a Washington broadcast lawyer who will prepare an answer to the complaint and file it for you, but you can expect to spend several days in Washington testifying before an FCC hearing. If the FCC finds that the complaint is justified, you might be issued a "cease and desist" order, or assessed a fine, or your license might be suspended or revoked. Even complaints that, in the FCC's opinion, have no real merit are kept in the records of your station and may be brought up at renewal time.

When the time comes to renew your license, you must inform your viewers that they have the right to challenge your renewal. The renewal application is at least as bulky and as complicated as the original application. Once again, anyone may file a competing application, asking that the license be taken away from you and given to them, and anyone may file a challenge asking that renewal be denied. But relax; before these petitions are considered, the FCC must find that you have failed to operate in the public interest. Otherwise, the competing applicants and challengers are given short shrift.

However, you must still satisfy the commission that you have operated in the public interest and that you will continue to do so. The catch is that "operating in the public interest" has no precise definition, and the standards of acceptable performance are subject to change at any time.

In spite of everything, the FCC is traditionally reluctant to take a license away from a TV station. During 1976 the commission considered 318 applications for license renewals for TV stations; 314, or 98.7 percent, were granted. Of the other four, one was denied outright, two were given short-term renewals (in essence, probation), and one was still being considered at the end of the fiscal year. Between 1972 and 1976, there were 12 TV license renewals denied out of 1,685 renewal applications; that is about 0.7 percent denied.

Critics of the FCC and of television in general often point to these statistics as proof that the FCC is more interested in protecting the industry than in serving the public. However, that is not necessarily true. The barriers to entering the TV business are so high, and the regulations for licensees are so formidable, that very few incompetent or irresponsible operators can hold licenses in the first place. If the system works properly, there should not be many instances when a renewal would have to be denied.

Broadcasters themselves, as might be expected, feel that the barriers to entry are entirely too high and the regulations on licensees are altogether too formidable. They complain that the relatively short license period, the burdensome requirements for renewal applications and the constant threat of complaints and challenges make their business riskier than it ought to be. It is not comfortable to know that your $10-million-a-year business could be wiped out at any time. Rep. Lionel Van Deerlin of California, chairman of the House Subcommittee on Communications, has introduced a series of proposed replacements for the old Communications Act of 1934. Each time Van Deerlin has proposed that television licenses should be perpetual—no renewal required. There still could be challenges and complaints, but they would be subject to stiff requirements and limitations. Only the most flagrant cases of abuse could result in the revocation of a broadcast license. Van Deerlin's bills have never gotten out of his subcommittee (because of other controversial provisions), but it is entirely possible that Congress will pass a new Communications Act sometime during the 1980s that will relieve broadcasters of the uncertainties and costs of frequent license renewals.

A more difficult issue is the question of whether licensees should be permitted to sell their license. If a license confers no ownership rights, it is hard to see how the FCC can justify permitting the license to be sold, and no one denies that approving a transfer does just that.

Certainly, a station owner has the right to sell his business, including the physical facilities, contracts, good will and interests in programs. However, if a licensee chooses to get out of the business, for whatever reason, perhaps the FCC should require that the license be abandoned. Anyone could then apply for the license, just as if it had never been issued, and competing applications would be judged according to their comparative merits. The winning applicant could then offer to buy the current licensee's business, but would not be obligated to do so. In any case, the license itself would have no monetary value as a business asset.

Such a proposal arouses sheer horror within the industry. Multistation owners could not trade their stations around as if they were baseball cards. Small operators could not become big operators by buying up the licenses of other small operators. Station owners could not let their physical facilities deteriorate and then retire and live off the proceeds of selling their license.

Whether license transfers will be permitted under the new communications law—if and when Congress passes such a law—remains to be seen. So far, none of the Van Deerlin bills have significantly changed the present practice. However, it is one of the many issues that must be resolved before a new law will be enacted.

The Local TV Station of the Future

Whatever changes may take place in the communications law and the regulation of broadcasting probably will not have as much direct, visible impact on the local station as the economic and technological changes that are already underway.

As television technology continues to become more sophisticated and less expensive, local program production will become more creative. Already, many stations are using the new portable videotape recorders and minicameras not only for electronic news gathering, but for the production of news, documentary, public affairs and even entertainment programs outside of the studio. The whole community becomes an accessible location for local productions. Some stations have invested in portable microwave transmitters that permit live broadcasting from "remote" locations (that is, anywhere outside the studio). Fancier switcher-SEGs, character generators and other studio production equipment, much of which costs less than the conventional gear of a decade ago, can give local productions nearly the same glossy, professional appearance of network productions, without inflating the cost.

Local stations will have to find some way to keep their audiences' interest, and more local production may be the only solution. Cable systems with thirty or more channels, mostly filled with movies, sports and the same kind of syndicated fare available from the local broadcaster, will give the local station a kind of intense competition that has never been faced before. Pushing the network button will no longer solve all of the local broadcaster's problems. A steady diet of off-network reruns will look pretty puny next to the high-quality offerings of the satellite-based "instant networks"—not to mention the scarifying prospect of direct satellite-to-home transmission.

One way for the local station to compete would be to offer what these other sources cannot—locally produced programs aimed at specific segments of the community. However, that sort of thing can be expensive, and traditionally it has not attracted large enough audiences to appeal to advertisers. At the same time, advertisers will enjoy the option of spending their money on the new media instead of the friendly local TV station.

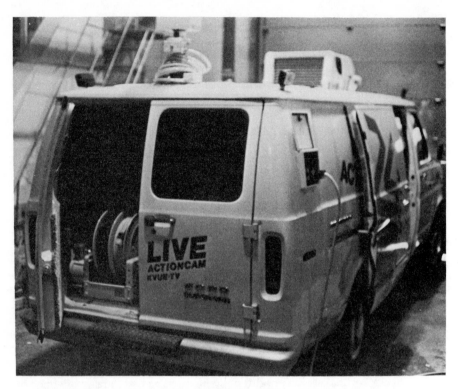

A mobile production unit for a local station. This custom-built van houses two portable cameras, a small switcher, recorders and miscellaneous audio gear. A telescoping mast (just above the back doors) can lift a microwave antenna to a height of 30 feet, so that a signal can be transmitted back to the studio from as much as 20 miles away. Most local stations have comparable equipment; this unit cost about $130,000. Again, however, such costly equipment is rarely used. (Photo by the author, courtesy KVUE-TV)

There are perilous days ahead for television broadcasters. Those who survive will do so by finding ways to compete in an entirely different economic and social environment from what they have known for the past thirty years. Some, we may be sure, will not survive. On the other hand, when the television industry first began, both radio and motion pictures were similarly threatened with extinction. The early 1950s were not happy days for the folks who owned radio stations or movie theaters. Today, however, both of those industries have not only risen from the ashes, they have soared to new heights of prosperity and popularity. They have discovered ways to offer what television does not, and they have transformed themselves accordingly.

Now it is the television broadcasters' turn to do the same. It will not be easy, especially since the last place the local station owner will find any help is the major commercial networks. They are going to have their own troubles.

Chapter

5

The Commercial Networks

What is a network and why do networks exist? There is no mention of networks in the Federal Communications Act of 1934, although they certainly existed when the act was passed. The Federal Communications Commission often seems to pretend that they do not exist; since the FCC has no power to regulate them directly, it reaches them indirectly by regulating what their own stations and affiliates can do.

Strictly speaking, a network is simply a group of broadcasting stations that have been connected by one means or another so that they can transmit the same programs. A network exists only through that connection, and through the contractual agreement between the stations to create that connection.

The first radio network consisted of three stations, all owned by American Telephone and Telegraph: one in Washington, DC, one in New York and one in San Francisco. On March 4, 1921, the Washington station broadcast President Harding's inaugural address. The broadcast was picked up and transmitted by telephone lines to the New York and San Francisco stations, where it was re-broadcast. Two years later, AT&T established a "permanent" network, using the same procedure to tie together its stations in New York, Washington and Providence. Programs could originate at any of the three stations, but the New York station soon assumed the responsibility for producing most of the network's programming. By the time President Calvin Coolidge was inaugurated in 1925, there were 21 stations in the network.

The Harding inauguration exemplified the first purpose of a radio network: to transmit live events at the time of their actual occurrence. For the first time in human history, the general public could "attend" important events thousands of miles away. This is so much a commonplace of our daily lives that we rarely appreciate its significance, but perhaps it is the single most revolutionary product of science and technology since the invention of a practical printing press. Radio alone makes an entire community witness to an event, but it is the radio (and, later, television) network that creates what Marshall McLuhan dubbed "the global village."

Television was deliberately created by the radio networks, and so it is hardly surprising that our television system was conceived in terms of a network from the very beginning. Now, a little more than thirty years after its birth, the monster is taking off on its own and the networks, like Mary Shelley's poor Dr. Frankenstein, can do little more than worry and gnash their teeth.

The concept of the network, whether for radio or television, could be fully justified if it did nothing more than permit the whole nation (or, for that matter, the whole world) to observe contemporary events. However, there are only so many contemporary events that are worthy of the whole nation's attention. Days and even weeks can go by without a single event of such transcendent importance, and even then, some events occur before the network cameras and microphones can be put into position.

There are, of course, other purposes for a network. Radio and television stations earn profits by transmitting programs that entertain large numbers of people. Creating twenty hours of television programs every day would be a prodigious undertaking if every TV station had to do it alone. Without networks, there simply would not be very many stations, and those that did exist would broadcast for only a few hours each day. Most stations barely manage to produce three hours of their own programming a day; the rest of the time is filled by the networks and syndicated shows.

By serving as many as 200 television stations at a time, the networks can amass the economic resources to produce 12 to 14 hours of programs every day. Of course, even the networks do not actually perform the production of that many programs; most are produced by other entities under contract to the networks. The networks themselves produce three or four hours of news programs each day, around 15 to 20 hours of sports programs each weekend, and four to six hours of serial dramas ("soap operas"), talk shows and other entertainment programs on weekdays. The film studios of Hollywood produce the rest.

The cost of producing television programs can vary widely. Game shows and variety shows may cost about $50,000 per hour, while a prime-time filmed adventure series can cost about $600,000 an hour. ABC's *Battlestar Galactica* (actually produced by Universal Studios) set a short-lived record with a budget of about $1.2 million per episode, but that figure is a little deceiving since each episode was intended to run at least twice, making the net cost something less than $600,000 per showing. The same, of course, is true for most prime-time shows, but it is not true for most daytime shows (variety, game and talk shows and soap operas). They run only once.

Nearly all prime-time television adventure and drama shows are produced by a handful of studios: Universal, Columbia, Paramount, Warner Brothers and very few others. Prime-time comedy shows are produced by a different group: MTM (Grant Tinker and his wife, Mary Tyler Moore); T.A.T. Communications (Norman Lear, who is often associated in a separate company with Bud Yorkin, Tandem Productions); and Desilu Productions (Desi Arnaz and his former wife, Lucille Ball), among many others. Some of the other companies that have been important program suppliers include: Filmways, David Wolper Productions, 20th Century Fox, United Artists, Mark VII, Ltd. (Jack Webb's company), Thomas-Spelling Productions, Irwin Allen Productions, Metromedia Producers, Quinn Martin Productions, and the leading game-show producers, Chuck Barris Productions and Goodson-Todman Productions. Each of these companies usually has at least one new series on the network schedules each year. Dozens of other independent producing companies come and go. A few producers have had as many as five or six shows on the networks simultaneously.

Hard as this may be to believe, producing prime-time television programs for the major commercial networks is invariably a money-*losing* proposition. When a network agrees to buy a series of programs from any of these independent producers, the contract calls for the network to play the program twice and to pay an amount equivalent to about 80 percent of the budgeted cost of each episode. The network has the right to cancel the contract at any time, literally on a moment's notice, and to pay for only those programs that have been completed; the network may or may not pay for programs partially completed or those on which filming has not begun.

Why would the producers agree to accept a guaranteed 20 percent loss (and often much more than that, since costs often exceed the budget)? Is it some tax-dodge scheme? Not quite, although the losses on unsuccessful programs can be subtracted from the profits on successful shows at tax time. There are profits because the rights to the shows revert to the producers after the network has had its two plays. The producers can then sell the program anywhere outside the United States for a fraction of the original production cost, and in only a few sales can recover the original investment. If a program is reasonably successful in this country, it is often highly marketable throughout most of the world.

Furthermore, if a show is successful enough to last for three years or more on one of the U.S. networks, there will be a sufficient number of episodes available (at least 60) to sell the series on a syndicated basis to independent stations and to network affiliates for showing during nonnetwork hours (primarily afternoons and weekends). Local stations pay anywhere from $50 to $50,000 for each episode of a syndicated series. It is not hard to figure the profits from a series of 60 episodes that is sold to, say, 100 stations; that would mean a minimum of around three million dollars *each time* the entire series is played. In fact, most syndication contracts call for a minimum of two plays per year per episode, and many stations "strip" their syndicated off-network series, running the same program five days a week and repeating the whole series two or three times in a year. Most of the revenue received from syndication is pure profit to the producer, although there is some expense involved in the distribution of the programs (mostly on film) and modest "residual" payments must be made to the actors, director and writers of each episode.

The bottom line is that the networks not only supply original programs to their affiliated stations, but, in effect, they underwrite a large part of the programs that wind up in syndication. Often the networks take a small interest in the programs produced for them, so they share in the proceeds of syndication when the programs are successful.

Soap operas, game shows and one-shot specials ordinarily are not rerun and have little or no value for later syndication, so the full cost must be paid by the network on their first run.

This economic system developed during the early 1960s, when the major commercial networks first took control over the whole process of program production. Before that, most programs were produced and owned by individual sponsors. That pattern was established in the early days of the radio networks; an advertiser would contract for a half hour or an hour of broadcast time and would supply both the program and the commercials. Thus there were radio shows like *The Lux Hour* and the *Lucky Strike Hour,* and, when television began, the *U.S. Steel Hour* and the *Camel News Caravan.*

The pattern began to change in the late 1950s when the costs of television production grew so great that individual sponsorship became financially impractical. For a while, the advertising agencies (which served as brokers, "packaging" programs for their clients and buying the network time) solved the problem by arranging co-sponsorships, with two or three of their clients sharing the costs and commercial time within a program. However, these arrangements grew unwieldy. Then the quiz-show scandals in 1959 (when the producers of several popular quiz programs were accused of feeding answers to the sponsors' favored contestants) brought demands that the networks exercise more direct control over the programs they transmitted.

Today it is comparatively rare for a single sponsor to underwrite an entire program. One exception is the Hallmark Greeting Card Company, which continues to produce about half a dozen programs each year in its *Hallmark Hall of Fame* series. Hallmark's advertising department contracts with the producers of the program and buys the necessary time from the network (NBC), just as it has done since 1952. Otherwise, there are few instances of single sponsorship, and those few cases usually result from a situation in which the network has bought a program that, for one reason or another, is unlikely to attract a mass audience but may draw a specialized audience that would be appropriate for a particular advertiser; Xerox, IBM and Bell Telephone are especially interested in programs of higher than average quality that presumably appeal to wealthier, better educated audiences.

The change from a sponsor-centered system to the present network-centered system placed the networks in the role of advertising brokers as well as program producers. In this role, the networks sell commercial time to a great variety of advertisers and schedule the commercials within the programs. Some advertisers buy "packages" of commercial spots that are to be scattered throughout each week's schedule, more or less at the network's discretion. Other advertisers buy selected spots within particular programs. Either way, it is up to the networks' sales departments to fill all of the available spots in every program on their schedules. They do a good job of it; in recent years, all three major networks have sold out at least 80 percent of their available spots for the entire coming year before the start of the new season in September. Although there can be last-minute cancellations and occasionally sponsors will abandon a show that promises to be both unpopular and controversial, it is rare these days for even low-mass-appeal news programs and documentaries to have unsold commercial time; of course, the networks do not always get the price they want on every show.

What the networks are selling, ultimately, is commercial time on their affiliated stations. A network buys twelve to fourteen hours per day of the local station's broadcasting time (minus the two minutes per half hour that are left to local commercials); the network then pays the local station for this time at a highly discounted rate, compared to what the station would charge anyone else for a single half-hour or hour program period. Usually the network's station compensation averages about 40 percent of the station's published rates, although the published rates are somewhat imaginary since local stations rarely sell a half-hour or hour period of time to anyone else.

Having bought time from the local stations at wholesale rates, the network then fills most of the time with programs and sells the remaining time as 30-second commercial spots. The "retail" price for a half-minute network spot may be anywhere from $10,000 for a daytime program to about $120,000 for a moderately popular prime-time show. A program like the *Super Bowl* or the *Olympics,* virtually guaranteed to produce an enormous viewing audience, commands prices of $200,000 and more per 30-second spot.

The networks are allowed to run up to six minutes of commercials per hour during the evening and up to 12 minutes during the daytime. Thus, an average prime-time program that cost about $600,000 to produce may bring $1,440,000 in revenue to the network. About 10 percent, or $140,000, will be divided among the network's 200 or so affiliates as station compensation; the average figure is perhaps $700 per station, but by far the bulk of the station compensation goes to the network's largest stations (that is, the stations in the largest markets—including the network's own five stations), so the compensation received by the typical, medium-sized station is a good deal less.

Still, the network has taken in $1.4 million and has spent $600,000 on production and $140,000 on station comp; what about the rest? Well, a fair-sized chunk will be paid to AT&T for the use of the telephone system to transmit the program to the affiliates; that may cost $50,000 or more for a single hour. Commissions to advertising agencies, salesmen and other intermediaries may shrink the revenue by 25 percent or more. But when it is all added up, the network is left with a gross profit of around $250,000 per hour. And that is for a moderately successful show; big hits earn more. On the other hand, unsuccessful shows can lose money just as fast, and there are some shows that each network produces with no expectation of making any profit—news specials and documentaries, for instance—in order to fulfill their "public service" obligations.

To summarize, the television networks function in three distinct roles: first, as a medium for the dissemination of information, especially in transmitting live, significant events; second, as suppliers of programming for affiliated stations; third, as advertising brokers for affiliated stations. All three functions have been present since television began, but the networks' roles, their relationships with their affiliates, and their relationships with one another have changed in important ways over the past 30 years.

The Evolution of the TV Networks

Until the early 1950s there were four networks: NBC, CBS, DuMont and ABC. Almost all network programs were transmitted live from New York, Chicago, or, to a lesser extent, Los Angeles.

The first important change in the television industry was the ABC-Paramount Theaters merger in 1953. Until then, ABC, which had been established a decade earlier when the federal government ordered NBC to dispose of its "Blue Network," had straggled far behind NBC and CBS in entering the television market.

During the 1930s, the major motion picture studios had developed a highly integrated industry. The studios "owned" nearly all of the talent (actors, directors, writers and technicians) under long-term contracts; they financed the production of nearly all movies; and they owned most of the movie theaters in the country, as well as the distribution companies that supplied movies to the theaters. Paramount Pictures, Inc., was one participant in this tightly organized industry, and it prospered. However, the federal government objected to these cozy arrangements and, in the early 1940s, began suing the studios for violations of the anti-trust laws. In 1950, such a suit against Paramount was settled when the studio agreed to sell off its theater chain and distribution company. The theater chain became United Paramount Theaters, whose president, Leonard Goldenson, had been an important executive at Paramount Pictures.

Paramount was one major studio that had seen in television not only a rival but an opportunity; some of the earliest television licenses had been issued to Paramount. From the first, the studio had reasoned that it probably could not beat 'em and might as well join 'em. Nevertheless, Paramount went along with the other major studios during the late 1940s in refusing to sell its recent films to television and in threatening to blacklist any performer who worked in the new medium.

When the theater unit was set adrift in 1950, Goldenson had to face the possibility that television would destroy the movie business, a prospect that had been widely predicted. Rather than become an executive of nothing, he began to explore forging a connection with the new medium. Those efforts led to the merger with ABC.

For ABC, the merger meant, more than anything else, an instant infusion of desperately needed cash—some $25 million. It also meant a small measure of respectability. ABC's founder and chief executive, Edward J. Noble, probably did not fully comprehend all the consequences that would flow from the merger.

Goldenson, even though he had most recently been in charge of the exhibition end of Paramount's business, had worked in the film industry since the early 1930s. He knew a great deal about how the industry operated, and he certainly knew most of the key people who made it operate. As president of ABC-Paramount Theaters, he was in a position to drag the movie industry into television, willing or not. Previously, only a few of the smaller studios, like Republic, had been willing to unload their outdated, low-quality films on TV. Goldenson saw that something much better was needed: filmed programs, produced by the movie studios specifically for use on television. The problem was to find a studio willing to stoop so low.

He found it in Walt Disney Productions. Disney was not a party to the major studios' TV blacklist, and some say that he had already concluded that television was to become the dominant entertainment medium in America. Whether or not he had that much prescience, he clearly had a problem: as a relatively small-time film producer catering to a relatively specialized market, he had to get the maximum return from each film he produced. Unquestionably, Disney had some successes, but he also had his share of box-office disasters, among which were *Fantasia* and *Sleeping Beauty*.

Television, in Disney's eyes, offered an opportunity to get some more mileage out of his accumulated backlog of short subjects and animated cartoons, and perhaps a chance to recover some of the losses on feature-length films that had failed at the box office. Furthermore, every appearance of a Disney product on TV would amount to advertising for Disney's theater products.

Not long after assuming control of ABC-Paramount, Goldenson approached Disney (as well as other studio heads). Disney was more than receptive; a deal quickly took shape. In October 1954 the deal materialized as a new ABC series, *Disneyland.* It was ABC's first prime-time hit show.

The show itself was a pastiche of old Disney cartoons and short subjects, "hosted" by Walt himself. Soon Disney began to devote entire hour-long shows to the promotion of his elaborate amusement park, Disneyland, a project he had dreamed about for fully a decade. A curious three-way symbiosis developed: the TV show, *Disneyland,* depended for its popularity on the Disney movies; the amusement park was promoted by the TV show; and the market value of the movies was considerably enhanced by both the amusement park and the TV show. In a broad sense, it was all advertising.

By 1956 Disney had begun producing new, original material specifically for the TV series (having exhausted the usable old films). But long before that, he had breached the dam, and television already was being flooded with filmed series produced by the major studios.

After Disney, the next Hollywood studio to find accommodation with television was Warner Brothers, again through the efforts of Leonard Goldenson, and again to the immense profit of ABC. Some of the early Warner made-for-TV shows were *Cheyenne, 77 Sunset Strip* and *Hawaiian Eye* Meanwhile, Paramount Pictures made its own deal with NBC, as did Universal Pictures, and CBS began to find that all of the major studios were eager to supply new series. By 1956, barely two years after the first Disney show, live television in prime-time was dead; the filmed series took over and, with minor exceptions, has held sway ever since.

Another important consequence of the ABC-Paramount Theaters merger was the demise of the DuMont network. Before 1953, DuMont and ABC had been nearly equal competitors. DuMont had a slight edge in the number of affiliates, but ABC had the advantage of an established (though modest) radio network as a dependable cash source. The merger obviously made ABC much more formidable, and when Goldenson began lining up Hollywood studios to produce programs, DuMont threw in the towel. The DuMont network folded in 1955, and most of its affiliates quickly turned to ABC.

Since then, there have been sporadic attempts to start a "fourth network" —that is, a network capable of competing with the three established commercial networks. Some very wealthy people have lost a great deal of money in these attempts.

Starting a television network is theoretically simple. First, you have to have programs, preferably something unique and highly appealing to a mass audience. Next, you must get local TV stations to agree to act as affiliates: that is, to show your programs. If you can get enough affiliates lined up, you can sell commercial time to advertisers. Then you have to arrange with AT&T or some other common carrier to transmit your programs to the affiliates. All four of these requirements impose some serious burdens.

Getting the programs is fairly easy, although it is also the most expensive part. Very few program producers are likely to go to the considerable expense of producing shows without payment in advance, or at least guaranteed. One alternative is to contract with whoever owns the rights to a sports event; usually the rights can be obtained for a modest advance fee, with the balance to be paid if and when the event actually is used. Unfortunately, there are not very many sports events of broad public appeal that have not already been bought up by the major networks.

Lining up affiliates is the hardest part of forming a new network. There are not very many independent stations, and the more successful ones are so profitable with their usual programming (syndicated old movies and off-network shows) that they are not terribly eager to give up their time for an uncertain venture. Network affiliated stations could agree to carry the programs in place of their usual fare, but that is not likely except in the major networks' weakest time periods—which means strong competition for your program from the other local stations. Getting a sufficient number of stations to line up at the same time is a herculean task. It is also expensive, since you must promise adequate station compensation.

If you have attractive programming to offer, and if you have lined up a sufficient number of affiliated stations (at least fifty, preferably a hundred), and if your affiliated stations have sufficiently large markets to produce an aggregate audience of respectable size, you may be able to find sponsors willing to put up enough money to make the whole venture worthwhile. In fact, finding sponsors might be the *easiest* part of the whole business; national advertisers simply cannot get enough time on the major networks, which is one reason the price for major-network commercials keeps going up. In recent years, some of the larger national advertisers and their agencies have repeatedly called for the creation of a "fourth network" to give them new advertising outlets (and to provide some price competition with the Big Three).

Finally, having the programs, affiliates and sponsors all lined up, you must negotiate for the physical connection of your network. Although I have referred several times to the use of "telephone lines" to transmit TV programs, in fact the distribution system only partly depends on telephone *wires;* mostly the system consists of microwave links from city to city. (Nearly all long-distance telephone calls also travel by microwave rather than by wire.) AT&T only has a certain number of microwave channels available for television, and those channels are almost entirely bought up by the major networks. There are other telecommunications common carriers that can provide microwave transmission services, but they only operate between a few major cities. You may find that there simply is no available service to some of your affiliated stations, or that establishing the service will cost a small fortune—payable in advance, please. Or you may find that some of the AT&T lines are available only on a "pre-emptible" basis: you can use them only as long as no one else (such as NBC, CBS or ABC) wants them, but you can be pre-empted at any time. If you're pre-empted in the middle of your program, too bad.

Discouraged yet? Well, you are not alone; so are most of the people who have tried to start a new network. The most successful "fourth networks" have been the Hughes Television Network (HTN) and Television Sports, Inc. (TVS), both of which specialize in basketball games and other sports events that, until recently, were not considered to be of sufficiently broad interest for the major networks. However, since 1975 or thereabouts, even these specialized networks have found themselves in increasingly heated competition with the major networks; TVS and NBC finally worked out an arrangement whereby TVS, which had bought long-term rights to nearly all college basketball contests, would actually provide some of its programs to NBC.

Other than HTN and TVS, and a couple of other equally specialized networks that function only sporadically, all efforts to establish another commercial network have been doomed to failure—until the past few years, when communications satellites have completely changed the economics of network transmission. Now, suddenly, there are more than a dozen television networks, some operating part-time and some full-time for highly specialized audiences. But we will find out how this has come about later, in Chapter 9.

The rapid conversion from mostly live programming to almost all filmed series took place between 1955 and 1956. The next major event in network television's history was the rise and fall of the quiz show. Quiz shows had always been a staple of television fare, but they generally had been relegated to the daytime hours. A quiz show is pretty cheap to produce, no matter how lavish the prizes may seem, and its built-in dramatic tension has terrific mass appeal.

The big-money, prime-time quiz shows began with *The $64,000 Question,* which premiered in June 1955. Each show had a single sponsor; *$64,000 Question* and its spin-off, *$64,000 Challenge,* were owned by Revlon. By 1957 there were half a dozen imitators but there seemed to be no limit to the genre's popularity. Then, in 1958, a disgruntled contestant claimed that the shows were rigged, that some contestants were being fed the right answers in advance. These charges led to congressional hearings; some of the show's producers admitted that they had "helped" certain contestants fend off their opponents because the "winners" were popular with the viewing audience, which boosted ratings, which pleased the sponsors.

The quiz show scandals badly tarnished the networks' reputation and brought to a rapid end the practice of selling entire half-hour or hour blocks of time to individual sponsors. The scandals could not have come at a worse time for the networks, which were busily putting together the immense capital necessary for the conversion to color. NBC had begun scheduling some programs in color in 1954, and by 1956 its entire prime-time schedule was in color (a fact which the network did not allow to escape public notice, since each color program was preceded by the original "NBC peacock"). CBS also began limited color programming in 1954, but moved much more slowly toward an all-color schedule. ABC struggled valiantly to catch up.

At the same time, the rapid introduction of videotape technology spelled the end of nearly all live programming daytime and evening. Before 1960, most of the daytime quiz shows and soap operas had been live, but video tape made that costly and logistically nightmarish practice no longer necessary. After 1960, even the few remaining programs that were nominally live (the news programs in particular) were actually taped during their original, East Coast transmission, then played back at times more convenient to the network in the Mountain and Pacific time zones.

By 1966 all three networks had finally made the conversion to full color for all programs, and the distinction between live and live-via-videotape had become a matter for semantic debate. Meanwhile, however, the television industry had begun to mature in some important ways. One of these was in its coverage of genuinely live, spontaneous events.

Television was there in Dallas on that horrifying day in November 1963 and covered every aspect of President Kennedy's assassination and the subsequent events with a thoroughness, professionalism and dignity that more than made up for the quiz-show scandals of recent memory. Television found new ways to make the presidential campaign of 1964, and especially the major party conventions, vivid and exciting. The campaigns and conventions of 1960, 1956 and even 1952 had been covered, too, but not as thoroughly and not with such techniques as handheld live cameras and computer projections of the election results.

Television seemed to be nearly everywhere with ABC's *Wide World of Sports,* which began in 1961 and, under the masterful direction of Roone Arledge and Edgar Scherick, not only introduced dozens of new production techniques to television audiences but also introduced dozens of neglected sports to the American public.

And television went to 'Nam.

The war in Vietnam had simmered for several years before television and print journalists became aware of it in 1963. After President Kennedy was assassinated, the events in that distant Southeast Asian land grew more and more ominous, and there were growing numbers of American reporters and camera operators assigned to Saigon and outlying points. As the U.S. military commitment grew, so did television's coverage; by 1967 hardly a day passed without new film footage from swamps, jungles, mountain passes and seaports with unpronounceable names. "Body counts" and "free-fire zones" were discussed with disarming familiarity by TV anchormen. Back home, the rising tide of protest also came before the cameras and microphones. Television covered the peace marches and demonstrations, as it had begun to cover civil rights marches and demonstrations a few years earlier. The one, in fact, seemed to blend into the other.

As the decade grew ever bloodier, television brought the gore into American living rooms, where it simply could not be ignored. For everyone who lived through that decade, there is a litany of places that corresponds to a series of television images: Selma, Birmingham, Newark, Watts, Grant Park, Los Angeles' Ambassador Hotel, Da Nang, the motel in Memphis and My Lai. There is not much chronology to these images; it is hard to remember in what order they came. But the images themselves were seared into a nation's consciousness and, in some cases, conscience.

There were, of course, other images as well. The U.S. space program provided its share: Alan Shepard's suborbital flight in May, 1961; John Glenn's first orbital flight in February, 1962; Ed White's first "spacewalk" in 1965; and, of course, the ultimate spectacle of Neil Armstrong and Edwin Aldrin cavorting on the Moon, in July, 1969.

And the 1968 Olympics in Mexico City, a splendid frolic before the more portentous political conventions.

The television coverage of all these events more than fulfilled the medium's original promise as a means of providing communication of significant events to the whole nation. The routine, day-in and day-out fare of television became, in the 1960s, situation comedies and "action dramas"—violence-laced adventure stories and melodramas. These became the primary form of entertainment for millions of people. But for those same millions, and for others who ordinarily would not deign to watch the "boob tube," television became an indispensable window to the world, however beautiful or ugly it might be.

One of the most significant events in the television industry during the 1960s was the one that did not take place: the merger of ABC and the International Telephone and Telegraph Company (ITT).

In spite of its many innovations and contributions to the industry, ABC was so far behind the other two networks during the early 1960s that many observers referred to the industry as a "two-and-a-half network system." The conversion to full color very nearly drove the network into bankruptcy. Goldenson sold off some of ABC's subsidiary properties, including its share in Disneyland, but that was not enough. Along came ITT, one of the largest corporations in the world, with heavy involvement in telecommunications in almost every country except the United States. Merging with ABC would give ITT a large-scale entry into the U.S. market; merging with ITT would give ABC what it desperately needed— almost limitless cash resources. It seemed a marriage made in Wall Street heaven.

The ABC-ITT merger was first proposed in 1965. The FCC (which had to approve the deal because ABC's owned-and-operated stations—the one consistently profitable part of the network—were involved) thought about it for more than a year, but finally approved in December 1966. However, before the bride and groom could begin their celebration, the Justice Department intervened.

Television's coverage of the U.S. "space spectaculars," such as astronaut Edward H. White's first "space walk" in 1965, exemplified the kind of service that the medium can provide at its best. (Photo courtesy of NASA.)

The Justice Department was never entirely clear about its reasons for objecting to the merger. ABC simply was not big enough to arouse problems under the anti-trust laws, and anyway, RCA was competitively equal to ITT. Publicly, the Justice Department expressed concern over a multinational company with its many foreign interests having access to an important news medium. Of course, ITT was and is a U.S. corporation; its headquarters are in New York City. But somehow, that was not the point. Of course, both RCA (and its wholly owned subsidiary, NBC) and Columbia had, and still have, diverse interests in other countries, but somehow that too was beside the point.

At Justice's insistence, the FCC ordered a re-hearing in March 1967. The outcome was the same: the commission could find no good reason to forbid the merger (or license transfer) and could see several reasons to approve it. However, the Justice Department threatened to take the issue to court, and it was obvious that the court case would drag on for years through appeal after appeal. In January 1968 ITT called off the whole deal.

Why did Lyndon Johnson's Justice Department intervene in the ABC-ITT deal? Perhaps it was because of ITT's persistent meddling in the internal affairs of the countries where it did business; perhaps it was because of ITT's attempts to co-opt the Central Intelligence Agency as a partner in its meddling. Or perhaps it was merely because ITT's high executives were staunch supporters of the Republican Party. Whatever the real reasons may have been, Justice's action devastated the jilted bride, ABC.

After the merger was aborted, there was nothing for ABC to do but pick itself up, dust itself off and go back to work. There were several attempts in 1968 and afterward to take over the struggling network (Howard Hughes was one suitor; another was Norton Simon), but Goldenson and his colleagues decided to go it alone. They had what was left of a $25 million loan from ITT in early 1967, and they were able to borrow a little more from banks and institutional investors in 1968. Their highly successful and profitable coverage of the Mexico City Olympics that summer boosted the network's ratings, prestige and spirits. Goldenson, by this time chairman of American Broadcasting Companies (parent of the TV network and various other enterprises), hired Elton Rule as the company's president, and the two vowed that ABC would stand on its own two feet.

Meanwhile, NBC and CBS were not resting on their laurels while ABC sorted out its financial affairs. CBS dominated the ratings with its endless skein of low-brow comedies: *The Beverly Hillbillies, Gomer Pyle, USMC, Green Acres, The Lucy Show* and countless others. NBC countered with a long list of action-adventure and drama series: *Bonanza, I Spy, Daniel Boone, Ironside* and *The Man from U.N.C.L.E.,* to name a few. However, NBC's biggest success was outside of prime time, with news (*The Today Show,* the *Huntley-Brinkley Report*), soap operas (*Days of Our Lives, The Doctors*), and the perennial *Tonight Show Starring Johnny Carson.*

NBC also had found that it was profitable to run not-too-old movies in prime time, a practice that the other networks emulated. Unfortunately, by the mid-60s the supply of fairly recent movies that were considered acceptable for television's mass audience had become very thin. In 1966 NBC announced a deal with Universal Studios to develop an entire series of new "movies for television." These were to be "feature-length" (that is 90 minutes to two hours long), with "film star" casts and the production values normally associated with theatrical films. Of course, NBC was not prepared to invest the kind of money Hollywood often spends on a theatrical film; budgets would be strictly limited, but still a bit more than the networks spent on routine series.

The made-for-TV movies, offered under the title *World Premiere*, were successful enough that the other two networks quickly followed suit. CBS relied mainly on its practice of outbidding the other two networks for Hollywood films that had been successful at the box office, but ABC enthusiastically embraced the concept pioneered for NBC—and beat them at their own game, with its *Movie of the Week* series of 90-minute potboilers, what Hollywood in the 1930s would have called "B pictures" (or worse).

The success of the made-for-TV movies was another step in the blurring of the distinction between television and motion pictures. The average viewer would be hard-pressed to describe the difference between a *World Premiere* made-for-TV film and a theatrical movie of comparable quality, shown the following week in the same time period. Meanwhile, filmed adventure and drama series on all three networks grew progressively longer. During the late 1950s the majority of filmed series were in half-hour lengths; in the early 1960s, the hour length grew more popular for westerns and dramas. By the mid-60s, nearly all non-comedy shows were an hour long. Then NBC began to experiment with 90-minute series shows, and found that the audience accepted them. Today, only situation comedies continue to be produced in half-hour form; the majority of action and dramatic programs are an hour long, with frequent 90-minute or two-hour "special episodes."

To see just how obscure the distinction between "movie" and "TV show" has become, consider the case of *Battlestar Galactica* and *Buck Rogers*.

In 1977 George Lucas's film, *Star Wars*, was an enormous sensation and commercial success, quickly surpassing all previous holders of the record for box-office profits. The television networks, always eager to spot a trend, sensed that science fiction might have a market.

ABC ordered up a pilot, to be produced by Universal, based on the Buck Rogers comic strip of the 1930s. The pilot, duly produced, was *Buck Rogers in the 25th Century*. It was not very good, as even the network executives could tell; they did not bother to schedule it as a *Movie of the Week*. Instead, they ordered another pilot, with an entirely different premise and cast, but using some of the costly special effects that had been developed for Buck Rogers. The new show was *Battlestar Galactica*. After an immoderate amount of special promotion, *Galactica* was run as a *Movie of the Week*. Enough people watched to encourage the network; they ordered it to be developed as a series. The series premiered in September 1978. It was neither a hit nor a flop, but only modestly successful in spite of its comparatively high budget.

Meanwhile, Universal decided not to let the *Buck Rogers* pilot merely gather dust, so the studio released it as a theatrical film. The film did reasonably well; it certainly was no *Star Wars*, but it did better than the flock of cheap science fiction flicks that had flooded the market after *Star Wars*.

In 1979 ABC decided that *Galactica* was simply too costly for its lackluster ratings, so the series was canceled. However, Fred Silverman, who had been the ABC head of programming when the *Buck Rogers-Battlestar Galactica* decisions were first made, had become president of NBC and he desperately needed potentially popular new programs. He went back to Universal and suggested that the studio try again to develop a series based on Buck Rogers. New scripts were ordered; NBC bought the series and scheduled it to begin in the fall. The series would lead off with the original pilot, which now had finished its run in the theaters and could be presented as a "major motion picture."

Meanwhile, Universal released the original *Galactica* pilot as a theatrical movie, and it, too, did reasonably well, considering that it had already been on TV twice.

What is a movie and what is a TV show? Evidently, on the basis of the *Buck Rogers-Battlestar Galactica* experience, there really is no difference any more.

During the 1970s, the three major commercial networks consolidated their gains and reached the pinnacle of their success. There were no major changes in their structure; successful programs came and went, as did network executives, and the fortunes of the three networks rose and fell to some extent, but all three were increasingly profitable, powerful and secure. They also faced a host of new threats.

The chief threats to the commercial networks were cable television and communications satellites. These, however, were not the only clouds on TV's horizon.

Television has always had its critics. From the very first, the medium has been treated with unbridled contempt by those who regard TV shows as puerile, vulgar and even downright immoral. In 1961 FCC chairman Newton N. Minow characterized the medium as "a vast wasteland" in a blistering speech before the National Association of Broadcasters, who were not especially amused. A later member of the commission, Nicholas Johnson, wasted no opportunity or excuse to scold the industry for what he regarded as its multiple failings.

Members of Congress also have gotten in their licks. Rep. Oren Harris chaired the hearings on the quiz-show scandals in 1959 and became a devoted critic of the medium. During the late 1960s and early 1970s, Harris was over-shadowed by Sen. John O. Pastore of Rhode Island, chairman of the Senate subcommittee on communications. Pastore feared that television's violent action programs might be harmful to viewers, and he persuaded the surgeon general of the Public Health Service to investigate that possibility. After an $8 million-study, the surgeon general concluded that violent television programs certainly could damage susceptible children and might have deleterious effects on adults as well. Armed with this evidence, Pastore bullied the networks into reducing the amount of violence in all programs and, in particular, all but eliminating violence from the first hour of prime time each evening—what came to be known as "family viewing time."

Pastore retired in 1976, leaving his subcommittee chairmanship to the less flamboyant Ernest Hollings of South Carolina. The focus shifted abruptly back to the House of Representatives, where Lionel Van Deerlin announced that the time had come to rewrite the Communications Act of 1934.

Van Deerlin's three attempts to rewrite the 1934 Act met with disaster. Each time, he tried to satisfy both the critics of the medium and the captains of the industry. He offered perpetual broadcasting licenses—no renewal necessary —but he also demanded that broadcasters pay a "spectrum fee" for their use of the electromagnetic spectrum, proportional to their revenues. He proposed to relax the "equal time rule" (which requires broadcasters to provide roughly equal time to political candidates if they provide any broadcast time to a single candidate) and the "fairness doctrine" (which requires broadcasters to air all sides of controversial issues). However, he also proposed to make station and network accounting practices subject to FCC review; in the past, the FCC has merely collected statistics without going too deeply into the stations' books, and without bothering the networks at all.

Van Deerlin's bills never went beyond subcommittee hearings, where they were shredded by critics on all sides. Actually, his proposals for broadcasting were not too far from what the industry wanted, but his proposals for cable TV and communications satellites gave the networks fits.

Nevertheless, Van Deerlin's efforts were not entirely in vain. They stimulated others to consider the weaknesses of the obsolete Communications Act, and they did address most of the significant issues in the communications industry. Sen. Hollings, at the urging of the television and telephone industries, came up with an alternative bill that essentially crystallized the status quo and tidied up some of the problems in the 1934 Act. Sen. Barry Goldwater introduced another variation, one that was even more generous to the industry.

As of this writing, Rep. Van Deerlin has declared that he will not try again to rewrite the entire Communications Act, but that he will continue to work on communications reform in a piecemeal fashion. The Hollings and Goldwater bills do not appear likely to win passage in the Senate before the 1980 election season, and they certainly will not be considered then. However, the movement for communications reform will not go away; sometime during the coming decade, the ancient Communications Act almost certainly will be thoroughly revised, either piece by piece or all at once. At this point, it is simply impossible to predict the outcome of this process, but it is not likely that the present structure of the television system will remain unchanged.

While fending off critics and prospective competitors, the networks were also busily engaged in their own intramural rivalry. The ratings races of the 1950s and 1960s seem tame and genteel in comparison to the pitched battles of the 1970s.

As the decade began, CBS was the undisputed ratings champion, with NBC a dogged second and ABC still trailing far behind. By the end of the decade, ABC had vaulted into the lead, trailed closely by CBS and NBC. Over a year's time, often less than two ratings points separated the three networks, yet NBC was ridiculed for its haplessness just as ABC had been in the past.

The funny thing is, the whole ratings game is played with loaded dice.

The Ratings and the Networks

There are two major television ratings services, the A. C. Nielsen Company and Arbitron. Both use essentially the same techniques to determine what people are watching on TV, but Nielsen monitors more homes on a continuous basis, and therefore the Nielsen ratings are relied upon more heavily in the industry.

Nielsen places its Audimeter in about 1,200 homes across the country. It is a simple recording device that indicates whether a TV set is on or off and, if it is on, to what channel it is tuned. These homes are supposedly chosen in such a way that they accurately represent the population of the whole nation. The Audimeters transmit their recordings by telephone lines to a computer in Florida, which analyzes what the "Nielsen families" are watching and projects those statistics into two figures for the national audience: the *rating* and the *share*.

A rating is the percent of the entire population that is watching a given program at a given time. Ratings are computed for each 15-minute period throughout the day; the rating for an entire half-hour or hour-long program is the average of those 15-minute figures.

A share is the percent of the audience that is actually watching television who are watching a given program. Thus, if only 75 percent of the public is watching television at all, and one-third of them are watching *Buckskin Sagas*, the rating for the program would be 25 but the share would be 33.

Only national (that is, major network) programs are rated continuously. The procedure is different for local stations and their programs. Four times each year, both Nielsen and Arbitron send diaries to randomly selected homes in each of the 200 television markets across the country. (There are television stations outside of these 200 markets but their programs are not rated by the major survey companies, evidently because no one really cares.) Viewers are supposed to keep an accurate account of their television viewing for two weeks, recording what they watch, who watches it and so forth, in the diary. The diary is then returned to the survey company, whose computers analyze the results and report ratings and shares on a station-by-station basis. In the past, these local ratings, or "sweeps," have been conducted only four times a year, in September, November, February and May, but recently there has been some agitation for either year-round sweeps in all markets, or sweeps at different times in different markets.

The importance of the ratings, of course, is that advertisers pay for commercial time—at both the network and local levels—according to the number of people watching. Obviously, advertisers would not be happy if they were forced to rely on someone's mere guesses about the size of the audience being reached with their expensive commercials, so they rely entirely on the ratings.

The catch is that, first, the ratings tell only who watched in the past—not who will watch in the future, when the next advertising campaign is planned. Second, the ratings (except the local sweeps) tell only that so many TV sets were turned on, not who was watching. Third, the accuracy, reliability, and validity of the ratings themselves are very much subject to question.

Even the Nielsen Company itself only claims that its ratings are accurate to within 1.8 points—plus or minus. In other words, if they say that a show has a rating of 20, in fact 21.8 percent of the population might be watching—or 18.2 percent. There are about 74 million households in the United States that have one or more TV sets, so each rating point (one percent of the total TV population) presumably equals 740,000 households. At an average price of five dollars per thousand, for a 30-second commercial, a ratings point is worth $3,700 per commercial, or about $44,000 per hour program (12 half-minute commercials).

Of course, the actual price of network commercial time is not calculated in quite that straightforward a manner. The higher a show's rating, the more advertisers will want to put their commercials on it, and so the price goes up. On the other hand, advertisers may shun a low-rated show, forcing the networks to offer its commercial time at bargain prices. These tendencies merely reinforce the ratings, making them even more important than they otherwise would be.

The networks undeniably want to reap the maximum economic benefit from every moment of their broadcast schedule, and so there is constant pressure to achieve the highest possible rating with every program. While it is certainly understandable that the networks seek their own economic self-interest, the effects for the viewers are often bewildering.

Any show that has a rating of 25 or more is a certified hit and is very unlikely to be canceled—unless it has less than a 30 share for its time period. Any show that has a rating of 15 or less is a loser and is sure to be canceled—unless it has more than a 30 share for its time period. The real battle is waged over those shows whose ratings run between 15 and 25 and whose shares are something under 30. The network's thinking is that, all else being equal, any show that is reasonably competitive should draw at least 30 percent of the audience that is watching something at any given time, or, in other words, a 30 share. The rating, however, depends on how many people are watching TV at all, and how many are (necessarily or by choice) doing something else. Thus, a daytime show rarely has as high a rating as a prime-time show because relatively few people are watching TV at all.

The rating reflects, indirectly, the total number of people watching a program, while the share reflects only the percentage of the available audience. The decision to buy commercial time on a particular show is made only on the basis of the ratings; the share doesn't make much difference to the advertiser. (Other factors also may affect the advertiser's decision. In the late 1960s and early 1970s, television and advertising people talked a lot about "demographics," or the composition of the audience by age, sex, ethnicity, income and other factors. The idea was that an advertiser should spend money only on those programs that reach a particular audience. However, most national advertisers want to reach as many people as possible with only minimal regard for demographic factors; anyway, it turned out that the most careful demographic studies were not much more useful than the obvious supposition that soap operas attract mostly women and football games attract mostly men.)

The ratings, then, have almost nothing to do with a program's real popularity. A more significant factor is the number of stations that carry the show. Obviously, the network with the fewest affiliates cannot hope to achieve ratings equal to the larger networks unless its programs draw a substantially higher share of the available audience at any given time. Throughout its history, ABC has suffered under just this handicap; during the 1970s, ABC generally had from fifteen to thirty fewer affiliates than NBC and CBS. Furthermore, ABC's affiliates were more often UHF stations (which typically draw smaller audiences than VHF stations) than were those of the other two networks. CBS had both the most affiliates and the most VHF affiliates, an advantage that would have been even more lopsided but for one fact: the CBS chain included more stations in small cities with sparse rural audiences. That is why CBS, for many years, maintained its ratings dominance with a schedule of rural-oriented situation comedies. Only the increasing urbanization of the American population, and some shrewd juggling of the affiliate line-up by ABC, enabled ABC to reach the position of ratings supremacy it enjoyed between 1976 and 1979.

Now it is NBC's turn to fight the ratings odds. Since 1976, more than a dozen NBC affiliates have switched to ABC. The three networks are now almost equal in the number of affiliates (at last report, ABC was still slightly behind), but NBC's stations apparently reach a somewhat smaller potential audience. Thus, even if all three networks carried identical programs and the public selected channels purely at random, statistical probability would put ABC and CBS in a virtual tie for first place with NBC trailing behind.

The Future of the Networks

Left to their own devices, the three major commercial television networks could continue indefinitely as they are now. Ratings leadership probably would alternate among the three of them as they found new programs with exceptional appeal, or as they juggled their affiliate line-ups. Most assuredly, all three would continue to make a great deal of money. In 1977 advertisers spent about $3.5 billion on the networks and another $4.1 billion on local stations. The three major networks share about half a billion dollars in pre-tax profits each year.

Unfortunately for the networks they will not be left alone. Cable television systems will continue to make inroads into the audience, taking viewers away from the network programs. Communications satellites increasingly provide cable systems with programs that are at least equal to the network shows in audience appeal, but the satellites are already doing more than that: satellite-borne programs are being fed to new, highly specialized broadcasting networks, such as the Christian Broadcasting Network (CBN) and the Spanish International Network (SIN), again pulling viewers away from the networks. Soon there will be direct satellite transmission of programs to local TV stations that, until now, have relied entirely on the networks for programming. If network affiliates have access to three or four or a dozen program sources, the networks may be very hard pressed to keep the affiliates in line. Direct satellite-to-home broadcasting, of course, would completely eliminate the present network-affiliate relationship.

In short, the networks will lose some part of their audience, which means above all a loss of revenue: advertisers will not pay to reach people who are watching something else. It remains to be seen how far this tendency will go. By 1985, it seems likely that the major networks will have experienced at least a 10 to 15 percent loss of audience, and by 1990 the loss may be closer to 30 percent.

It is more than just a matter of losing numbers of viewers, though. The new program sources appeal to specialized audiences who are not entirely satisfied with network fare. Some of these specialized audiences are the very people who are most avidly sought by national advertisers: people who have better than average incomes and education, for instance. Unless the major networks find ways to appeal more strongly to these specialized audiences, they could wind up with an audience composed largely of the poor, the elderly and the poorly educated—not an attractive market to many advertisers.

The networks almost certainly will continue for many years to serve as the primary source of instantaneous coverage of significant live events. Unfortunately, that service has not been very profitable for the networks in the past; even though coverage of a space mission or a political convention usually attracts a large audience, the costs of the coverage swallow most of the revenues.

These are troubled times for network executives, who cannot help but see manifold dangers ahead. There is an excellent chance that the three great networks, built in the legacy of the golden age of radio, have already entered their decline and will not last out the present century.

However, that applies only to the commercial networks. The fate of public television may be entirely different.

Chapter
6

The Bemused Bridesmaid: Non-commercial TV

"Always the bridesmaid, never the bride." That classic definition of frustration aptly describes the role that non-commercial broadcasting has played in our nation's television system. It is actually a role inherited from the earliest days of radio.

No more than two or three countries in all the world permit their broadcasting systems to be dominated by commercial interests. In nearly all countries, West and East, industrialized and "developing," broadcasting is the exclusive province of a governmental agency or of a quasi-governmental public agency like the British Broadcasting Corporation. Where private, commercial broadcasting is permitted at all, it is either distinctly secondary to the government-sponsored service, or it is closely supervised by the government. Nowhere else is public broadcasting (that is, non-commercial broadcasting) relegated to a distant second place.

The reasons are only partly ideological. There has never been a moment in the history of broadcasting when our own government, representatives of the broadcasting industry or anyone else has declared, "Broadcasting should be primarily for the purpose of generating private profits." On the contrary: the broadcasting system from its inception has been based, at least in theory and rhetoric, on the principles that the use of the airwaves is a public trust and that all broadcasters must justify their licensure by serving the "public interest, convenience and necessity." It is simply a matter of historical circumstance that the means of providing this service has been placed in private hands whose first priority has been private gain.

The Dismal History of Non-commercial Radio

The first broadcasters were, in fact, non-commercial. Several years before Pittsburgh's KDKA was licensed as a commercial broadcasting station, a number of colleges and universities operated broadcasting stations on an experimental basis. In fact, the first license ever issued to a radio station for purposes other than radiotelegraphy or ship-to-shore transmission was granted in 1912 to St. Joseph's College in Philadelphia. The University of Wisconsin, the University of Minnesota and Latter Day Saints University in Salt Lake City were among a number of educational institutions that held experimental licenses before 1920.

After KDKA went on the air and was issued a regular broadcasting license, many of the college stations applied for and received the same privilege. There was a great deal of enthusiastic talk about the impact that radio would have on education; some educators thought it would be comparable to the advent of the printing press. The state-supported agricultural colleges of the Midwest and Great Plains were especially fervent in their hopes for radio; they saw it as a means of bringing culture, enlightenment and scientific farming techniques to the rural hinterlands.

Initially, only two channels were allocated to radio broadcasting, and Secretary of Commerce Hoover had no authority to assign licenses to a particular channel or to regulate the hours during which a licensee could broadcast or the power of a licensee's transmitter. In 1923 a federal court ruled that Hoover could not even refuse to issue a license; anyone who applied, and who met the minimum criteria, had to be given one. The inevitable result was sheer chaos.

The educational broadcasters, most of whom were operating with outmoded equipment that had been hand-built for experimentation, and all of whom were handicapped by limited finances and personnel, found themselves shoved aside by commercial entrepreneurs. Commercial stations, with their essentially unlimited transmitting power and erratic hours of operation, simply overrode the weaker educational stations' signals. Complaints to Hoover were unavailing since his hands were tied. He did increase the number of channels from two to 96, and he organized a series of conferences with broadcasters in an effort to promote self-regulation by the industry. Unfortunately, each increase in the availability of channels merely encouraged a flood of new license applications, and in the economically frenzied 1920s "self-regulation" was an empty promise. Furthermore, as Citizen's Band operators have discovered more recently, it only takes one irresponsible broadcaster to monopolize an entire channel and deprive everyone else of its use.

By the mid-20s, educational broadcasters began to clamor for stronger, more effective federal regulation, and especially for radio channels dedicated to educational use. At first, the commercial broadcasters opposed any sort of regulation, but by the decade's end it had become clear to the major forces in the industry—AT&T, RCA, Westinghouse and a few others—that more regulation was indispensable. In 1927 Congress finally passed the Federal Radio Act, creating the Federal Radio Commission to "advise" the secretary of commerce on such matters as licensing standards and frequency allocation. The educators were disappointed, however, that the Radio Act did not contain the dedicated channel allocation they expected to receive. Regulation achieved just the opposite of the effect educators had hoped.

The FRC's immediate solution to the problem of overcrowded channels was to increase slightly the number of available frequencies, and then to assign stations to particular frequencies, hours of operation and limited transmitter power. All well and good, but unfortunately, the FRC had limited enforcement powers and virtually no staff. In order to encourage voluntary compliance with its rules, the FRC gave the largest, wealthiest stations the most favorable frequencies and allowed them to operate 24 hours a day with essentially unlimited power. Smaller, weaker stations were given correspondingly less favored treatment—and the smallest, weakest stations were those of the colleges. For a while, it actually looked like the FRC would begin revoking the licenses of the weakest stations. Intensive lobbying by the educational broadcasters and their supporters kept that from happening, but otherwise their standing rapidly deteriorated.

Meanwhile, both commercial and non-commercial broadcasters continued to seek permanent, stronger regulation to protect their diverse interests. The FRC had been created as a temporary advisory board, and its existence had to be renewed each year; it was given virtually no funding by Congress. Furthermore, Congress's expectations for the FRC were pretty unrealistic. Among other things, the FRC was expected to reorganize the burgeoning radio industry to "equalize" the geographic distribution of stations. This would have required the elimination of the super-powerful "clear channel stations" and the revocation of the licenses of some of the favored stations in the East in order to open up frequencies for new stations in the less populous West, and the FRC simply did not have the political muscle, the statutory authority or the enforcement resources to do anything of the sort.

By 1930, there was general agreement that the 1927 Radio Act simply was not sufficient. Unfortunately, Congress's attention was absorbed by the unfolding economic disaster of the Great Depression, and radio regulation took a very low spot on the list of priorities.

The educational broadcasters and their few allies organized their first major, sustained lobbying campaign. They no longer begged: they demanded frequencies of their own, with reasonable regulation of operating hours and transmitter power to enable them to reach their intended audiences, and they wanted their frequencies to be in the standard broadcasting band. (It had been suggested that a separate band of frequencies be set aside for educators, but that would have meant that listeners could not receive the educational stations on standard radio receivers.)

The commercial broadcasters insisted that separate educational channels were unwise because they would take frequencies away from licensees who could make better use of them (that is, themselves). They also maintained that there was no need for separate educational stations since the commercial stations were more than willing to share their facilities with educators. Many commercial stations did carry educational and cultural programs, often produced by local educational institutions, on their schedules.

When President Roosevelt took office in 1932, he decided that the entire fragmentary, disorganized system of federal communications regulation should be consolidated, streamlined and made more effective. To accomplish this, he would have to reduce to a minimum the number of controversial issues that would distract Congress from the main task: the establishment of a single, independent federal communications regulatory agency. Therefore, Roosevelt persuaded the educators to hold off on their demands, to support his proposed Federal Communications Commission, and, once the FCC had come into existence, to let it arbitrate their problems with the commercial broadcasters. He repeatedly assured the educators that he understood and sympathized with their needs. The educators therefore stood aside and made only a minor effort to influence the content of the Federal Communications Act of 1934; they waited and took their case to the newly formed FCC. As it turned out, they had once again been outmaneuvered.

At first, it looked like the FCC would give serious heed to the plight of the educational broadcasters. Only a few months after final passage of the Communications Act, the FCC convened a conference on the subject. However, it soon became apparent that the new commission was not interested in the idea of reserving certain frequencies for educational use. The educators themselves were divided, some insisting that only a separate allocation would protect them and assure them of access to their audience, while others feared that a separate allocation would become a "ghetto" of frequencies that the public would largely ignore. Those educators who had developed a good working relationship with commercial broadcasters spoke glowingly of the commercial stations' cooperation and willingness to devote several hours a day to educational and cultural programming. The commercial broadcasters repeatedly insisted that they would carry all the educational programs anyone wanted to transmit; in fact, according to the broadcasters, educators had failed to make use of all the opportunities they had been offered.

Furthermore, at the FCC's conference on non-commercial broadcasting, representatives of religious, labor and various other organizations showed up, each demanding that they, too, be given a special allocation of frequencies or some other special consideration. Representatives of the government, some of whom had already demonstrated their interest in promoting non-commercial broadcasting, offered conflicting opinions on what should be done. Ultimately, the FCC did what one would expect it to do under the circumstances: nothing.

Thereafter, the FCC answered all demands, requests and pleas from non-commercial broadcasters with the solution that had been offered before: use the free time available on the commercial stations. Indeed, the commercial stations made it a point to include a few hours of non-commercial programming in their daily schedules, if only to demonstrate their commitment to public service as responsible trustees of the airwaves.

Throughout the middle and late 1930s, the FCC continued to make token efforts to appease non-commercial broadcasters, especially educators. However, during this same period commercial broadcasting enjoyed phenomenal growth. The time available for non-commercial programs declined drastically because those "public service" hours had always been unsold portions of the broadcast schedule. The common practice then was to sell half-hour or longer blocks of time to single sponsors, who provided both the program and the commercials. Unsold blocks were given to non-commercial users at, in essence, no loss to the station. When sponsors began to buy more and more broadcasting time, the non-commercial users found their programs shunted to less and less desirable time periods—or they were shut out altogether. Mozart and elementary physics gave way to Serutan and soap powders.

In 1936 Major Edwin Armstrong petitioned the FCC to allocate frequencies for broadcasting with his frequency modulation (FM) system. By this time, the radio networks were already clamoring for the allocation of frequencies for television, and the FCC was nearly driven to distraction by the advocates of both new services. The educators and other parties interested in non-commercial radio hooked up with Armstrong, who welcomed their support. Their tacit agreement was very simple: the non-commercial broadcasters (or would-be broadcasters) would lobby for an FM radio service, and in return Armstrong would lobby for the reservation of non-commercial frequencies in the new service. The FCC, for its part, not only encouraged the educators to take an interest in FM, but almost insisted on it. The educators were wary at first, for fear that FM would turn out to be a sad substitute for AM frequencies they still cherished, but by 1938 the educators had acceded to the inevitable.

Then the FCC did something altogether uncharacteristic: it established a new radio service that no one had asked for. In January 1938 the commission announced that 25 channels in a frequency band far above the standard AM commercial band would be available *only* for non-commercial educational radio. Licensees in this band had to be educational institutions. They were authorized to transmit by AM, but they could request special permission to broadcast by FM if they preferred.

Unfortunately, no one was manufacturing transmitters or receivers to operate at the frequencies allocated to this new service, and there were serious questions about the technological feasibility of using it. A few school systems experimented with the system, but most waited for something better.

In 1940 the FCC finally established an FM commercial radio service. The frequencies for this new service were in a band just above the non-commercial educational band, and 35 channels were allocated to FM. Five more non-commercial educational channels were dropped into the spectrum space between the band allocated in 1938 and the new FM band. Thus, under this scheme, there would be 30 non-commercial educational channels, from 41 to 43 megahertz, and 35 commercial channels, from 43 to 50 megahertz. The lowermost 25 channels could be either AM or FM, but the rest were to be FM only.

Before the educators could begin to make effective use of this unexpected new opportunity, World War II intervened. Commercial broadcasters soaked up the new FM channels with alacrity, but the educators were content to wait out the war. The FCC was astonished and angered by the educators' apparent indifference, and came close to wiping out the 30 educational channels altogether. However, they waited; there was still the matter of television to resolve.

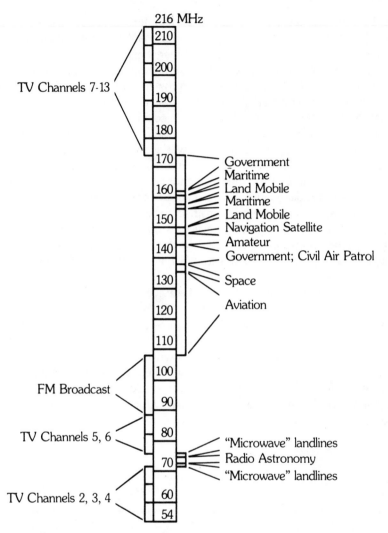

VHF Television, FM Broadcasting and Other Uses of the VHF Spectrum. This is one of the "busiest" frequency bands in the electromagnetic spectrum, as the list of users to the right of the column suggests. If the FCC's original plans for television had been carried out, all TV stations would move to the UHF band (512 to 806 MHz) and this "prime real estate" would be available to the various other users whose frequencies now are overcrowded.

In 1945 after a series of hearings and conferences, the FCC announced a general reallocation of frequencies above the AM commercial band. The FM service was moved bodily from its 41-50 megahertz portion of the spectrum to the band from 88 to 108 megahertz. The bottom of this band, from 88 to 92 megahertz, was permanently reserved for 20 non-commercial educational channels; the remaining 80 channels were allocated to commercial broadcasting. At the time, there were only a dozen or so educational stations using the 41-43 megahertz band and the original FM commercial service had never really gotten established, in part because the war soaked up most of the capital that might have been used for such new ventures, and in part because the major radio networks ignored FM. They were more intent on getting television started. The original FM radio channels were turned over to the land mobile service, and television was given the spectrum from 48 to 88 megahertz and from 174 to 216 megahertz. (Three years later, television's channel one, from 48 to 54 megahertz, was taken away and returned to the mobile radio service, which also occupies the spectrum from 108 to 174 megahertz along with miscellaneous other services.)

Although the relocation of the FM service was somewhat disruptive to the stations that were already in operation, for many of them it meant merely modifying their existing transmitters; of course, virtually all FM receivers had to be replaced, since they were not designed for the new frequencies. However, at least the educators finally had their very own channels, and the radio manufacturers agreed to build receivers that would accept the entire band from 88 to 108 megahertz. Thus the educational stations could ride on the coattails of the commercial (FM) stations as their popularity increased.

TV for Education

Meanwhile, television had come into being, a fact that the educators ignored. The U.S. Commissioner of Education, John W. Studebaker, politely asked the FCC to set aside two television channels for educational use, and there were a few similar requests from public school authorities, but nothing like the intense lobbying that had been needed to bring about reserved radio channels. Besides, the FCC was busy trying to choose between the various competing television systems. When the commission finally settled that issue in January 1945, it also declared that there was not enough interest on the part of educators to warrant reserved channels. However, the FCC promised to give educational broadcasters equal consideration for licenses, and, if enough interest developed in the future, to consider setting aside a few channels for their use.

Actually, the FCC's allocation of 13 VHF television channels (formally adopted in May, 1945) was supposed to be merely a temporary expedient until the technology for UHF television could be made practical. The commission clearly anticipated that *all* television service would be shifted to the UHF band at some future date, and there would be enough channels at the higher frequencies to satisfy educators and everyone else. Within three short years, it became apparent that that was not going to happen: VHF's popularity had vastly exceeded everyone's expectations, to the point that receiver manufacturers could not keep up with the demand and there were about three times as many license applicants as there could ever be VHF stations. Virtually none of the applicants, however, proposed to broadcast non-commercially.

The FCC then imposed its freeze on licensing, a freeze that lasted four years while the commission reconsidered the whole business of television. Reluctantly, they concluded that moving the television service entirely to UHF would not be practical (mainly because there would be howls of outrage from all the people who had bought comparatively expensive VHF receivers).

During the freeze, two members of the commission did their utmost to drag non-commercial broadcasters into television. The single person most responsible for the creation of an educational television service was Commissioner Frieda B. Hennock, who begged, cajoled, scolded and threatened educators and fellow commissioners, insisting that there be a reservation of television channels for education. She spoke to every organization that would have her, testified before Congress, wrote articles for magazines, published pamphlets and brochures, and, according to some witnesses, screamed and wept during the commission's closed-door sessions; the intensity of her passion for educational television evidently came close to hysteria at times. In any case, she certainly made her point. Educators slowly awakened to the prospects she held out, and the other members of the FCC were not about to disappoint her. In April 1952 the FCC formally established the UHF television service, which would provide 70 channels. At the same time, the commission revised its table of assignments for the VHF service. Under the new table, there would be potentially 242 non-commercial, educational television stations, 80 of which would be in the VHF band and the rest in the UHF band. Ms. Hennock complained that there should have been more educational station assignments and that more of them should have been VHF, but she had won as much as she could.

Licenses were issued immediately to half a dozen applicants for educational television stations. New organizations sprung up to promote educational TV, and several philanthropic foundations pledged millions of dollars to the new medium. The National Educational Television and Radio Center was formed in Michigan to develop programs for non-commercial broadcasting. In June 1953 the first educational television station, KUHT in Houston, Texas, actually went on the air; seventeen other stations followed shortly thereafter and the FCC was still processing another 30 applications.

However, this initial flurry of activity proved to be misleading. Some of the first stations to go on the air went off within a few months; they had neither the funds nor the technical expertise to keep going. What had been a steady flow of applications dropped off to a mere trickle. Educators had discovered the unpleasant facts of television life: first, that it is an awesomely expensive business; second, that creating programs to fill the broadcasting schedule requires an enormous variety of creative and technical talents; third, and most damaging, that no one was watching those UHF channels.

The early days of UHF were plagued by the near-total lack of television receivers capable of accepting the UHF signal. Without an audience, there was not much point in transmitting programs even for non-commercial purposes. Since a large part of the population already had invested in VHF receivers, and were at least reasonably satisfied with the limited programming available on VHF stations, the demand for UHF sets was not large enough to appeal to manufacturers. The few available UHF receivers were grossly overpriced and inferior in design.

In a few years, there were converters available that could translate UHF signals into VHF frequencies; their cost was reasonable, eventually getting down to around $20 to $30, and some people were willing to buy them—especially in areas where one or two of the network-affiliated stations had been stuck in the UHF band. However, the persisting attitude, among both broadcasters and the public, that UHF is somehow inferior to VHF did nothing to boost the fortunes of educational television.

Early educational programming was almost uniformly dreadful. Loaded with good intentions and no money, and having almost no capability to record programs, the broadcasters transmitted endless hours of college professors lecturing in front of a blackboard. There was nothing that even resembled a network of educational stations; some stations exchanged filmed programs, but even these were rare, and video tape had not yet come onto the market. Even when videotape equipment became available in 1956, it was far too costly for most educational stations. As late as 1970, the majority of educational TV stations had no videotape equipment.

The NETRC was almost the only organization attempting to produce and distribute educational programs on a nationwide basis; it also acted as a program exchange service, whenever a local station managed to produce a program worthy of being exchanged.

These discouraging circumstances severely hindered the development of educational television in the mid-50s, to the point that the FCC began in 1957 to reassign some of the educational stations to commercial licensees. This practice stopped quickly when some influential members of Congress objected, but the FCC was plainly annoyed with the educators and greatly pressured by the commercial broadcasters to give them more channels.

The All-Channel Receiver Act of 1963, requiring television manufacturers to include UHF tuning circuits in all receivers, helped to solve the educational stations' problems. Eventually, as the old VHF-only sets wore out and were replaced, most of the audience could at least pick up the UHF signal if they wished.

In 1964 the FCC created another new service for educators: the Instructional Television Fixed Service (ITFS). This service was to be reserved exclusively for educational institutions, to enable them to transmit programs from a central point to any number of classrooms over a fairly large geographic area. The ITFS operates at frequencies of around 2.5 gigahertz—what are usually called "microwave" frequencies—so they cannot be picked up by regular TV receivers, but the signal can be converted to ordinary VHF frequencies by special receiving equipment. In short, ITFS serves as a private television communications system for educational organizations. Once again, the proposal caught educators flat-footed: they had not asked for this new boon. This time, however, they recovered quickly enough to thank the commission and to apply for licenses in the new service.

The commission was well aware that the lack of money was by far the biggest barrier to a well-established national system of educational television. On its own initiative, the commission began to encourage large foundations to support non-commercial television, and began to sound out Congress on the possibility of opening the federal purse to educational broadcasters. However, there were other forces already at work on the problem, and one of those forces was the formidable Lyndon Baines Johnson.

The main control room of KLRU-TV, the PBS station in Austin, Texas.
KLRU (and its sister station, KLRN-TV, which primarily serves San
Antonio) enjoys far better facilities than most PBS stations; they are leased,
at nominal rates, from the University of Texas. In return, the station's staff
supervises student interns from the Department of Radio-Television-Film,
who thereby get real "on-the-job" training in addition to their classroom
work. (Photo by the author, courtesy KLRU-TV and the University of
Texas Communications Center)

As early as 1957, Johnson had helped educational broadcasters put together a bill to provide federal funds for the construction of educational TV stations, but the bill had never gotten through Congress. It was reintroduced in 1958, 1959, 1960, 1961 and 1962; it finally passed in April 1962 and was signed by President Kennedy a few weeks later. The Educational Television Facilities Act simply authorized the Department of Health, Education and Welfare to give grants to non-commercial television stations for the purchase and installation of broadcasting equipment. No money was appropriated until the following year, but between 1963 and 1968 more than $30 million was funneled into educational TV. The act, which was later retitled the Educational Broadcasting Facilities Act and, later still, the Public Telecommunications Facilities Act, continues to be one of the primary sources of funds for the construction of educational television and radio systems (including ITFS systems and, though rarely, cable systems). Thanks largely to this one measure, educational television stations now reach almost 90 percent of the U.S. population.

After Johnson became president, his "Great Society" series of antipoverty and education programs frequently included funds for educational television. The National Defense Education Act, passed in 1958, had offered some money for schools to purchase television receivers and related equipment, and the U.S. Office of Education had responded by reorganizing its Audiovisual Aids to Education program into the Educational Media Branch. But this was just the beginning. No fewer than six antipoverty and education acts passed in 1964 and 1965 allowed some funds to be spent either to purchase receiving equipment for the schools or to promote broadcasting more directly, by constructing and building television transmitters and studios and by paying for the production of programs.

The federal government was not the only source of desperately needed funds for educational television. Several philanthropic foundations had come up with money for station equipment and for the production of programs. The FCC decided to permit non-commercial broadcasters to give a brief credit to supporters before and after each program; this simple measure, while it forbade mentioning any commercial product, encouraged large corporations to invest in educational television as a subtle form of advertising.

Undeniably, the single most important contributor to educational television was the Ford Foundation, which began plowing money into non-commercial broadcasting in 1952 and, at last count, had spent more than $300 million on the medium. Some of the Ford money went into station construction, especially in the early days before the Educational Television Facilities Act. However, the great bulk of Ford's money was spent on the production and distribution of programs. Ford was a major supporter of NETRC, which moved from Michigan to New York City in 1959 and, a few years later, truncated its name to National Educational Television (NET). Ford also helped provide seed money and continuing funds to individual stations, enabling them to serve as "national production centers."

The cavernous main studio at KLRU/KLRN, which currently houses the set of the popular series, *Austin City Limits*. Other KLRN/KLRU productions have been carried nationally by PBS, including the children's shows, *Carrascolendas* and *Khan-Du*. This studio is said to be the largest and best-equipped television studio outside of New York and Hollywood. (Photo by the author, courtesy KLRU-TV and the University of Texas Communications Center)

Still, the educational stations were not tied together into any sort of network. Program distribution meant circulating programs on film or, less often, video tape; this meant that it was simply impossible for all stations to show a given program simultaneously, even had they wanted to. Furthermore, films and tapes sometimes got lost in the mail, or showed up the day after they had been scheduled.

A proposed solution came from a thoroughly unexpected source: ABC. The network, whose fortunes in 1965 had not yet begun to improve, asked the FCC for permission to build a communications satellite. ABC would use the satellite to distribute its own programs, would sell time on one or two other satellite channels, and would provide at least one channel free of charge to educational broadcasters.

This proposal was stunning at the time. The first commercial communications satellite (AT&T's *Telstar*) had been launched only two years before, and the first communications satellite to be put into a permanent, geosynchronous orbit was barely a year old. However, ABC's idea was not an exercise in science fiction. The network correctly calculated that it could recover the cost of its satellite just from the savings it would incur by transmitting its programs nationally without using the expensive AT&T telephone system; any revenues it received from leasing additional channels would be mostly profit, and giving a free channel to educational television would be taken as an expression of public spirit.

Unfortunately, Congress had chartered the Communications Satellite Corporation in 1962 to develop the technology and commercial applications of such devices. Comsat (one of whose major stockholders, not incidentally, was AT&T) insisted that it had been given a monopoly over domestic communications satellites. The FCC, unsure of its authority—much less of the long-term consequences of ABC's proposal—invited comment.

One of the first to comment was the Ford Foundation, who suggested going ABC one better. Ford wanted to establish a non-profit corporation that would operate a network of several domestic communications satellites; the satellite channels would be leased to the television networks, the telephone company and anyone else who wanted to use them. Not only would the rates for television transmission by satellite be lower than the corresponding rate for use of the telephone landlines, but the new corporation's profits would be used to subsidize educational television.

AT&T immediately cried "foul," as did Comsat. The telephone company claimed that depriving it of the revenue from carrying the television networks' programs would drive up its costs, and therefore its prices, for other users of the long-distance system. However, all three commercial networks endorsed the Ford Foundation proposal, as did the Johnson administration and representatives of the educational broadcasters. Comsat grudgingly conceded that Ford had a good idea, but still insisted that it should operate any domestic satellite system—and offered free channels for educational television, as well as some funds for non-commercial programs out of its projected revenues.

Considering the unanimity of agreement on the Ford Foundation's proposal, it seemed only a matter of time before the entire television industry would be shifted to satellites, with an enormous dividend for educational television. AT&T's opposition was not a significant factor, especially after it was learned that its transmission of the TV networks actually was being subsidized by other long-distance telephone services, rather than the other way around.

But the Ford Foundation's bird-in-the-sky vision came to nothing because of an unfortunate coincidence. At almost the same time as the ABC proposal, President Johnson had arranged for the Carnegie Corporation—another foundation that had long supported educational broadcasting—to conduct a major study of the medium's long-term future. The study had not yet gotten underway when the Ford Foundation's response to ABC's idea was announced. Everyone agreed that no decision should be made until the Carnegie study was completed.

The Butterfly Emerges: Public TV

The Carnegie Corporation established a Carnegie Commission on Educational Television in November 1965. The commission, chaired by MIT president James R. Killian, Jr., issued its report in January 1967. Briefly, the Carnegie Commission recommended that educational television be transformed into a new beast, which it called "public television," and become more than just lectures and instructional programs, but instead a major cultural resource for the entire public. Toward this end, the Carnegie Commission recommended that the federal government establish an independent, nonprofit Corporation for Public Television that would receive money from the government and other sources and distribute these funds to individual stations and independent production centers like NET. The report also mentioned the possibility of using communications satellites for the benefit of public television, but there was no strong endorsement of the ABC, Ford Foundation or Comsat proposals. In fact, all three of the satellite proposals were effectively dead.

The Carnegie Commission's proposals went into considerable detail about how much money the proposed Corporation for Public Television should have, where the money should come from, and how it should be distributed. There were also recommendations concerning the Educational Broadcasting Facilities Act (it should be extended) and miscellaneous other matters.

The Ford Foundation, notwithstanding the fact that its own proposals had been shelved, vigorously supported the Carnegie Commission's findings. So did the educational broadcasters. Most important, so did President Johnson. The Public Broadcasting Act of 1967, establishing the Corporation for Public Broadcasting (the name change reflected a belated recognition that educational radio should be included), was introduced in both houses of Congress in March. It finally passed with minor amendments in October and was signed into law in November. The Carnegie Corporation, Ford Foundation, United Auto Workers, Communications Workers of America and various other organizations immediately put up several million dollars to get the CPB started and to augment its nine million dollar interim federal budget; even the CBS television network kicked in a million dollars.

Then everything ground to a halt. President Johnson was increasingly preoccupied with the Vietnam War and the rising protests at home. Months passed before he got around to nominating a full slate of directors, and more months went by while the Senate dallied over confirming Johnson's appointments. The corporation did not get around to hiring a president until March 1969 —nearly a year and a half after the Public Broadcasting Act had been passed. Congress fussed and fretted over appropriations for the CPB and finally came up with only five million of the promised nine million dollars.

Meanwhile, however, the FCC moved forward on its own to provide the CPB with the one thing public broadcasting had never had: a mechanism for a national network. In essence, the FCC simply acted on its own authority, instructing AT&T to make landlines available on a limited basis at a sharp discount from the regular price. AT&T complied, but not eagerly.

The Ford Foundation also went ahead on its own; it established the Public Broadcasting Laboratory as a new program production center. The Ford plan was that PBL would produce new programs and use the AT&T "interconnection" one evening per week to distribute the programs to all public television stations. NET, also with Ford money, would continue to produce and acquire programs and would distribute them over the interconnection four evenings a week. The stations could broadcast the programs as they were being sent down the telephone system, or could videotape them for transmission at a later time, or could substitute other programming as they wished. Ford also awarded a large grant to the Children's Television Workshop (CTW), which also had received money from the U.S. Office of Education and other sources.

This flurry of activity, in spite of the CPB's slow start, brought public television to the center of attention in 1967 and 1968. PBL's Sunday evening program, in a news-magazine format, attracted a good deal of popularity. The cooking-show host of WGBH's *French Chef,* Julia Child, attained a national audience overnight, even though her series had been available to educational stations since 1962; suddenly, through NET and the interconnection, she was a star.

The CPB finally got itself organized and began to function in 1969. Congress kept feeding it modest doses of money, but probably the infant agency could not have absorbed much more at the time. One issue that CPB addressed almost immediately was interconnection; the FCC had established it only as an "experiment," clearly intending CPB to pick up the ball. CPB did so and established the Public Broadcasting Service as an independent agency whose sole function would be to manage the interconnection, acquiring programs from the various production centers and other sources and sending them out via the telephone lines. NET, whose staff thought this should be their function, went into a prolonged sulk and finally merged with the New York City public television station, WNDT, which then changed its name to WNET. PBL ceased to exist.

By January 1970, it seemed that the millenium had come for noncommercial broadcasting. The CPB had even taken educational radio under its wing, forming National Public Radio and a program production and distribution service for the 425 or so educational radio stations across the country.

But there were darker days on the horizon.

The Nixon Blitzkrieg

In January 1969, Richard M. Nixon had become President. Within a matter of months, his vice president, Spiro Agnew, had launched a series of vitriolic attacks against the news media. The Federal Bureau of Investigation began to "investigate" reporters for the New York *Times* and CBS. The Internal Revenue Service questioned whether certain NET programs were intended to "influence legislation," and, if so, whether NET's tax-exempt status should be revoked.

In September 1970 President Nixon established the Office of Telecommunications Policy and appointed Clay T. Whitehead as its director. OTP was the successor to the White House office that had been responsible for coordinating the various radio frequencies allocated to the government. However, Whitehead perceived his charter to be much broader; he became the principal administration spokesman on all telecommunications policy matters.

Each year between 1970 and 1974, when President Nixon resigned in disgrace, the U.S. Office of Education asked for considerably less money for the Public Broadcasting Facilities program than Congress had authorized; indeed, each year Congress appropriated more than the Nixon administration requested. The same was true with respect to appropriations for the CPB. It was clear to everyone (as it had been even before President Nixon took office) that CPB and public broadcasting generally had to be free of annual appropriations in order for the broadcasters to plan on a long-term basis, and in order to fend off political interference. Public broadcasting was soon to find out just what "political interference" could mean.

The first direct salvo came in October 1970 when Whitehead complained to the National Association of Educational Broadcasters, at its convention, that the CPB and PBS had "over-centralized" public broadcasting, creating a "fourth network" and, in some vague way, depriving local stations of their autonomy. Furthermore, he declared that public broadcasting had been "captured" by the "liberal Eastern establishment," as evidenced by the news and public affairs programs carried by PBS (some of which had been critical of the Nixon administration). According to Whitehead, public broadcasting was doomed unless it disavowed such programming and returned more control to the individual stations.

Soon after that, Nixon spokesmen called attention to the presence on the CPB staff and at the various production centers of individuals whom they regarded as "liberals." Among them were the respected television journalists Sander Vanocur and Robert MacNeil. According to the administration, these individuals and several CPB executives were being paid excessive salaries (although each had taken a substantial reduction in income when they had left their jobs in commercial broadcasting and other private industry). The critics went so far as to complain about the quality of the interior decor in the CPB offices: it was too rich, they said.

These attacks had the intended effects. First, they made it increasingly difficult for public broadcasting supporters in Congress to defend the CPB. Second, the criticisms touched on some raw nerves and unhealed wounds, creating and widening disagreements within the medium. Many public broadcasters were, indeed, concerned about the idea that PBS might become a "fourth network," which they did not want; they had struggled to keep their stations alive during a long period when they were alone in the wilderness, and they intended to maintain their autonomy.

The Nixon administration used its criticisms to justify the continued use of one-year appropriations, rather than giving the CPB and public broadcasting the multi-year appropriations it needed to establish its independence and to plan properly for its continued growth. In 1972 the attacks on public broadcasting grew even more rabid. The CPB executives and congressional supporters tried to achieve some reasonable compromise or accommodation, but that turned out to be impossible. PBS abandoned virtually all of its news and public affairs programming, and CPB rearranged its policies to give local station managers a greater voice in the system. It was all in vain. Congress finally passed a two-year appropriation and President Nixon promptly vetoed it. In his veto message, the President recited all of the criticisms that his own spokesmen had raised, and justified the veto on the grounds that public broadcasting obviously was too controversial to be trusted with more than a one-year appropriation. Congress meekly introduced such a bill, passed it, and sent it to the President for his signature.

The president and chairman of CPB promptly resigned in protest, as did a number of other public broadcasting officials. President Nixon just as promptly filled the vacancies with his own people. However, he underestimated his nominee for chairman of the CPB board, Thomas B. Curtis, a former Representative from Missouri. Curtis, though he shared some of Nixon's prejudices against public broadcasting, was fundamentally sympathetic to the medium and was intelligent enough to recognize the ploys of Nixon's henchmen.

Henry W. Loomis, Curtis's choice as president of CPB, was more clearly a Nixon camp follower; he quickly began to dismantle the program distribution system that had been painstakingly put together, involving CPB as the source of production funds and PBS as the agent for program acquisition as well as manager of the interconnection. Under Loomis's plan, PBS would be confined to the status of bookkeeper in charge of the interconnection and CPB would be merely a passive conduit of funds, which would flow directly to the individual stations. The stations presumably would use these funds to either produce or to buy programs, and would arrange among themselves to order their transmission over the AT&T lines; PBS would do little more than help coordinate and keep track of the stations' requests for interconnection.

Such an unwieldy system was obviously impractical, but it had some appeal to the more independent-minded stations. PBS officials responded angrily, charging CPB with undermining the entire public broadcasting system. Some of the station managers cursed both their houses, CPB for knuckling under to the Nixon administration and forcing the cancellation of the public affairs programs (which were among the more popular of public broadcasting's offerings) and PBS for taking it upon itself to choose what programs to send and when to send them—that is, acting like a network.

In March 1973 Patrick Buchanan, one of President Nixon's assistants and advisers, appeared on Dick Cavett's late-night talk show on ABC and not only admitted, but chortled over the administration's success in throttling public broadcasting and fomenting dissension within the medium. According to Buchanan, the entire, well-orchestrated campaign of harassment and intimidation was in retaliation for public broadcasting's failure to give unswerving loyalty to the President—in short, critical public affairs programs. Buchanan had good reason to be pleased, since all those programs were no more.

Buchanan's performance was appalling to the viewing audience, many of whom had little inkling of what was going on in public broadcasting. But Buchanan had gone one step too far; public broadcasters reacted swiftly, closing ranks between the station managers and PBS. The CPB continued to parrot the Nixon line, and shortly thereafter announced that it would no longer fund any public affairs programming. However, Ralph B. Rogers, chairman of the board of the Dallas public television station, KERA, and formerly an executive of Texas Instruments, brought together his counterparts at the other public stations, along with their station managers, representatives of the National Association of Educational Broadcasters (NAEB), and others who accurately perceived the threat to the medium. This ad hoc consortium worked out an entirely new structure for PBS and created a new entity, the Station Program Cooperative (SPC).

The basic idea behind the SPC is quite simple: the stations themselves should control the acquisition of programs through what amounts to a marketplace. Anyone may propose to develop and produce a program, or series of programs, for public television. The proposals are assembled by PBS into a catalog that is sent out to all the participating stations. The stations decide which programs they might be interested in carrying. PBS then calculates, on the basis of the proposed program budget and the number of stations that have indicated an interest, the cost per station for each program. The stations then decide which programs they are willing and able to buy, using the funds they have received (or expect to receive) from the CPB, foundations and local contributions. If enough stations are willing to fund a program, it gets produced; otherwise, it does not. In addition, programs can be produced entirely with funds from foundations or government agencies (such as the U.S. Office of Education or the National Endowment for the Humanities, both of which spend several million dollars a year on public television programs); a few programs may be funded directly by the CPB.

PBS continues to manage the interconnection and other program distribution mechanisms, including the largest program exchange library for public television. However, the stations are not obligated to show the programs they have chosen at the times selected by PBS to transmit each program down the telephone lines. The stations may tape programs for later use, or not show the programs at all. PBS obligingly transmits most programs at two or more times each week, for the convenience of those stations that have limited taping facilities.

President Nixon's rapid descent into the quagmire of the Watergate scandal, and his subsequent resignation, brought an end to the organized attack on public broadcasting, although some Nixon loyalists continue even today to regard PBS and the medium in general with suspicion. Tom Curtis, chairman of the board of directors at CPB, resigned in protest of the Nixon administration's constant interference; the remaining board members chose James R. Killian, Jr., who had headed the prestigious Carnegie Commission on Educational Television, to succeed Curtis. Sen. John Pastore persuaded the Senate to appropriate funds for the CPB for two years and for the educational broadcasting facilities program for five years. The bill passed the House with minor modifications and was eventually signed by President Nixon in August 1973. By that time, public television was broadcasting daily coverage of the Senate's Watergate hearings.

The SPC went into effect in 1974. At first, it proved to be a cumbersome and time-consuming procedure, but as the participants have become accustomed to it and refinements have been made, the system has proven remarkably successful. The stations have at least the option of freely choosing most of their programs without having to bear all of the costs alone. In essence, PBS operates more as a syndicator than as a network. However, the use of the telephone-line interconnection permitted most stations to show prime-time programs simultaneously, an important factor for the promotion of programs through national advertising. Thus, since 1974 public broadcasting has enjoyed the best of both worlds: that of network affiliation, and that of syndication to independent stations. Meanwhile, PBS quickly began to prepare for the satellite age.

The original ABC, Ford Foundation and Comsat proposals to give public broadcasting a "free ride" on someone else's satellite may have been forgotten by everyone else, but not by PBS. In 1976 PBS announced a new plan to transmit its programs via *Westar*, a domestic commercial communications satellite that had been launched by Western Union in 1974. (The FCC had earlier decided that neither Comsat nor AT&T could operate domestic communications satellites on a common carrier basis. Comsat was restricted to serving international communications, and AT&T could operate satellites only to supplement its telephone landlines.)

In less than three years, the PBS satellite system was completely installed and in operation. Almost 150 earth stations (to receive signals from the satellite) had been built, serving 163 PBS stations. PBS leased four satellite channels, thereby making it possible to transmit four different programs simultaneously so that the stations could choose whichever program they liked and ignore the rest or tape them for later use.

The system also provides six "uplinks," or transmitters to the satellite. Although most programs originate at the main PBS facility near Washington, DC, the regional centers can transmit programs directly to the satellite for distribution to the entire network.

Besides giving PBS enormously greater flexibility in distributing programs, the satellite network has cut the cost of program distribution drastically; all four satellite channels, available to PBS 24 hours a day, cost less than the system had been paying AT&T for part-time use of a single landline interconnection. Furthermore, the landline interconnection, under the terms of the discount agreement developed by the FCC in 1968, was subject to pre-emption whenever the lines were needed for commercial broadcasting. AT&T had eventually added new lines to its system, thereby reducing the frequent need for pre-emption, but pre-emptions still occurred occasionally and were both a great irritant and an impediment to PBS in its efforts to establish some sort of national public broadcasting service.

There is a curious irony in the fact that public broadcasting has moved to satellite transmission well ahead of the commercial networks, even though it was one of the commercial networks, ABC, which first suggested it. The major networks have been slow to make the same move for a number of reasons, which will be explored more fully in Chapter 9, while PBS had neither the long-standing investment in the landline system nor the financial resources to absorb the heavy expense of landline transmissions.

As America enters the 1980s, television is still predominantly a commercial medium and the three major commercial networks continue to monopolize the public's attention and interest. The total budget for public television, including the local budgets for all public television stations plus the budgets of the CPB and PBS (including the operation of the satellite distribution system) and all other funds expended on program production, does not equal the *profits* of the three commercial networks. Nevertheless, the poor bridesmaid has grown accustomed to her role and is making the most of it.

The tremendous flexibility of the Station Program Cooperative, combined with the versatility and economy of the satellite distribution system, may prove to be more than the foundation for public television's future. They may also provide the major commercial networks with a pattern for their own response to the difficult days ahead. As television's audience becomes more fragmented and specialized, the commercial networks will either adapt or perish. Public broadcasting has already confronted those alternatives and has shown an amazing capacity to adapt.

As for public broadcasting's own future, it seems to be secure. Congress now appropriates funds for the CPB and for public broadcasting facilities construction on at least a three- to five-year basis, and there is growing sentiment to establish some kind of permanent mechanism that would give public broadcasting adequate funds with complete independence from the political process.

The only cloud on the horizon is the fact that public television is tied to broadcasting, and it is inextricably a part of the television broadcasting system. There are challenges to the whole idea of broadcasting as the principal means of distributing television signals, and if these challenges are successful it is conceivable that public television could be pulled down along with commercial television. Public television's survival skills may yet face their sternest test; the challenger is cable.

Part
III

Cable
Television

Chapter
7

Cable: The Dream and the Nightmare

All television distribution systems rely on the principle of the modulated carrier, as explained in Chapter 1. The information signal (that is, the composite video signal) is used to modulate a carrier signal, which can be separately amplified without introducing an objectionable amount of noise into the information signal, and which can be used to energize an antenna to transmit the signal through the air.

Basic Cable Technology

There is also another way to distribute a modulated carrier. This method is sometimes called a wire waveguide, but the more common term is *coaxial cable.*

A coaxial cable consists of a solid wire or a hollow tube that serves as the conductor for the modulated carrier. Around this conductor is either solid insulating material or, in most heavy cables, an air space maintained by insulated supports placed along the conductor. A second conductor, usually made of braided wire, surrounds the insulating material or air space; this second conductor serves as a ground for the current in the main conductor, and also acts to shield the main conductor from any magnetic fields in the environment. Finally, there is an insulating sheath of plastic or rubber covering the entire cable.

The coaxial cable acts as nothing more nor less than a pipeline for the modulated carrier. At any point, the cable can be tapped to draw off the current and feed it to a receiving device (such as a TV set). Amplifiers can be placed along the cable to keep the carrier signal up to the desired strength.

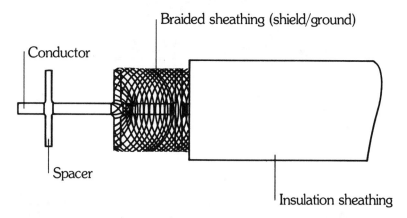

Coaxial Cable. Electrical signals, at radio frequencies, follow the conductor; the braided sheathing serves both as a ground and as a shield, cutting off interfering radio signals. Smaller coaxial cables usually have solid insulating material between the conductor and the sheathing; larger cables use air as the insulator and have plastic spacers to keep the conductor centered in the insulating space.

Most important, any number of modulated carriers can be accommodated by a single coaxial cable, as long as they are transmitted on separate frequencies. In theory, there is no limit to the frequency bandwidth that can be transmitted down a coaxial cable. In practice, however, the size of the cable's main conductor, the size of the insulating material or space around the conductor, and the characteristics of the secondary conductor (the shield) all affect the bandwidth that the cable can handle successfully, and there are also technical limitations on the design of amplifiers and other important parts of a cable distribution system. Still, even the cheapest, most unsophisticated coaxial cable can easily accommodate a bandwidth of at least 60 megahertz, or the equivalent of ten television channels. The type of coaxial cable most commonly used by cable television systems in the late 1950s and early 1960s could handle between 20 and 30 television channels; more modern cables are capable of carrying fifty or sixty television channels with no difficulty.

Cable television was invented in the late 1940s, when the television industry first began. There are various claims to the title of originator of cable television. Some authorities say that the first cable system was built in Astoria, Oregon, while others claim that it originated in Pennsylvania. In fact, it probably developed independently in several different places at about the same time. Wherever people were sufficiently interested in watching television, but there was no local television station to satisfy that interest, someone (perhaps a local appliance dealer who wanted to add television sets to his inventory) would hit on the basic concept of cable television. By erecting a large antenna on the highest point in town, preferably on a mountaintop, and amplifying the weak signal received from some distant television station, the signal could be distributed by coaxial cable to people's homes, usually for a modest fee.

Because the early cable systems aspired to do no more than this, they were often called community antenna television systems, or CATV. During the FCC's television licensing freeze, from 1948 to 1952, the CATV industry began to boom; there were many small towns, and even some good-sized cities, that had no television service and only distant prospects of acquiring any. To this day, there are thousands of cable systems in remote areas that function as no more than CATV systems, offering anywhere from three to six channels of television programs from the nearest cities—which may be a hundred miles away, beyond mountains or other geographic barriers.

Main components of the CATV system are the master antenna, or a group of antennae on a single large tower; demodulators, which strip the carrier signal away from the composite video signal; amplifiers, bringing the video signal up to an acceptable level; and modulators, which supply a new carrier signal to be modulated by the composite video. All of these components together are known as the "head end."

In a few systems, the antenna is located some distance away from the head end. This may necessitate the use of demodulators, amplifiers and modulators at the antenna base, transferring the received signals to an intermediate carrier that takes the signal to the head end, where the signal is once again demodulated, amplified, cleaned up by signal processors and re-modulated for transmission through the cable system. For obvious reasons, this kind of complication is avoided whenever possible.

Beyond the head end, the several signals are carried by one or more mains or trunks, then through a branching series of distribution lines, and finally to the individual subscribers. The line from the distribution cable to the subscriber's TV set is known as a "drop." Along the entire network, at regular intervals, line amplifiers restore the modulated carrier signals to their required strength. In cable terminology, incidentally, the subscriber's TV set—or any other device that ultimately receives signals from the cable—is known as a "terminal."

There is nothing much more to basic cable technology than that. However, a great deal can be added to the basics. For example, a studio can be built at the head end; programs produced in the studio, or played on a videotape recorder or a film chain, can be fed into a modulator and transmitted down the cable system just the same as a signal from the master antenna. Or signals can be received from very distant television stations, hundreds or even thousands of miles away, over microwave transmission systems operated by independent common carriers (by FCC decree, AT&T has been prohibited from entering this business). Or signals can be received from communications satellites through an earth station at the head end. All of these signals can be added to the signals from local and nearby television broadcasting stations, and all can be fed down the cable to subscribers. At the subscriber's "terminal," or TV set, there is no intrinsic difference between the signals received from a local TV station, an origination studio at the head end, or from a distant station via a satellite in outer space.

Much more than just television signals can be transmitted through a cable television system. The frequency bandwidth of one television channel could be used instead to carry about 30 stereo FM radio channels. Or about 600 low-grade voice radio channels, comparable to Citizen's Band signals. Or several thousand simple on-off or digital pulse signals, which might be used to operate various automatic devices. For example, the cable service could transmit a pulsing signal that would automatically regulate the clocks in your home, or that would sound an alarm in the event of a natural disaster or some other threatening event.

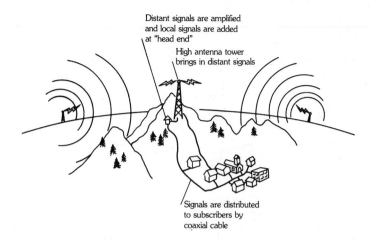

Distant signals are amplified
and local signals are added
at "head end"

High antenna tower
brings in distant signals

Signals are distributed
to subscribers by
coaxial cable

The CATV Concept. A high antenna tower, often on a mountaintop or tall building, brings in distant TV (and FM radio) signals; these signals are amplified, and sometimes locally originated signals are added, at the "head end"; all signals are distributed by coaxial cables to subscribers, who otherwise would be limited to the few nearby signals they could receive via rooftop antennas.

Signals can flow through a coaxial cable in both directions, as long as they are on different frequencies. Thus it is possible for an origination studio to be located anywhere in the system. Programs can be transmitted "upstream" toward the head end and "downstream" toward more distant subscribers just as easily as if the studio were at the head end. Or signals can be transmitted from the individual subscribers back toward the head end. These "feedback signals" can be used for an astonishing variety of purposes. Subscribers could use a simple push-button device to respond to a program they are watching, to vote in a survey or referendum, or even to purchase some product that is being displayed on their TV sets. Or the feedback signals can be used to transmit, for instance, burglar or fire alarm signals to a central security office, or to monitor an electric, water or gas meter.

There is one serious misconception about so-called two-way cable television. The fact that you subscribe to a cable television service that has some two-way capability does *not* mean that the folks down at the cable company can see you through your TV set. A television receiver is strictly a one-way device; a moment's reflection on the technology of television will show why this is

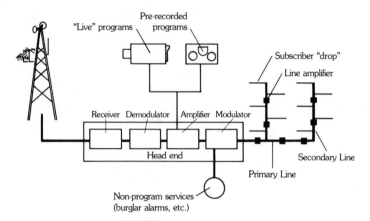

"Live" programs
Pre-recorded programs
Subscriber "drop"
Line amplifier
Receiver Demodulator Amplifier Modulator
Head end
Secondary Line
Primary Line
Non-program services (burglar alarms, etc.)

The components of a Cable Television System. Signals received at the tower are tuned through an ordinary TV receiver; the carrier is removed in a demodulator; the signal is amplified and "processed" to restore it nearly to studio quality; a new carrier frequency is inserted in a modulator; the signal is fed into the coaxial distribution systems. "Live" programs and pre-recorded programs (on video tape or film) also can be introduced at the amplifier stage and given their own carrier channels. Non-program services, such as burglar alarms, also may be fed into the system on their own frequencies (separate from the television channels). One important factor in determining the system's capabilities is the quality of the line amplifiers, which are placed throughout the distribution system to keep the multiple signals up to their proper strength.

inescapably true. A cathode ray tube—the "picture tube" in the TV—simply cannot be used as a pickup tube, nor vice versa. In order for the cable company to spy on you, they would have to install a camera and transmitter, or some other monitoring device, in your home and chances are you would be aware of any attempt to do that. Furthermore, no cable company can install the necessary equipment to monitor your electric meter or to provide a burglar alarm service without your knowledge and permission. I mention this because some people have gotten unduly worked up over the prospect that two-way cable would somehow lead to invasions of their privacy in the "Big Brother" sense.

There is one catch in two-way cable, and it explains why relatively few cable systems offer these capabilities. The amplifiers and modulators at the head end and the line amplifiers that are placed along the cable are active electronic devices, and they are carefully designed to eliminate, as much as possible, unwanted electric signals or "noise." Quite often, line amplifiers are designed to transmit signals only in one direction. More modern line amplifiers are able to carry signals in both directions, at least at certain frequencies, and most competently managed cable systems have installed two-way amplifiers in the newer portions of their system. However, older systems and the older portions of large systems may have line amplifiers that are strictly one-way in design. In order to offer feedback services, the cable system operator would have to replace all those one-way amplifiers, and that could be very costly.

Still, the majority of cable systems do have at least a limited two-way capability, even if they do not offer any two-way services at present. Like any other business operators, cable system owners will offer whatever services their customers demand. However, cable system operators are not known for their aggressive marketing or for being innovative (with some noteworthy exceptions). They have been extremely slow in exploiting the potential of cable technology, and many of the services offered by cable systems have been prompted more by the insistence of the customers or of regulatory agencies than by the ingenuity and salesmanship of the operators.

On the other hand, it must be said in the operator's defense that offering new services is not always a simple matter of connecting up a few wires; sometimes a very large capital investment is required, with uncertain prospects for a profit. Most cable subscribers have not demanded anything more than three or four channels of conventional television service; the demand for more exotic services has come from a relatively small part of the market. And regulatory agencies have not consistently promoted the expansion of cable services. For a while it seemed that the FCC was determined to eliminate cable television except as a supplementary service to bring the major networks' signals to remote audiences: the original CATV concept.

The regulation of cable television has its own peculiarly fascinating history. Almost from its earliest days, cable television has been subjected to heavier regulation than just about any other nascent technology, and that regulation has often been inconsistent in its purposes as well as its effects. Part of the reason has been a persistent uncertainty, in the minds of regulators, about the ultimate benefits and eventual costs (in terms other than monetary considerations) of cable.

The technology of cable does not sound terribly ominous, and it may be a little hard to imagine that presumably sane, level-headed people would come unglued at mention of the word. In fact, the prospect of cable television terrifies and infuriates many people. At the other extreme, there are those who become rapturous over visions of cable as an electronic cornucopia.

The greatest and most persistent foes of cable have been the captains of the present television industry: the network executives and local station owners. They regard cable as an interloper, parasite and thief—and those are some of the more generous terms used.

Cable's Threat to Broadcasting

As long as cable systems stuck to their original task, delivering a few distant broadcast signals to the hinterlands, the broadcasters raised few objections. After all, the early CATV systems merely added a few more miles to the market coverage of the nearest broadcasting station. Cable was not perceived as a threat of any consequence.

The first inkling of trouble came from the operators of struggling UHF stations. After the FCC opened up channels 14 through 83 and assigned most of the UHF channels to smaller communities, there was an initial rush for licenses. But almost every attempt to start a UHF station ended in a sea of red ink, because few people could receive the UHF signals. Furthermore, the networks avoided offering affiliation agreements to the UHF stations whenever possible, leaving them with precious little in the way of programs.

The UHF broadcasters, however, settled on cable as the scapegoat for their problems. They claimed that cable systems imported VHF signals from distant cities, which amounted to unfair competition since the cable system paid nothing to the distant station and in effect, "sold" the distant station's programs to local subscribers. Since those distant stations often included network affiliates, according to the UHF broadcasters, the cable systems were discouraging the networks from affiliating with UHF stations, and therefore undermining the whole plan to develop UHF television.

The FCC accepted these arguments, at least in part. The commission was determined to see UHF succeed, and anything that might harm that effort, including cable, was suspect. The problem was that the FCC had no legal authority to stop cable or to impose any sort of regulations on it. In 1958 the FCC began its first official inquiry into the cable business, and, after nearly a year, concluded that it could do nothing.

However, at about the same time, the Carter Mountain Transmission Company applied for permission to carry several television signals by microwave to a group of cable systems in rural Wyoming. The owners of a UHF station in Riverton, Wyoming, objected. The FCC intervened on the side of the broadcaster, denying Carter Mountain's application. Carter Mountain sued, and the suit eventually reached the Supreme Court. But the court refused to hear the case, saying that the FCC obviously had the right to deny an application for a microwave service if it would interfere with another FCC-regulated service.

The Carter Mountain case provided a very slim basis for FCC regulation of cable systems if they imported distant signals by microwave, which was becoming an important part of cable technology in the late 1950s. More important, the Carter Mountain case firmly established the principle that the FCC should regulate cable in such a manner as to protect the existing system of television broadcasting.

By 1962, when Congress passed the All Channel Receiver Act requiring TV manufacturers to include UHF circuits in new sets, and UHF-to-VHF converters were more widely available than they had been, the threat from cable seemed to be diminishing. However, cable technology had begun to evolve away from its earlier CATV identity. Not only were more cable systems importing stations from very distant cities, using microwave systems whenever the FCC would permit it, some cable operators had begun producing their own local programs or running syndicated old movies and off-network re-runs on otherwise unused channels.

The FCC took another look at the rapidly developing cable industry in 1965. Broadcasters again raised the charges of "unfair competition," and claimed that the cable systems were "parasites" using distant stations' signals (and programs) without paying for them. Using the Carter Mountain case as a precedent, the FCC declared its intention to regulate any cable system that imported one or more signals by microwave. The regulations, however, were not severe; they merely required the cable operator to carry the signals of all local broadcasting stations and to "black out" any distant signal if it carried the same program as a local station. This provision was the first *program exclusivity* or *non-duplication rule;* later on, the rules got more complicated and much more troublesome.

The broadcasters were far from satisfied. They wanted cable stopped altogether, something the FCC was not about to do. However, in 1966 the commission took the next step: it asserted jurisdiction over all cable systems, on the grounds that their use of broadcast signals might cause harm to the whole television system. The 1966 rules not only required cable systems to carry local broadcast signals, but also required them to carry the signal of any broadcast station that was "significantly viewed" within the cable system's market. By "significantly viewed," the FCC meant that a substantial number of people ordinarily watched the station without cable. Thus, for example, a cable system might be required to carry the signal of a station in a city fifty or more miles away, if the station could demonstrate that a substantial number of people in the cable system's potential market area were among the station's audience.

Furthermore, the 1966 rules limited the number of distant signals that could be carried by a cable system. Cable systems in the 100 largest television markets were required to apply for permission to carry *any* distant signals, and had to show that doing so would not harm a local station.

These rules had two immediate effects: first, the FCC was inundated with applications from cable systems for permission to carry distant signals; second, since the backlog of applications quickly reached epic proportions, the booming cable business came to a screeching halt. In 1968 the FCC suspended the hearing process and, in effect, "froze" the cable business in its tracks. Even though new cable systems in smaller markets were not subject to the same rules, the uncertainty about what the FCC would do next served to inhibit the whole industry.

The FCC's next step reassured no one. In 1969 the commission decided that cable systems ought to earn their right to use broadcasters' signals by providing some sort of public service to their communities, in the form of locally originated programming. Some cable companies had already begun local origination; some had found it very lucrative, others had not.

Up to this point, the FCC's slowly evolving regulatory scheme seemed to be aimed primarily at protecting broadcasters. After the 1965 rules were issued, several cable companies sued the commission, claiming that it had overstepped its legal authority. The suits were consolidated into one case which reached the Supreme Court in 1968. The court quickly declared that the FCC had the authority to regulate cable "to the extent that such regulation is reasonably ancillary to its responsibilities for the regulation of television broadcasting." The vague term, *reasonably ancillary,* seemed to give the commission almost unlimited authority since just about anything a cable system might do could have some effect on broadcasting.

The 1969 rules, however, had added a new element: the requirement of local origination. That rule troubled broadcasters quite a bit, since it meant that the local cable system now would be a direct competitor.

From a broadcaster's point of view, competition with a cable system is inherently unfair because of the cable operator's economic advantage. A broadcaster may spend five million dollars to build a studio, transmitter and related facilities and at least that much every year for operating expenses, all to transmit one television signal at any given moment. From this single stream, the owner must derive enough revenue to cover those heavy costs and produce a profit. At the same time, the broadcaster is obligated, under the terms of the FCC license, to serve local needs.

Since both local advertising revenue and the station compensation received from a network are dependent on audience size, the broadcaster must attain the largest possible audience for every minute of the broadcast day.

The cable system directly attacks the broadcaster's audience base, and the weapon in this attack is the signal imported from a station in some distant city. Those signals contain not only network programs, which are not much competition since the local stations carry the same shows, but also old movies, off-network series and other syndicated fare.

When a local station owner buys or leases a syndicated "package," he is supposed to have the exclusive use of the program for a given period of time in his market. If he buys, say, *Adam-12*, no one else in the same market can run *Adam-12* for three to five years. Anyone who wants to watch old re-runs of *Adam-12* will have to watch his station.

But what happens when the cable system imports a distant station that also carries *Adam-12?* Now all of the *Adam-12* fans can choose to watch their favorite show on either the local channel or the distant channel—or can watch both, ignoring the local station's programs while the distant station is resurrecting the escapades of Pete and Jim.

As far as the broadcaster is concerned, the "exclusive" right to show *Adam-12* has been undermined and the audience has been stolen by the cable operator.

When cable systems begin originating their own programming, the economics of cable versus broadcasting become even more significant.

Generally speaking, it does not matter to the cable system operator whether a viewer is watching one channel or another. The cable operator's primary source of revenue is the subscriber's monthly fee, usually in the range of five to twelve dollars. This fee is more than enough to cover the original investment in the cable system and the relatively modest operating costs. If the cable operator decides to put programs on an unused channel, the additional cost is negligible. A cable origination studio can be built very nicely for well under $100,000, because the equipment does not have to meet the rigidly high standards required for broadcast equipment. The cable operator can even get away with hiring lower-paid, less highly qualified technicians. If the "local origination" will consist entirely of old movies and off-network re-runs, the "studio" can be nothing more than an inexpensive film chain and a couple of small videotape recorders.

Some cable operators are content to write off the minimal expense of their "local origination programming" against their subscriber revenues. Others sell advertising time, just as the local broadcaster does but usually at lower rates. Even if the local origination channel does not attract a very large audience, the cable operator can still make money at it, offer a little extra inducement to prospective subscribers, and even fulfill some of the obligation to serve local needs that is supposed to be borne by broadcasters. In essence, the 1969 FCC rules were intended to put a similar obligation on the cable operators.

The Midwest Video Corporation was one cable system operator that did not like the 1969 rules at all. Midwest Video owned a dozen or so small and medium-sized cable systems in the Midwest and Southwest, including a half-interest in the cable company in Austin, Texas (the other half is owned by the LBJ Company). Midwest also was one of the companies that sued the FCC over the 1965 cable rules. This time, Midwest contended that the local origination rule went beyond the FCC's authority since it was not "reasonably ancillary" to regulation of broadcasting. Midwest regarded this as confiscation of a property right, without due process or appropriate compensation. Midwest also claimed that the FCC's rules violated the First, Fifth and other amendments to the Constitution.

Once again, the case worked its way to the Supreme Court, and once again the court upheld the FCC's authority—although this time, Chief Justice Warren Burger warned the commission that it was venturing onto thin ice, that its "ancillary to broadcasting" theory could not be used to justify too many rules.

Meanwhile, however, the FCC had been busily reconsidering the whole business once again, as it promised to do when the 1969 rules were announced. But the FCC had been listening not only to the cable operators and the broadcasters. Cable suddenly had acquired a certain popularity it had never sought.

Cable's Weird Friends

It might be supposed that the cable system operators, faced with the intransigence of the networks and broadcasters, would be happy to have support wherever they could find it. Not so! Some cable operators have spent at least as much time and energy fighting off their presumed allies as their outright enemies.

One irony of the whole cable controversy has been the fact that about half of all the cable systems in the United States, including virtually all of the larger ones, are owned by companies that also own television stations. The networks themselves are forbidden by FCC rules to own cable systems. However, the slow advance of cable has been propelled largely by a score or so of multibillion-dollar media conglomerates that own television stations, radio stations, newspapers, magazines and diverse other enterprises. Taft Broadcasting, for example, owns not only television stations and cable systems but the Hanna-Barbera cartoon studios and a chain of amusement parks. One of the largest cable system operators is Time, Inc., a fact of considerable importance to the growth of pay-cable.

The people who run cable systems are by no means flamboyant entrepreneurs. They are engineers, lawyers and good gray executives whose backgrounds and corporate loyalties are, more often than not, in broadcasting. Small wonder, then, that the cable people often seem eager to climb into bed with their avowed enemies, and adamant in shunning the attentions of their most ardent suitors.

Something must be said, too, about the nature of cable's weird friends. One of the seemingly innumerable complications in the story is the politicization of the controversy over cable's role in our national communications system.

In 1964 a previously unremarkable scholar named Marshall McLuhan published a book, *Understanding Media: The Extensions of Man.* It was in this book that McLuhan set out the theory summarized by the phrase, "The medium is the message." Although McLuhan said very little about cable, he did say a lot about television. He was remorselessly critical of commercial TV's programs but praised the medium itself. In McLuhan's view, television could be the means to overcome war, poverty, ignorance, bigotry and apparently everything except hemorrhoids. He spoke of a "global village" in which all of mankind could live in peace, entertained and enlightened by the magic of the phosphorescent tube.

A few years after McLuhan had burst from his academic chrysalis and fluttered into the public's consciousness, a number of articles appeared in influential magazines about the ultimate potential of cable technology. The articles were written by young journalists and scholars who had taken McLuhan to heart; they envisioned "wired cities" with hundreds of television channels, interconnected by trunk cables and satellites to form a "wired nation" with limitless forms and varieties of communication services.

The theme of television's redemptive power was soon taken up by politically oriented academics in the late 1960s, that most political of decades. The litany went something like this:

—Television has vast power to influence people, thanks to its sensation of immediacy and what McLuhan called its "coolness."

—This power has been corrupted and abused by the venal capitalists who monopolize the television system by owning the three commercial networks and almost all of the local stations.

—Cable, because of its potential ability to deliver dozens or even hundreds of channels to every home, is the savior of American television. All that remains is to ensure that the same greedy capitalists do not control all the new channels and subvert them to their nasty, profit-making ends.

The "media-freaks" with their visionary dreams of a wired Utopia cared little about distant signal importation or market fragmentation. They were much more interested in seeing that at least a few of every cable system's channels were set aside for non-commercial, *public access programming*. They were convinced that if only "ordinary people" like themselves could get their hands on the means of communication, a revolution would surely follow.

The idea that every cable system should devote at least one channel to "public access" was offered first to Canada's counterpart of the FCC, the Canadian Radio-Television Commission. In 1971 the CRTC embraced the concept with some enthusiasm. Meanwhile, the same idea was being peddled to the FCC by McLuhanite scholars and political activists. Given that hoary agency's traditional inclination to favor commercial interests over radical innovators, the likelihood that the FCC would look kindly on the concept of "public access" seemed remote. But that failed to take into account one Nicholas Johnson.

The Fox in the Henhouse

The period from 1968 to 1972 was an interesting one for the Federal Communications Commission. The future of cable television was only one of many divisive issues on the agenda. The Justice Department continued its age-old efforts to break up the leviathan monopolies of the telephone industry. Spiro Agnew attacked the news media right and left, demanding "responsibility" and threatening disaster. President Nixon "reorganized" the White House Office of Telecommunications Policy, politicizing it and making it an instrument of terror against broadcasters and anyone else who ran afoul of the president.

And through it all could be heard the clamoring voice of Nicholas Johnson, Commissioner. He was one of President Lyndon Johnson's (no relation) appointees to the commission. A young lawyer, he had been expected to serve as just another of the establishment flacks who have usually populated the FCC. Instead, Johnson turned out to be the fox in the henhouse. He adopted the media freaks' manifesto and appointed himself as official FCC gadfly.

Of course, Johnson was only one of seven commissioners and could have been outvoted at every turn. However, he was gifted with eloquence and the willingness to expose his opinions in public, come what may. He stormed meetings of the broadcasters, cable system operators and anyone else who would have him. He criticized, complained and heaped contempt on all sides.

Johnson played an important role in persuading his fellow commissioners to adopt the 1969 rules, with their startling local-origination requirement. However, these were to be merely "interim rules" until a permanent set of regulations could be developed. That momentous event took another three years.

In 1972 the FCC issued its Cable Television Report and Order, a regulatory scheme that was supposed to please everyone. The "freeze" was over.

There were technical standards covering signal quality, to please consumers who complained that they sometimes paid for cable service and got nothing but fuzzy pictures. There were provisions allowing state and local governments to impose their own franchise requirements (which some states and most municipal governments had already done). There were even restrictions on the fees that telephone and utility companies could charge the cable operators for the rental of space on the utilities' poles. Previously, the telephone companies—who were forbidden by the FCC to offer cable television service—had charged outrageous fees for pole attachments.

These, however, were the small print. The big issues were the signal carriage rules and access.

The 1972 Report and Order offered an elaborate schedule that defined which broadcast signals a cable system had to carry, which it could carry, and which it could not carry. A cable system had to carry all local stations' signals unless a local broadcaster specifically requested otherwise; signals from "significantly viewed" stations had to be carried also. After that, the system could carry a certain number of distant stations, the number depending on the size of the cable system's market. The bigger the market, the more signals a cable system could import. Exemptions were made for certain kinds of "special interest" stations, such as foreign language stations, whose signals otherwise would not have been carried.

At the same time, cable systems were required to provide four distinct types of access:

—*Public access*, a channel on which anyone could present any kind of program he, she or they liked, free of charge, on a first-come-first-served basis.

—*Political access*, a channel on which candidates for office could appear, or present programs on their own behalf, free of charge but on an "equal-time" basis.

—*Governmental/educational access*, one or more channels for use by local governmental and educational agencies, free of charge initially but subject to a "nominal" fee after five years.

—*Leased access*, a channel that could be leased or rented by independent producers of television programs, for a "reasonable" fee, on a first-come-first-served basis; presumably, the leasees could recoup their expenses by selling advertising time.

The cable systems also were required to provide "facilities" for the various access users at "reasonable" rates. These facilities supposedly would consist of a local origination studio and other production equipment. All four types of access could be combined on one channel until the demand for time grew to the point that additional channels would be needed.

The media freaks were ecstatic. All across the country, tyro TV technicians, college professors of communications, denizens of counter-culture communes and socially aware clergymen joined forces to establish public access groups. In some communities, the cable system turned over a channel, or at least a few hours on a channel that otherwise would be carrying duplicated network programs, to a volunteer-run "public access council." Other cable operators kept control over the access channels, doling out time to the various producing groups that sprung up like daisies in a pasture.

There was no specific requirement that cable operators originate their own programming, but the 1969 local-origination rule was not specifically rescinded, either.

Some 300 independent video enthusiasts attended the second annual convention, in Austin, of the National Federation of Local Cable Programmers (NFLCP). Most of the members are involved in producing programs for cable systems' public access channels; a major topic at this 1979 meeting was the Supreme Court's decision eliminating the FCC's requirement that cable systems offer free channels for public use. Representatives of several major cable system operators reassured the NFLCP members that their commitment to public access did not depend on the abandoned FCC rules. (Photo by the author, courtesy NFLCP)

The 1972 rules included another important provision: an expanded program exclusivity rule.

In essence, the rules said that a cable system could not import from a distant station a program that was being carried on a local broadcasting station during the same week. As before, these rules affected syndicated programs much more than network programs. However, the precise way that the rules were to be applied depended on the size of the cable system and the nature of the program involved. Several years later, when the rules were being reconsidered, one member of the FCC said:

> "One might suppose that so complex a regulatory structure must reflect a set of equally complex economic factors that have been studied and found to have important bearing on the economic impact of duplicated programming. But so far as I can ascertain, the rules reflect reality in about the same way a Tibetan mandala depicts the universe."

Nevertheless, the rules pleased two constituencies: the producers of syndicated programs, who had feared that the marketability of their "product" would be undermined if they could not guarantee exclusivity to the local stations, and the manufacturers of automatic video switchers, who sold several thousand of those devices to cable operators.

Nicholas Johnson's influence can be seen throughout the Cable Television Report and Order of 1972. He was almost singlehandedly responsible for the access provisions, and his opinions carried considerable weight in the drafting of the signal carriage provisions (although these were not his major interests). After the rules were issued, he began to exhort the media freaks to take full advantage of the access rules and he rode herd on the cable operators who were less than enthusiastic about implementing those provisions.

Unfortunately, Johnson's term ended shortly after the cable rules were promulgated, and, to no one's surprise, President Nixon chose not to reappoint him. He continued to serve for several months into 1973 before Nixon appointed his successor, James Quello. After Johnson finally left the FCC, he became chairman of the National Citizens Committee for Broadcasting, a public-interest lobbying group. He reorganized and revitalized the NCCB and, as of this writing, continues to serve as one of its most outspoken and activist leaders.

The 1972 Rules Revisited

Broadcasters were reasonably satisfied with the regulatory scheme embodied in the 1972 Report and Order, and the media freaks were given most of what they wanted. The cable system operators were outraged. The distant-signal rules and exclusivity provisions would ruin their business, they claimed, and the access rules amounted to a giveaway of their property.

Not all cable operators reacted with antagonism toward the access rules. American Television and Communications Corporation (the Time, Inc., cable TV subsidiary) not only implemented the rules but, in some cases, went far beyond them, providing free studios, free "drops" to community centers and schools and extensive assistance to access producers. Cablevision, Daniels and Associates, an operator of numerous systems, also went to great lengths to ensure that schools and other public agencies were able to make good use of the access channels. In many cases, municipal franchising authorities used the FCC's rules as the basis for franchise provisions guaranteeing not only that channels would be available, but that studios and production funds also would be provided.

different approach. Midwest Video sued again, claiming that its property rights were infringed upon and that the signal carriage and access rules were violations of the First and Fifth amendments to the Constitution.

Meanwhile, in 1974 the FCC issued a "clarification" of the 1972 rules. The old local-origination rule was officially discarded and the access rules were interpreted to mean that the cable operator would have quite a bit of control over who could use the channels and for what purposes. Also, the cable operators were not expected to provide full-fledged studios for access use; as the FCC interpreted its own rules, a Port-a-pak and a minicamera would suffice to satisfy the obligation to provide "production equipment" for access users.

Another provision of the 1972 rules, which would have required all cable systems with more than 3,500 subscribers to offer at least 20 channels, was riddled with exceptions. All systems that had existed prior to 1972 were given five years in which to comply with this requirement. In 1976, that five-year deadline was indefinitely postponed, and the rule that required all cable systems to obtain from their local franchising authority a "certificate of compliance," stating that the operators were in compliance with the 1972 rules, was abandoned.

All of these changes in 1976 were predicated on the cable operators' argument that the rules were so burdensome that the industry's growth was being stunted. Indeed, in 1973 and 1974 there was a marked slowdown in the expansion of existing cable systems and in the establishment of new ones. Of course, those were recession years; most American businesses experienced the same decline. By 1976 the cable industry, like the rest of American industry, had recovered nicely; in fact, cable was booming. Nevertheless, the FCC was convinced that, in its agonizing efforts to be fair to everyone, it had unjustly penalized the cable industry and hindered its development. By this time, too, the FCC had begun to realize that cable was not merely an adjunct to broadcasting, that it was a medium in its own right and that it had a right to compete freely with the existing broadcasting system.

Meanwhile, the Midwest Video suit to overturn the access rules finally came to trial in the Eighth U.S. Circuit Court in St. Louis. The trial took months; Midwest Video was joined by Teleprompter and several smaller cable operators, while the American Civil Liberties Union, the Black Media Coalition and several access producer groups filed briefs in support of the access rules. The decision, which finally came early in 1978, was a stunning victory for Midwest Video and the cable operators. The court declared that the FCC had clearly overstepped its authority, that the access rules could not be justified as being "reasonably ancillary to the regulation of broadcasting," and that the rules probably violated the cable operator's constitutional rights.

For several weeks afterward, it was not clear whether the FCC would even bother to appeal the Circuit Court ruling. However, the ACLU and other interested parties would not give up so easily; finally, the FCC did file an appeal. The Supreme Court wasted little time settling the matter: in January 1979 it affirmed the Circuit Court's ruling that the FCC had exceeded its legal authority. The access rules were no more. (The Supreme Court did not rule on the constitutional issue since the question of jurisdiction was a more immediate issue and, once it was settled, no further decision was necessary.)

By then, the FCC had little taste for such radical notions as public access, anyway. Under its new chairman, Charles Ferris, the commission had gradually adopted the currently fashionable belief that free competition, not governmental regulation, is the consumer's best friend. In June 1977 the FCC announced that it would undertake yet another review of its cable television regulations. This time, however, the commission would attempt to discover exactly how the economic structure of the cable industry worked, and how it was related to the broadcasting and program syndication industries.

This *Inquiry into the Economic Relationship between Television Broadcasting and Cable Television,* and the companion *Inquiry into Cable Television Syndicated Program Exclusivity Rules,* took nearly two years to complete. The commission itself sponsored some economic studies, but relied primarily on the various interests—the broadcasters, the cable operators, the syndicators and such organizations as NCCB—to supply research data. Among those who filed comments, most of which included reports on research of one sort or another, were the Corporation for Public Broadcasting, ABC, the Association of Maximum Service Telecasters (an anti-cable lobby), various local station owners and multistation operators, the Commissioner of Baseball, The National Association of Broadcasters, the National Cable Television Association, PBS, the U.S. Department of Justice, and a consortium of 67 cable system operators.

The final report, released May 7, 1979, concluded that there was no evidence that cable systems damaged broadcasters in any significant way, or might do so in the future. The FCC discovered that no matter how many distant signals a cable system imported, the effect on local stations' audiences was less than the effect of the competition among the local broadcasters themselves. Even in a "worst-case" situation, assuming the continued growth of cable until more than 50 percent of all homes subscribe to a cable system, the FCC believed that broadcasters would lose no more than 10 percent of their audiences. Thus, there seemed to be no real reason to continue the bizarre mosaic of signal carriage rules that the commission had begun with the Carter Mountain decision in 1962.

The program exclusivity inquiry came to similar conclusions. In a report released the same day, May 7, 1979, the commission declared that syndicators were not unreasonably injured if cable systems carried programs from distant stations in spite of the local broadcasters' contractual right to exclusivity. Nor was the local broadcaster injured, according to the FCC. More important, as far as the commission was concerned, the elimination of the program exclusivity rules would mean that much greater diversity of choices for the consumer. The commission concluded, "Assessing the facts developed in this report against our criteria for ascertaining the public interest points unambiguously toward the elimination of the rules." However, since many local broadcasters had signed up for syndicated programs with the expectation of exclusivity, the commission held off on actually abandoning the rules until it could consider whether some sort of "grandfathering" or transitional phase should be employed to soften the blow. As of this writing, the rules are still at least partially in effect, but they are almost certain to be removed within a year or so.

With the signal carriage rules abandoned, the program exclusivity rules on the way out, and the access rules overturned by the Supreme Court, there is not much left of the grand scheme of the 1972 Cable Television Report and Order. Many observers expect the FCC to give up altogether, and leave the regulation of cable television entirely up to local franchising authorities. Others expect the issue to come up again when Congress finally gets around to revising the 1934 Communications Act.

When Rep. Lionel Van Deerlin drafted his two successive versions of a new Communications Act, in both instances he provided for the complete deregulation of cable. The second Van Deerlin bill appeared to preclude even local regulation, although it was not clear whether Van Deerlin meant to go that far. In any case, neither bill got beyond Van Deerlin's own House Subcommittee on Communications, and it is not likely that Congress will consider the matter any further during the 1980 election year. Still, the 1934 Act is a dinosaur and it certainly must be replaced sooner or later. How Congress will treat cable in the new law depends on several factors: first, of course, the relative lobbying strength of the various interested parties; second, the progress of the cable industry now that it is essentially free of federal regulation and able to compete head-on with broadcasting; and, third, the extent of the interest shown by the public. So far, the general public has remained blissfully unaware of the entire controversy, and as long as that remains true, the issues will continue to be decided by the special interests.

Cable most certainly will continue to grow. As of June 1979 there were 4,059 cable systems in operation in the United States, with about 14,250,000 subscribers—roughly 15 percent of all households that have TV sets. In terms of audience size, cable television is about where non-commercial broadcasting was in 1960. However, non-commercial broadcasting was struggling to stay afloat in 1960; cable television today is thriving. One very big reason is the rapid development of pay-cable.

The Coin Box in the Living Room

According to many critics, the reason for commercial television's inability to offer a steady diet of culturally and intellectually uplifting programs is the medium's dependence on advertising. Advertisers naturally want the largest possible audience, which broadcasters supply by programming for the lowest common denominator. If only the advertisers could be eliminated, so goes the theory, television could offer an unlimited variety of vastly superior programs.

The same argument has been used to justify non-commercial broadcasting. Unfortunately, eliminating the advertiser also eliminates a crucial ingredient in television: money. Public television's solution is to beg for money from the government, philanthropic institutions and individual viewers.

Pay television is another solution. Commercial TV programs cost advertisers something on the order of five cents per viewer per hour. If viewers could be induced to pay directly for the programs they watch at a higher rate— say, a dollar or so per hour—it would be possible to produce and transmit programs that would appeal to a smaller audience. Presumably, these special-interest programs would be of vastly superior quality; they would have to be, in order to get viewers to part with cash out-of-pocket.

The catch is that some way must be found of delivering programs only to those viewers who are willing to pay.

This can be done by broadcasting a "scrambled" signal. There are several techniques that can be used. The program can be broadcast at a frequency that regular TV sets cannot receive, or the ordinary carrier signal can be disrupted by a second signal. In either case, the subscriber must have an "unscrambler" that converts the signal to a conventional carrier frequency. In some pay-television systems, the "unscrambler" is offered for a specified monthly fee that the viewer must pay whether or not he watches any particular program on the pay-TV channel. In other systems, the "unscrambler" contains a coin box, not unlike the TV sets in cheap motels: the viewer must drop a quarter, or whatever amount, into the coin box in order to receive a program. More sophisticated systems simply record a viewer's use of the "unscrambler," on which basis a monthly bill can be prepared.

Several attempts were made during the late 1960s and early 1970s to establish pay-television broadcasting systems. All were dismal failures; there simply were not enough people willing to pay a monthly fee or a per-program fee, no matter what kind of "superior" programs were offered. The more successful of these experimental systems relied heavily on a schedule of recent movies and sports events—essentially the same sort of thing that commercial television already offers.

Even though pay-TV looked like a dud, commercial broadcasters reacted to the mere concept as if it were a threat to truth, justice and the American way. The networks and their affiliates lobbied desperately to keep the FCC from licensing pay-TV stations. When this failed, the broadcasters unleashed a barrage of advertising to persuade prospective viewers that pay-TV was immoral, fattening and/or Communist-inspired. The battle against pay-television often reached the same level of hysteria as an anti-fluoridation campaign. Sometimes, though not often, the scare tactics worked. The voters of California approved a referendum to prohibit pay-TV entirely; however, the California Supreme Court ruled that the voters did not have the right.

Why such vigorous opposition to an unsuccessful experiment? Simply because the broadcasters feared that pay-TV, if it once established a foothold in the industry, would compete with "free TV" for the most popular programs, especially recent movies and such sports events as the World Series and Super Bowl. The broadcasters reasoned that a pay-TV system with even a relatively small number of subscribers could afford to pay premium rates for such "high quality" programs. Thus "free TV" might be left with only the cheapest, bottom-of-the-barrel programs. Since most viewers would feel compelled to pay a modest fee for the privilege of watching their favorite shows, "free TV" would be left with an audience composed entirely of the poor, who could not afford to pay for their entertainment.

Of course, under those circumstances, "free TV" could no longer lavish funds on such notorious money-losers as public service programs. Thus, pay-TV threatened not just the broadcasters' profits but the entire structure of American broadcasting—and was that not sacred?

Strangely enough, the broadcasters never offered any real proof that this "siphoning" would occur or that it would have the disastrous effects they predicted. Still, the FCC accepted the premise and applied it not only to over-the-air pay-television—but also to cable.

If cable operators could originate their own programs, it did not take much genius to realize that they could also ask their subscribers to pay extra for one or more channels of special programming. As with over-the-air pay-TV, a pay-cable system required some sort of "scrambling-unscrambling" device to keep non-subscribers from watching the pay channel, but such devices were readily available as early as 1960.

The earliest pay-cable systems were organized by some of the larger multi-system cable conglomerates, and their programming, predictably, consisted mostly of old movies and sports events. The FCC, heeding the complaints of the broadcasters, discouraged both over-the-air pay-TV and pay-cable as long as it could, but finally authorized experimental over-the-air systems in 1968. By that time, pay-cable systems also were in operation.

Pay-cable's greatest advantage over ordinary pay-TV is the relatively low cost of cable transmission—and the fact that most of the costs are already borne by the basic cable subscribers. The channel used for pay-cable otherwise would produce no revenue at all, so from the cable operator's point of view, anything the pay-cable channel earns beyond the cost of the programming is pure profit.

These glittering prospects attracted the attention of Time, Inc., which already owned not only the stable of extremely profitable magazines, but the chain of cable systems, American Television and Communications (ATC). Time, Inc., also was heavily involved in producing and distributing educational films and television programs, some of which were co-produced by Time-Life Films and the British Broadcasting Corporation for use on PBS. Among these exceptional programs were the *Forsythe Saga* series and Lord Kenneth Clark's *Civilisation*. After these programs have appeared on PBS, Time-Life Media, a distribution subsidiary, sells or rents copies to schools or anyone else who wants them.

Time, Inc., decided that pay-cable might be another major profit opportunity, so, in 1971 Home Box Office (HBO) was organized as a pay-cable subsidiary. HBO's role was to acquire or produce programs and to distribute them to local cable systems, including ATC's systems. The cable systems would transmit the programs on a "scrambled" channel and would collect a monthly subscription fee from anyone who wanted an "unscrambler"; the cable operator and HBO would split the subscription fee.

As with other pay-TV systems, HBO relied heavily on recent movies and sports events, with a few "cultural specials"—an occasional opera or a video tape of a nightclub act—thrown in for good measure.

Once again, the commercial broadcasters set up a howl. The FCC responded in 1972 by issuing a new set of rules covering both pay-TV (over-the-air) and pay-cable. Under the rules, a "subscription television" system could not carry any series programs (equivalent to commercial TV's prime-time shows), nor any movie more than two years old, nor any sports event that had appeared on "free TV" at least once during the previous three years. Movies older than ten years could be shown if they were genuinely "classics" of more than routine interest.

These rules were not entirely satisfactory to either the broadcasters, who wanted pay-TV eliminated altogether, or the cable operators, who wanted fewer restrictions. So, in the time-honored tradition of the industry, both sides sued the FCC. In 1978 the Supreme Court ruled that the "anti-siphoning" regulations were unjustified (since no one had ever proven that "free TV" would be harmed by "siphoning") and unconstitutional.

Meanwhile, however, the pay-cable industry had limped along under the 1972 rules. HBO was not the only pay-cable system, but it was one of the largest and most visible; it was also chronically unprofitable. Its programs were carried by landline from its New York City studios to a dozen or so cable systems in the southern New England-New York State area. By 1975 the system had attracted about a hundred thousand subscribers, but the turnover among subscribers was very high, indicating that not many people were satisfied to pay the $8 a month fee just to watch last year's movies and a few tennis matches. The cost of leasing the telephone landlines was horrendous.

Satellite transmission, by drastically reducing the cost of distributing programs, enabled pay-cable services to expand their program offerings beyond the usual diet of old movies. HBO, for example, offers "concert" performances by Sammy Davis, Jr., Steve Martin, Rich Little, magician Harry Blackstone and others. Showtime, HBO's main competitor, offers similar fare, while other pay-cable systems tend to specialize in a particular type of programming. (Photo courtesy HBO)

Then HBO discovered the switchboard in the sky: the communications satellites. In 1975 HBO announced that it would begin transmitting its program by satellite, and that it would "assist" any cable system operator to acquire an earth station if the operator would add the HBO service to his system. (At about this same time, the FCC announced that it would permit the use of comparatively small earth stations for receive-only purposes; this cut the cost of receiving satellite-relayed programming by more than half, and made HBO's proposal economically possible.)

By 1977 HBO was transmitting its programs to some 300 cable systems all over the United States. More than a million subscribers were paying the eight dollars a month, half of which is kept by the local cable operator. Out of its $4-million-per-month share, HBO paid less than a thousand dollars an hour for its use of the satellite—a small fraction of what the company had been paying for landline distribution to a mere dozen cable companies. HBO wiped out a five-year accumulation of deficits and began earning a net profit less than a year after beginning satellite distribution.

It can be said that the satellite saved HBO, and, with it, the whole idea of pay-cable. But, then, HBO did quite a bit for the communications satellite industry, too. In fact, HBO set off an explosion of satellite-borne television services, and the potential effects of that explosion have not yet been fully calculated, as we will see in the next chapter.

The RCA satellite transmission facility in New Jersey. Signals from HBO's studio in New York, along with signals from other pay-cable, "free" cable and various other sources, are transmitted up to the geosynchronous satellite hovering over the equator. (Photo courtesy RCA Corp.)

Chapter

8

Satellites, Cable and Television

On May 25, 1961, President John F. Kennedy informed the Congress that "this nation should commit itself to the goal, before this decade is out, of landing a man on the Moon and returning him safely to Earth." In fact, during 1969 *four* men, on two separate trips, landed on the Moon and returned safely to Earth, and they were later followed by eight others.

Whether the Apollo program was a good idea, whether it was worth the cost, and what the ultimate consequences might be, all remain questions of considerable controversy a decade later. But there can be little doubt that the United States has succeeded in putting its space technology to work in dozens of useful ways. One of those ways is the development of communications satellites. Even without all the other technological, political, social and economic developments we've talked about so far, communications satellites alone would be enough to thoroughly transform our national system of television communications.

The Physics of the Geosync Bird

Satellites, regardless of their uses or merits, are fascinating devices. Since the Soviet Union launched *Sputnik I* on October 4, 1957, several thousand operating satellites have been put into orbit around the Earth.

Most people thoroughly misunderstand the physical principle of the satellite. There is a popular misconception that a satellite, once it gets beyond the Earth's atmosphere into "outer space," is free of the Earth's gravity and merely cruises around the globe at will. Actually, most satellites never go entirely beyond the atmosphere, and no satellite ever goes beyond the reach of Earth's gravity; if it did, it would simply fly off into the universe. A satellite stays in orbit because it is constantly falling around the globe.

Imagine that you are standing somewhere on the equator, facing eastward, with a pea-shooter held parallel to the ground. If you fire a pea, it will fall to the ground some distance away, and the path it follows will be curved. The harder you blow through the pea-shooter, the farther the pea will travel, but its path always will be circular.

If you blow very, *very* hard, the pea might fly all the way past the horizon, around the Earth's curvature, and fall to the ground out of your sight. If you blow very, very, *very* hard, it might even travel halfway around the world before it fell to the ground.

Now, suppose you give one massive, prodigious blow into the pea-shooter, propelling the pea at a speed of just under 8 kilometers per second (about 17,900 miles per hour). The pea will now fly all the way around the Earth; it has achieved *circular velocity*, a speed sufficiently high that the curve of its falling path is the same as the curve of Earth's surface. In short, you have just put the pea in orbit. (Throughout this discussion, I will completely ignore the presence of the Earth's atmosphere so that we do not have to be concerned about winds, friction, and so forth.)

The same principle applies no matter how high the object is above the Earth's surface. The exact value of circular velocity (the speed required to maintain a circular orbit) declines somewhat at higher altitudes, but the rate of decline is very gradual—the Earth is awfully big and its gravitational field is very much a factor even at enormous distances. For instance, the Moon is approximately 240,000 miles from Earth but it must travel at about 2,300 miles per hour in order to stay in orbit; if it ever slowed down, it would fall on us. Still, the higher a satellite is placed in orbit, the slower it needs to go in order to stay in orbit. This produces a curious effect.

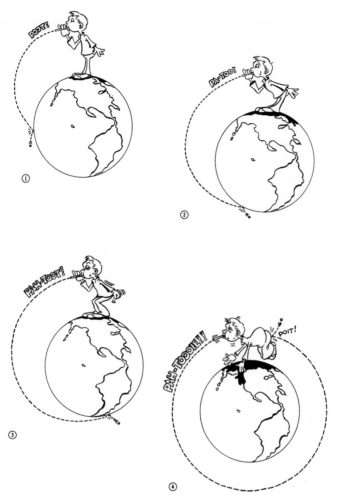

"Falling Around the World": How a Satellite Stays in Orbit. When a pea is blown from a peashooter, it follows a curved path back to the ground (1); if it is blown hard enough, the pea might follow a curved path a quarter of the way around the world (2), or even halfway around the world (3). A truly prodigious blow could propel the pea into a curved path all the way around the world; the pea is forever falling, but always traveling fast enough that it never gets to the ground (4). Of course, air resistance is ignored in this simplified explanation.

Suppose you have a jet-propelled car parked on the equator, facing eastward. The Earth itself is turning, west to east, at a speed of roughly 1,038 miles an hour (1,670 kilometers per hour). Imagine that the Earth is a smooth, solid globe with no obstructions for you to run into. You plant a flag at your starting point on the equator, rev up your jet engines, and zoom eastward at 17,900 miles per hour (28,800 kilometers per hour). It will take you approximately one hour and 24 minutes to go all the way around the world and return to your flag. Throughout the trip, as long as your jet-propelled car's wheels are touching the ground, the Earth's rotation is irrelevant: it is added to the car's speed, but the flag is also moving away from its original location at the same speed.

Now suppose that instead of a jet-propelled car, you use a rocket plane to make the same trip, skimming just above the earth's surface at 17,900 mph. This time, your trip will take a little longer because, by the time you have gone all the way around the Earth, the flag will have moved 1,443 miles (2,321 kilometers) to the east. It will take one hour and 28 minutes to complete the trip.

If an observer was standing near your flag, he would have to conclude that the rocket plane was going slower than the jet-propelled car, since the former took longer to make the same trip than the latter. However, the observer would certainly say that both vehicles had traveled from west to east faster than the Earth was turning.

Now suppose that you take your rocket plane up to an altitude of 100 miles (162 kilometers) above the Earth's surface and make the same trip again, still at 17,900 mph. At that altitude, you will have to go farther in order to get all the way around; a circular orbit at that altitude is about 25,530 miles (41,100 kilometers) long. If you fly at 17,900 mph, it will take 1.42 hours to go all the way around; meanwhile, however, your flag will have moved 1,480 miles to the east, which will take you another 0.08 hours to make up, for a total trip length of 1.5 hours—or one hour and 30 minutes. Nearly all manned space flights in Earth orbit have been at an average altitude of around 100 miles and have had an orbital period (the time it takes to go completely around the Earth with reference to a fixed point) of about 90 minutes.

Once again, the observer standing by your flag would say that the rocket plane at an altitude of 100 miles was traveling slower than it was at the surface, since it took longer to cover the same distance. In fact, the higher you go in your rocket plane, the slower you will seem (to an observer at a fixed point on the surface) to be traveling. Eventually, you will reach a point at which your rocket plane, even though its actual speed is equal to the circular velocity for its orbit, will appear to be standing still in relation to a fixed point on the Earth's surface. You would be in what is called a *geostationary* or *geosynchronous orbit*: geosync, for short.

The geosync orbit—there's only one—is at 22,300 miles (35,880 kilometers) above the surface. At that altitude, a little less than one-tenth of the way to the Moon, the circular velocity has already been reduced to 5,833 miles per hour (9,385 kilometers per hour, or 2.6 kilometers per second), or less than one-third of its value near the surface. This is important because it is highly desirable not only to put an object into this orbit, but to keep it there. There is no atmosphere to worry about at this altitude, but there are stray molecules of gas, bits of dust and the gravitational forces of the Moon, the Sun and other planets, all of which affect a satellite enough to slow it down and cause it to fall out of orbit eventually unless some acceleration is provided now and then. Fortunately, since the circular velocity is comparatively low, not much acceleration is needed.

The existence of a geosync orbit is not a recent discovery; Johannes Kepler calculated it back in the late sixteenth century, but of course he had no way of going up to check it out. That prospect had to await the development of rocket propulsion, of fuels sufficiently powerful to propel an object to such a great altitude at such tremendous speeds, and of automatic devices that would keep a rocket and a satellite on course. A Russian schoolteacher, Konstantin Tsiolkovsky, worked out the basic mechanics of orbital flight by rocket propulsion about 1898; his work, which was largely ignored by the rest of the world, was repeated by a German physicist, Hans Oberth, and an American engineer, Robert H. Goddard, during the period from 1905 to 1930. But of the three, only Oberth gave very much attention to the practical implications of space travel. In 1929 he suggested that technicians in "space stations" could relay messages to and from distant points on Earth's surface—by heliograph (radios, at that time, simply were not powerful enough to transmit across such great distances).

In 1945 Arthur C. Clarke, a British amateur astronomer and frequent science fiction writer, suggested that manned radio relay satellites could be placed in the geosync orbit. He calculated that three such satellites, spaced equally around the Earth, would be able to cover the entire planet, except for the small and virtually unpopulated areas at the North and South Poles. In a short story, "I Remember Babylon," Clarke worried that such communications satellites could be used to beam propaganda directly into people's homes. (Clarke, by the way, later wrote the screenplay for the brilliant Stanley Kubrick film, *2001: A Space Odyssey.*)

The first attempt to actually launch a communications satellite was made by the United States. In August 1960 the National Aeronautics and Space Administration (NASA) put *Echo I* into a circular orbit at an altitude of about 1,000 miles (1,600 kilometers). *Echo I* was really nothing more than a balloon with an aluminized skin that would reflect radio waves; this is known as a *passive relay.* Although it worked well enough, it was not very practical; since the satellite was not in a geosync orbit, it had to be tracked by antennae on the ground, and its reflective surface was not very efficient. An *Echo II* satellite also was launched, in January 1954, for further experiments, but it was the last passive-relay satellite used.

The first *active relay* was *Telstar I,* launched July 10, 1962. It did not just reflect radio waves; it received them through its own antenna, amplified the signal, and re-transmitted it back to the Earth. *Telstar* was interesting in another respect: it was the very first satellite developed and paid for by a commercial interest—the American Telephone and Telegraph Company. It was followed a few months later by another active-relay satellite, imaginatively called *Relay I,* built and owned by RCA. Both *Telstar* and *Relay* were low-orbit satellites, in orbits of about 100 miles.

On February 14, 1962, the first geosynchronous communications satellite, *Syncom I,* went into orbit. It was built by Hughes Aircraft Company for NASA. Unfortunately, it suffered a mechanical breakdown. However, a duplicate, *Syncom II,* went into geosync orbit in July 1963 and it worked just fine. A third *Syncom* was launched in August 1964 and was used to relay television pictures of the Tokyo Olympics.

The *Syncoms* were strictly experimental spacecraft, but the experiments were so successful that commercial development was only a matter of time—and not much time, at that. The U.S. Congress had established the Communications Satellite Corporation (Comsat) in 1962 with the specific responsibility for developing communications satellites on a commercial basis. At about the same time, the International Telecommunications Union (one of the agencies affiliated with the United Nations) encouraged its members to form their own communications satellite system, which they did: the International Telecommunications Satellite Consortium, or Intelsat.

Intelsat owns its entire system of geosync satellites, all of which have been built in the United States and launched by NASA at Intelsat's expense. Comsat provides technical assistance to Intelsat and manages the system. However, the member nations own their earth stations (except in the U.S., where the earth stations are owned by Comsat).

Comsat, in turn, is owned by stockholders, just like any other private corporation. When Comsat was established, half of its stock was sold to AT&T with the clear understanding that AT&T would gradually sell off its interest. Today, AT&T no longer owns any shares in Comsat.

The first satellite launched by NASA for Comsat and Intelsat was *Intelsat I,* nicknamed *Early Bird,* on April 6, 1965. It was a huge success.

The Flock in Outer Space

The great advantage of a communications satellite is cost. A landline system requires not only miles of cable (or microwave repeaters spaced roughly every thirty miles, depending on terrain), but switching facilities, amplifiers and a quantity of other gear, all of which demand constant electrical energy and frequent maintenance. A satellite may be fairly expensive to build, but it only has to be built once and launched once; after that, it will run for several years with no further attention. It draws its power from solar panels; a small quantity of fuel onboard supplies the rocket engines that keep the bird in its proper orbit. Best of all, a satellite is completely insensitive to the distance between the source of a signal and its destination. With a landline system, every mile between source and destination costs more money; with a satellite, it does not matter in the slightest whether the source and destination are a mile apart or a continent apart, as long as both are within range of the bird.

As of January 1, 1979, there were nearly four dozen communications satellites in geosync orbits around the globe. Why so many? Clarke's calculations—that only three geosync birds could cover the entire Earth—were not wrong. There are so many communications satellites because there are so many different uses for them, and no one satellite network can accommodate all of the radio channels required.

Early in 1979 there were plans for another 55 geosync satellites to be launched within two to five years. There was growing concern over the prospect of crowding the geosync orbit with so many birds that they would interfere with one another, and many space experts believe that by 1985 there will be a clear need to build gigantic "space platforms" to hold massive relay stations.

In addition to the Intelsat network, which now contains more than a dozen separate satellites, there are geosync satellites owned and operated by several individual nations (including Japan, France, Canada, and the USSR) and a number of regional consortia that serve the Middle East, the South Pacific island-nations and South America. There also are various experimental satellites in geosync orbit, and the Marisat group of navigational satellites used by both ships at sea and aircraft. By January 1978 there already were more than a hundred members in Intelsat; today the number has climbed to about 150. (The USSR runs a separate international system for eight nations, including Belgium —the only non-Communist member—and Cuba.)

Communications satellites began to affect American television as early as 1964, when the Olympic games were transmitted from Tokyo via *Syncom III.*

After that, the major networks frequently used Intelsat's birds to relay news and sports material from distant parts of the world. Unfortunately, the networks often found this to be more trouble and expense than it was worth. For several years, earth stations were few and far between, and, since they are almost always owned by national governments, using them involves all sorts of bureaucratic hassles. Furthermore, Intelsat deliberately set its rates very high at first, partly because of uncertainties over how long a given satellite would remain usable (and, therefore, how soon it would have to be replaced), and partly because the Western European governments already had a tremendous investment in the transoceanic cable communications system and they were not eager to see the satellite system compete too vigorously. For these and various other reasons, the Intelsat system to this day continues to be used more for telephone communications than television.

The real need was for a domestic communications satellite to serve only the United States. That is what AT&T and RCA had in mind when they built and launched their *Telstars* and *Relays*. But when they went to the FCC for permission to put up an operational system, they ran into the same brick wall that has greeted every new technology in communications.

The FCC could not decide who should run a domestic satellite system, and at first it evidently did not occur to them that there could be several competing systems. Comsat wanted to be given a blanket monopoly over the entire industry, but the commission was reluctant to do that. AT&T thought that it should be given the monopoly, since the satellite system would have to be coordinated with the existing landline system or the latter might be rendered obsolete overnight. But the FCC did not want to do that, either. Meanwhile, the FCC was being badgered by the European governments to protect their interests in the transoceanic cables.

The FCC finally concluded that Comsat should confine its operations to the international satellite system, at least for the time being. Meanwhile, AT&T, RCA and Western Union all were given permission to develop separate domestic satellite systems, subject to final authorization to put the systems into operation.

Of course, it takes a while to plan, build and launch a satellite, and the bird in orbit is fairly useless unless there is a network of earth stations to exchange signals with it. The first commercial domestic communications satellite was finally launched in April 1974 when Western Union put *Westar I* (built by Hughes Aircraft) in geosync orbit. *Westar II* followed in October 1974. RCA American Satellite was next, launching its *Satcom I* in December 1975 and *Satcom II* the following March. AT&T got its first *Comstar* into orbit in May 1976 and there are now two more *Comstars* in orbit and a "spare" waiting to be launched whenever needed. A third RCA *Satcom* was launched in late 1979 but failed to reach the geosync orbit. It either blew up or wandered off into the universe—no one really knows. A replacement, which would have been *Satcom IV*, should be launched by mid-1981. A third *Westar* should be in orbit by the time you read this.

RCA's *Satcom I*. This geosynchronous communications satellite, with its twin, *Satcom II*, and Western Union's *Westar* series, revolutionized cable television in the late 1970s. Just as the decade ended, *Satcom III* was launched—and promptly lost in space. However, a fourth *Satcom* is expected to be in orbit by mid-1981, to meet the clamoring demand for "instant-network" channels. (Artist's rendering courtesy RCA Corp.)

All three satellite systems are equally capable of relaying telephone, telegraph, computer data or television signals. Although, as Arthur Clarke pointed out, a satellite in geosync orbit could receive from and transmit to any point on about one-third of the globe, most satellites do not work that way. The larger their area of signal coverage, or what the engineers call their "footprint," the weaker the signal at any given point within that area—or the stronger the signal must be in order to be usable at any point within that area. A stronger signal requires more electrical power and heavier, more costly electronic devices in the satellite. By focusing the satellite's signal coverage area, through the use of directional antennae, the power requirement is reduced and, therefore, so is the expense. Thus, each satellite has its own distinctive "footprint." All of these domestic birds—the *Comstars, Westars* and *Satcoms*— can cover most of the 48 contiguous states, but their coverage beyond that area differs from one satellite to the next.

When AT&T launched its first *Comstar,* it asked the FCC for authorization to carry the same types of signals as the RCA and WU birds: private-line long-distance telephone service, high-speed data transmissions, teletype and television. By this time, however, both RCA and WU were actively trying to develop a market for television service and they were afraid that their efforts would be undermined by Ma Bell. The FCC agreed, and in July 1976 ordered AT&T to confine its satellite operations to telephone and telegraph services (including data), at least for a three-year period during which the other two systems would have a chance to establish their own markets. This decision, another of the FCC's attempts at Solomon-like arbitration of competing interests, had the direct effect of discouraging all three of the major commercial television networks from using communications satellites. After all, the networks had relied on AT&T for their interconnections since the 1920s, and even NBC—a subsidiary of RCA!—was not about to abandon that relationship. Besides, there was the difficult question of who was going to pay for the costly earth stations that each local broadcaster would need to receive the network signal via satellite.

Indeed, the earth station problem threatened the viability of all three domestic satellite systems. Each of the three companies—AT&T, RCA and WU —had to establish a number of earth stations in major cities around the country in order to use their satellites at all. In 1975, an earth station might cost anywhere from $75,000 to $150,000, depending on its location and other factors. One major determinant of the cost is the size of the earth station's antenna, and at that time the FCC would not authorize anyone to use an antenna less than ten meters (about 33 feet) in diameter.

The FCC helped matters immensely when it decided in 1976 that smaller antennae could be used on earth stations that would only receive television signals. The smaller antennae, only 4.5 or five meters in diameter (15 to 17 feet), reduced the cost of the earth station to around $25,000; since then, technological refinements have pushed the price down even further, to as little as $10,000 in some cases.

Still, the major networks were not especially interested in using either the RCA or WU domestic systems. Local broadcasters could see little point in buying earth stations at any price, since they already received their programs either at the networks' expense (via landline) or at the negligible expense of mailing syndicated program tapes and films. Besides, no one was transmitting programs to the satellites, so there was nothing to receive.

The deadlock was broken in 1975 when HBO, the Time, Inc., pay-cable subsidiary, announced that it would begin transmitting its programs via satellite to cable television systems across the country. Simultaneously, RCA announced that it would provide an earth station, either free or at greatly reduced cost, to any cable system that signed up for HBO. Suddenly the rush was on, and all across America satellite earth stations all but sprouted from the ground.

Of course, once a cable system had put up an earth station, it could receive not only HBO's programs but any other programs that were being relayed by the same satellite (*Satcom I,* in this case). Since the bird could handle up to 24 television channels, there seemed to be plenty of room for additional program sources.

What happened next all but defies description. In about a year's time, HBO had signed up more than 300 cable systems, which in turn hooked about a million subscribers to the pay channel. Meanwhile, Ted Turner, the flamboyant owner of an independent station in Atlanta, WTCG (now WTBS), as well as the Atlanta Braves baseball and the Atlanta Flames hockey teams, decided to offer his station's programming to the nation's cable viewers. He established a subsidiary, Southern Satellite Systems, which leased a *Satcom I* channel; any cable system that already had an earth station could use the WTCG signal for a token fee, and Southern Satellite would help finance an earth station if the cable company did not already have one.

The Spanish International Network (SIN), a struggling chain of Spanish-language stations in about a dozen cities from New York to San Diego, had gotten along by bicycling programs (that is, sending a tape or film from one station to the next) in the same manner as syndicators. Landline interconnections were just too expensive to be used for anything other than special occasions. Then there was *Westar*. SIN began transmitting its signal by the WU satellite in 1977. Overnight, literally, SIN became a true network, transmitting its programs (most of which are bought from Televisa, the Mexican privately owned, four-channel television service) simultaneously to all its affiliates. By 1979 the network had grown to 18 stations with more on the drawing boards. SIN was the only U.S. network in 1978 to carry, live, the entire World Cup international soccer championships from Argentina.

The Christian Broadcasting Network (CBN) had only three affiliates for its wall-to-wall fundamentalist programming in 1976; the network had been in operation since 1960 and seemed to be going nowhere, partly because of the limited availability of desirable broadcast licenses and partly because of the high cost of landline interconnection. Then CBN went on *Satcom I,* making its programs available free to any cable system that wanted them. Within a year, there were some 400 cable systems carrying evangelist Pat Robertson's *The 700 Club* and an assortment of other religion-oriented programs.

In May 1978 *Satellite Communications* magazine listed nine satellite-to-cable networks: Turner's WTCG, HBO, CBN, Americom Satellite Network (ASN, via *Westar*), Fanfare (a sports-oriented pay-cable service based in Houston), Madison Square Garden, PTL Television Network (another religious network), Showtime (a pay-cable service offered by Viacom, the leading syndicator of off-network series), and Robert Wold Company. The list overlooked SIN, but no matter; by the time it appeared, the list was already out of date. By the middle of 1979, 22 of *Satcom I's* channels were in use (the other two had quit working, and, unfortunately, RCA could not find a mechanic to go out and fix them). SIN thought it had a deal to lease a channel, but the deal fell through and the Spanish network sued RCA for reneging—the first lawsuit ever over the "right" to use a communications satellite.

The *Westars* also have filled up quickly with television networks, most of them serving cable systems, some—like CBN and its competitors, PTL and the Trinity Broadcasting Network—serving both broadcasters and cable systems. The Public Broadcasting Service (PBS) uses *Westar*. Group W (Westinghouse Broadcasting) announced that it would begin feeding its own stations with news and public affairs programs via *Westar,* beginning late in 1980.

Radio, too, has moved to the geosync orbit. Mutual Broadcasting began interconnecting by satellite in 1978; AP and UPI followed in early 1979, and by the end of the year, ABC, CBS and NBC were using *Satcom* instead of landlines to feed most of their affiliates. Of course, an antenna and earth station for a simple radio signal is not nearly as expensive as it is for television.

At last count, there were at least two dozen satellite-borne television networks in the United States. Most of these "instant networks" serve cable systems, either as a pay-cable service or, like the religious networks, free. There are also the "super-station" services, pioneered by Ted Turner's WTCG, which essentially do nothing more than distribute an independent broadcaster's signal across the entire country, usually for a nominal fee to the cable system operator.

Meanwhile, the three major networks continued to ignore what was happening 22,300 miles above the equator. There were, of course, any number of feasibility studies, market surveys and long executive memoes on the subject, but whenever the subject came up at meetings between the network brass and the affiliated station owners, the network executives brushed it aside: they planned to continue using the landline network for the foreseeable future.

Goodness knows, there is nothing *less* foreseeable than the future; most people have a hard enough time "foreseeing" the present. The networks might as well have chosen to ignore the existence of OPEC. But, then, these were the captains of a mighty—and mighty profitable—industry. They had little to gain (except lower transmission costs) by adopting the new technology, and much to lose.

A local broadcasting station, after all, would be in just the same position as a cable company once it got a hold of an earth station: it could take its signal from any source it liked, whenever it liked. In theory, of course, a local station is a partner in a network affiliation by free choice, and can change the relationship, through renegotiation. In fact, the networks control the affiliation relationship. A local station has four choices: ABC, CBS, NBC or independent. As an independent, a local station has a fairly broad range of choices from various syndicators and program packagers, but it must pay cold, hard cash for everything it buys, and the best pickings are concentrated in a very few hands. Affiliates of the major networks find the same thing true when they buy syndicated programs to fill their non-network hours.

It turned out to be one of those syndicators who finally broke the ice late in 1979. Viacom, primarily a packager of off-network series and formerly a subsidiary of CBS, offered to provide a free earth station to any local broadcaster who would sign a contract for a stipulated number of Viacom's programs over a certain period of time. Within a month, Viacom had more than a hundred takers.

Why Viacom? As the major packager of re-runs, it serves almost every local station in the country with at least one or two programs. Until it began using the satellite, those programs were "bicycled" from station to station. That is a lot less expensive than landline interconnection, which would not have been feasible anyway since the stations did not want to use the syndicated programs at the same hour of the day. However, "bicycling"—which means either sending tapes and films through the mail or by special courier—is still a costly business, and there is inevitably a certain percentage of lost tapes and films. The satellite would enable Viacom to transmit its programs to dozens of customers at once; they could tape them on their own equipment and simply erase the tapes afterward. That eliminates the cost of duplicate copies of each program, the expense of shipping them from place to place (a cost that was partially borne by the customers themselves), and the danger of lost materials. Even taking into consideration the cost of leasing a satellite channel and the pro-rated cost of providing an earth station to every subscriber, Viacom figured it would save money from the first day on.

It is hard to predict what will happen once local stations have their own earth stations. The Viacom offer was, of course, a limited one; perhaps two hundred or so local stations will get an earth station free from the syndicator. However, as with HBO, that is only the beginning. As soon as there are enough local broadcasters with earth stations, there will be other program services offered via satellite; that, in turn, will stimulate more local broadcasters to acquire an earth station.

In July 1979 the FCC lifted its moratorium on AT&T's domestic satellite, *Comstar*. The Bell System is now free to offer television interconnections via satellite. By a curious coincidence, the three major networks thereafter announced within a month that they were "re-evaluating" the feasibility of distributing their programs by satellite.

At about the same time, Comsat—still smarting under the ban on domestic operations imposed by the FCC—appealed to the commission to let it begin offering a pay-television service of its own direct from the satellite to the home.

Satellite-to-Home Broadcasting

When Arthur C. Clarke first envisioned communications satellites in the geosync orbit, he imagined that they would beam their signals directly to home receivers. One problem he foresaw—and the main point of his story, *I Remember Babylon*—was that direct satellite-to-home broadcasting would eliminate all the middlemen. He particularly worried that government agencies would have no control over what their citizens received. In his story, a geosync bird is used to transmit propaganda messages cleverly interwoven with subtle pornography. The porn attracts viewers, who unwittingly absorb the propaganda. Since the programs are transmitted from outside the nation's boundaries, there is nothing the government can do; jamming a satellite's broadcasts would be virtually impossible.

Considering the quality of today's commercial television, with its relentless "propaganda" for both commercial advertisers and ideological promoters interspersed with programs that frequently contain subtle and not-so-subtle pornography, it may be that Clarke's worst fears have come true without the benefit of satellites. The addition of satellite-to-home broadcasting could hardly make the situation much worse. On the other hand, satellite-to-home broadcasting might have some other unpleasant side effects that Clarke overlooked.

A satellite of the type Comsat proposes to use would carry four to six channels of television programs. Subscribing individuals would be given a special antenna, receiving equipment and converters that would shift the signals down to ordinary TV frequencies. According to Comsat, the proposed service could be operational by 1983.

Direct satellite broadcasting, obviously, bypasses both the local broadcasting station and the local cable system. Anyone who gains access to one of the satellite channels will have unfettered access to the nation's living rooms. The Comsat proposal indicates that various producers would supply programs under contract, leaving Comsat to determine what is transmitted. However, the same technology could be used on a "leased access" basis, whereby anyone who could afford to lease a channel, full- or part-time, would have one.

The technology already exists. In April 1978, the Japanese government-operated television network, NHK, launched *Yuri* (an acronym, in Japanese, for "Medium-scale Broadcasting Satellite for Experimental Purposes"; the acronym also translates into English as "Lily"). The satellite itself and the associated ground equipment were designed by the Japanese electronic giant, Toshiba, built by General Electric, and launched (for a fee) by NASA.

Yuri's two television channels can be received by anyone with the proper equipment. It requires only an antenna of one meter in diameter—slightly more than three feet. The antenna is mass-produced from a single stamping; it looks something like an oversize garbage can lid. Such a small antenna can be used because the satellite itself is considerably more powerful than the American domestic satellites; the stronger the signal, the smaller the antenna that is needed.

Two U.S. satellite systems also have demonstrated the feasibility of receiving satellite broadcasts directly on small earth stations; they are the *Applications Technology Satellites* (ATS) series and the *Hermes* series, the latter built and operated jointly by NASA and the Canadian government. One of the ATS birds—ATS-6—has been used at various times to deliver educational programs to remote areas of Alaska, the Rocky Mountains and India. The satellite was moved around from place to place in the geosync orbit for these purposes. When ATS-6 finally ran out of fuel, NASA shut it down, to the dismay of the government of India. Almost certainly, it will be replaced with a longer-lived bird.

It is not hard to see the economic advantage of direct satellite-to-home broadcasting. Not only does it eliminate the expensive long-distance landline network, it also eliminates the expense of local distribution, whether by broadcast or cable. A direct-broadcasting satellite is heavier and more complicated than a *Satcom* or *Westar,* but that is a one-time cost; after that, the only additional expense is the operation of the ground transmitter to send a signal up to the bird.

Direct satellite broadcasting raises a host of new questions. Who will have access to the bird? Who will be responsible for program content? Under our present broadcasting system, this is the immediate responsibility of the local broadcaster and the local cable system operator; they are liable for any obscenity, libel or unlawful matter. What would become of local broadcasters and cable operators in competition with satellite broadcasters? What would happen to the FCC's much-vaunted, long-cherished concept of localism? Would direct satellite broadcasting draw audiences away from local program sources to such an extent that local service would become impossible?

Of course, similar questions arose when cable television began to compete with local broadcasters, and again when pay-television and pay-cable became feasible. Local broadcasters have "cried wolf" so many times, perhaps they are not entitled to be taken seriously again. The FCC has officially concluded that neither regular cable services nor pay-cable services are likely to have any substantial effect on local broadcasting. At worst, the FCC believes that a local TV station might lose ten percent of its audience, and the commission does not consider that a big enough loss to warrant giving the local station any special protection. These conclusions are based on the most extensive economic studies ever performed in the field of telecommunications. However, that is no assurance that the conclusions are correct, or even that a ten percent audience loss is negligible.

Furthermore, there might be an accumulation factor that the FCC has not yet considered. If a local station loses ten percent of its audience to cable, five percent to home video devices, and another five percent to satellite broadcasters (just to pick numbers at random), that would mean a loss of fully one-fifth of its audience. By and large, audience size and revenues are directly proportional for a local broadcaster. Few businesses could absorb a loss of one-fifth of its revenue without drastic effects on its operations. Since public service and minority-interest programs are, for most stations, notorious money-losers, it stands to reason that they would be the first to be jettisoned.

The effects on the major commercial networks also could be substantial, if audience losses accumulate as I have suggested. Again, ratings determine revenues, and ratings are directly dependent on total audience—*not* audience share. A 20 percent decline in the total audience would be simply devastating for the commercial networks.

Bear in mind that I have no evidence that the new video technologies actually will draw away 20 percent of the television audience. The FCC says that cable systems might attract as much as ten percent of a station's audience, if about 50 percent of the homes in the station's market are hooked up to the cable and if various other factors are present. But that supposes that cable systems will continue to offer the relatively limited fare that has been available in the past. The economics of satellite-to-cable networking and of pay-cable are so attractive that surely cable will be able to provide superior programming in the future. As for the attractiveness of direct satellite-to-home broadcasting, obviously that remains to be seen. However, the economics are enough to make program suppliers drool. If sufficiently powerful satellites can be put into geosync orbit, and if adequate small-antenna earth stations can be produced at a cost people are willing to pay (probably somewhere between $500 and $1,000), and if the nagging question of who will control the channels can be resolved, the old saying, "the sky's the limit," may no longer apply.

And then there is still the joker in the deck: home video equipment. It may be that a great many people will choose to provide their own programming. But before taking up that subject, let us see how people are using video technology for all sorts of pragmatic purposes, in education, industry, medicine and other useful pursuits.

Part
IV

Private Television

Chapter
9

Television for for Practical Purposes

For most people, television is merely that magical box in the living room that provides an endless torrent of news, sports and entertainment. The viewer's role in this system is merely to receive, to watch and listen. Most viewers, in fact, have only a dim notion of where programs come from, and the distinction between locally produced programs, locally originated syndicated programs, and network programs is not apparent to them.

However, since the middle 1960s and the development of practical, comparatively inexpensive video production equipment, an entirely different kind of video has evolved.

Even in the early 1950s, while commercial television was still getting its feet on firm ground, a few large and wealthy institutions began to put television to work. There was no practical means of recording video programs at the time, so these early private television systems consisted of little more than a couple of cameras, a simple switcher and a cable network to a number of receivers. Since signals were not broadcast, and one had to be connected to the system in order to receive the programs, these systems were called *closed circuit television,* or CCTV. Today, the term CCTV is sometimes used loosely to refer to any non-broadcast television system.

The first CCTV systems were built in a few colleges, especially at medical schools where televised lectures and demonstrations could be transmitted to student laboratories scattered around the campus. The systems also were used in a very few large high schools and public-school districts, and in a few large industrial plants and corporate headquarters. The equipment used in these early private systems was the same used in broadcasting, because that was all that was available. It was, of course, frightfully expensive and it required the constant ministrations of highly trained technicians. Since all program transmissions were "live," scheduling was a real headache. Understandably, even the most enthusiastic proponents of video grew discouraged.

However, these early systems demonstrated both the need for television as a communications medium for practical purposes, and some of the prospective benefits. Manufacturers were encouraged to begin designing and producing equipment intended specifically for non-broadcast applications.

The introduction of videotape recording spurred these developments considerably. Now a school could record a lecture or demonstration and play it back repeatedly; a corporate executive could record a message to employees and distribute it to the company's various plants and offices. Scheduling problems did not entirely disappear, but at least there was a way to deal with them. Unfortunately, the early video recorders were still too costly, bulky and balky. Ampex's attempt to market a suitcase-sized portable quad recorder flopped. Then came the helical scan recorders, first appearing about 1962 in one-inch models and later (about 1965) in half-inch versions. Along with the much less expensive recorders, there were smaller, cheaper cameras as well. Suddenly television was practical for all sorts of utilitarian applications.

Suddenly, too, television was not just something watched at home for entertainment. It became a part of everyday, workaday life. And for growing numbers of people, television was something you could do for yourself: it was a medium of communications that anyone could use.

Television in the Business World

Among the first to install private television systems were the giant insurance companies; Mutual of Omaha began in 1967 and several others, including Prudential, State Farm and John Hancock, were not far behind. Their primary need was to provide continual training to enormous sales forces, as well as to claims personnel, underwriters and clerical staffs. Insurance is a complicated business and it is constantly changing as new policies are offered, old ones are modified, rates change, and so forth. Most insurance agents, if they work for one of the larger companies, spend almost as much time in training sessions of one kind or another as they do in actual selling. Much of this training requires studying and analyzing printed matter, but general principles can be helpfully explained in a videotaped program before (or while) the agents study the print material.

There were similar needs in the fast-growing, fast-changing data processing field, and it is no surprise that IBM quickly added television to its training curriculum. Texas Instruments also established a network of "Learning Centers" at its plants, relying heavily on video as the principal learning medium.

Staff training is probably the most common application of video in the business world. Wherever there are large numbers of personnel in plants or offices scattered over a large geographic area, or, in the case of manufacturing operations, spread out through several different work shifts, videotape recorded training programs have become all but indispensable. For example, Employers Insurance of Wausau produces programs on tape in its Wausau, Wisconsin, studio and distributes them to some 30 offices around the country for use in formal training sessions. In addition, agents in any of its local offices can obtain specific tapes from a library of more than 50 titles. Bloomingdale's, the New York fashion retailer, uses videotape programs to introduce new styles and fashion trends (as well as more mundane matters, such as how to operate a cash register) to its sales force in some 14 branch stores. Fisher Scientific Company, a manufacturer of sophisticated laboratory equipment, distributes training tapes to some 30 facilities around the world.

One major advantage of video for staff training is that any number of students can receive the same instruction, either simultaneously or individually. Training programs via videotape can be presented to classes of 10 to 100 or more students, or studied by a lone student in need of review, a make-up lesson or specialized information. Furthermore, once a program has been recorded, it can be used and re-used as long as the content is still accurate: a week, a month or several years.

Television in the classroom. Although television has not quite fulfilled the exuberant forecasts of the early 1960s, it has become a familiar feature of the school day, supplementing and extending the teacher's instruction. (Photo courtesy National Audio-Visual Association)

Television also can serve more immediate business needs. Corporate executives often discover that important information simply is not getting through to the people at the bottom of the hierarchy; policies are misinterpreted or ignored, lower-echelon employees have no sense of commitment to a common effort, and morale sags. Printed memoes are too easily overlooked or misunderstood; too often, they are simply stuffed in a filing cabinet without even being read. A number of companies have found that "TV newsletters," either on video tape or distributed "live" by CCTV, help to eliminate the gap between the upper and lower levels. The company president or branch manager is no longer a remote, faceless entity; he or she is a living, breathing person who carefully explains why a new policy is being implemented, why new rules must be enforced or how a new fringe benefit plan works. The "newsletter" format also can be used to familiarize employees with the functions and responsibilities of a company's various branches or divisions, and it can be used to give recognition to individual employees for outstanding work—or just to help break down the barriers of anonymity that too often characterize larger corporations. When employees see a video program about the bowling team's trophy, or the fellow in the Oshkosh plant whose hobby is woodcarving, or the secretary in Atlanta whose mother, grandmother and great-grandmother also worked for the company, the dark sea of depersonalization is parted—at least for the moment. Of course, the same content can be conveyed in a printed newsletter, but not with the impact and immediacy of television.

There are more mundane uses for television in industry, too. A few industrial plants use television cameras and monitors to keep an eye on automated production lines. Not only does this enable a single employee to watch several locations at once, but television cameras can give a view that no human observer could manage. The cameras can be built into the assembly line, or (with suitable protection) placed in dangerous locations, or designed to record images in the infrared or ultraviolet spectrums that are beyond human capacities. Cameras can even record x-ray images, allowing the observer to peer into finished products and make sure there are no flaws, broken parts or other quality problems.

A related application is the use of video security systems. Again, cameras can be mounted in dozens of locations, feeding signals to a single monitoring point. Some highly sophisticated low-light cameras can even produce a useful image by starlight. Not only can intruders or thieves be spotted without their knowledge, but the evidence can be recorded immediately on video-tape. Because tape is relatively inexpensive and eraseable, it is practical to record the signals from security cameras continuously in some cases, such as bank lobbies, where the use of motion picture film for the same purpose would be prohibitively expensive.

Some companies have found that television is just as persuasive a sales tool outside of the viewer's home as it is in the living room. General Motors, Ford and Chrysler all use videotaped training programs to instruct their dealers' mechanics on the intricacies of their products, and all three automakers also offer showroom sales programs to their dealers. Several manufacturers of do-it-yourself hardware and building materials have designed elaborate store displays that feature a television monitor and videocassette player. The display shows a tape demonstrating the use of an antiquing stain or a lock wrench, and presumably the customer will buy the product on-the-spot. The Broadway department store in Los Angeles produces its own point-of-sales tapes, giving customers consumer tips and extolling the virtues of various products; the company even replays its commercial TV spots in the store. Eli Lilly and Company, one of the world's largest pharmaceutical manufacturers, presents clinical programs (often, but not always, featuring the company's products) at medical conventions. The Eli Lilly booth often attracts the largest crowd in the exhibition hall because it is offering current scientific information in a highly palatable form.

All of these business applications of television have evolved just during the past fifteen years. Today, it is a rare company with more than a couple of hundred employees that does not have some sort of television studio facility and videotape playback equipment in all its major offices. The insurance and data processing industries have led the way. Most of the major manufacturing industries, retailing, consumer goods producers, and the hotel industry also have found private television to be an indispensable communication tool. New uses for television are being discovered almost every day.

One new application promises to become increasingly common in the near future: *teleconferencing,* or the use of two-way, live television for dialogue between individuals who are some distance apart.

There were a few attempts at teleconferencing in the late 1960s and early 1970s but without much success. The biggest barrier in the past has been the cost. There is nothing very exotic about the equipment needed for a teleconference: it is just the same as the equipment needed for a live one-way transmission, except that everything must be duplicated and signals must be sent in both directions. And that is the problem—sending the signals in both directions. Ordinarily that means tying up two landline channels (either using telephone wires or a microwave network), and that can be prohibitively expensive even if the distance between the two origination points is not very great. However, communications satellites offer an alternative that is not only less expensive to begin with, but that is almost entirely insensitive to distance.

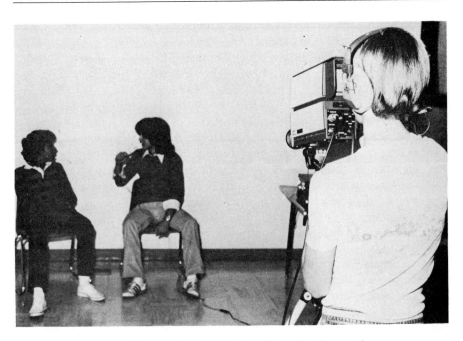

Not only are students seeing television in school, they frequently are producing television programs, using relatively inexpensive "industrial-type" cameras, recorders and related equipment. A generation of young people are learning to treat television not just as passive spectators, but as active participants. (Photo courtesy Texas Education Agency)

So far, teleconferencing has been used only on an experimental or "pilot project" basis. However, most of the experiments have been successful enough to encourage commercial development of teleconferencing services. Satellite Business Systems, Inc., which is owned jointly by IBM, Aetna Life Insurance Company and Comsat, has made a teleconferencing service one of the key features of its proposed satellite system, which otherwise would be devoted primarily to data transmissions. AT&T also has indicated that teleconferencing would be offered on its *Comstar* satellite when the FCC frees it from previous restrictions; in the past, AT&T has tried to sell what amounts to a teleconferencing service, using its "Picturephone" equipment and landlines, but has met stiff resistance to the cost. Both RCA and Western Union offer teleconferencing on their *Satcom* and *Westar* satellites. As of this writing, teleconferences have been held only sporadically, either on an experimental or demonstration basis, usually in connection with a convention or trade meeting.

For the near future, teleconferencing still will be fairly expensive; including the cost of satellite channels, the use of earth stations capable of both receiving and transmitting and the on-site television production equipment, the price for a one-hour teleconference in most cases will be in the range of $2,500 to $5,000. These costs will drop somewhat as teleconference services are more frequently used but it does not appear likely that the price ever will go much below $1,000 an hour. Obviously, at these prices, it will be a long while before business people "hook up" a teleconference as casually as they might make a telephone call. Even for the simplest kind of teleconference, involving one person at each end and using limited equipment (such as a small monitor with a built-in camera), the cost of transmitting the signals will keep two-way video communication out of ordinary, everyday use. However, it has been estimated that a corporate executive's time is worth between $500 and $1,000 per hour; if three or four executives can "meet" by teleconference and save themselves an hour of travel time apiece, the teleconference has more than paid for itself. The differences between "meeting" another person by two-way video and merely talking to the person by telephone are much greater than might be imagined, and of course video offers the opportunity to include all sorts of visual material (graphs, photos, etc.) that cannot be transmitted conveniently over the telephone.

In some cases, teleconferencing has proven to be literally a life-saver, and it may well be that its greatest use will be in the field of medicine.

Television in the World of Medicine

There is a standard scenario that explains rather clearly the potential for video communications in medicine. A patient in some remote location has contracted a rare disease, or has suffered a bizarre injury. Either there are no local medical resources at all, or the personnel available are not sufficiently qualified or familiar with the type of case the patient presents. A telephone call to a distant specialist probably would be inadequate; it just is not possible to express complicated information about symptoms and the patient's appearance in words alone. Instead, the patient is put before a television camera, and pictures—along with an explanation by the patient and medical personnel—are transmitted hundreds or thousands of miles away to a specialist. There is, of course, an audio feedback channel so that the specialist can ask pertinent questions, request more tests and, ultimately, suggest a course of treatment. In extreme cases, a local physician might even perform surgery while the distant specialist watches over his or her shoulder.

This is not just a scenario, nor is it a far-fetched episode from a prime-time TV drama. Already, patients' lives have been saved in the remote Alaskan bush, the sparsely populated Rocky Mountains, and swampland villages of rural Mississippi, among other places.

This kind of application of television to medicine might well be more common if there were more television origination facilities in remote areas of the world, and more medical specialists willing and able to serve as consultants in these circumstances. Unfortunately, getting the television equipment to all the places where it might be needed is almost as expensive as getting competent medical facilities to those places. Where there are no medical personnel at all, someone else must assume the responsibility for maintaining and operating the video equipment. If there are medical personnel in the area, they must add camera operation and transmitter maintenance to their list of skills, or find someone else to perform those chores.

And it is still expensive, even when the equipment is readily available. Whether landlines or satellite channels are used, transmitting a television signal over any distance will cost money, and someone must pay. So far, most of the experiments in remote-control medicine have used microwave systems or satellite channels that were provided by the government without charge or donated by the system operator. However, if these capabilities are to be provided to all of the rural areas where they might be needed, on a permanent basis, some better arrangement must be made to handle the cost.

Fortunately, medical emergencies are not the only good use for teleconferencing systems in medicine. If video communications systems can be used for a number of different purposes, the costs can be distributed among the various users and perhaps reduced substantially for all of them.

The most common use of television in medicine, as in business, is for training and education. Physicians and paramedical personnel are hard pressed to keep up with the constant flow of new medical discoveries and newly developed techniques; they also must participate in educational programs to improve or expand their skills, to learn a new specialty, or to freshen memories of knowledge gained years before. At one time, not very long ago, a "medical continuing education program" probably consisted of a pinochle game at the local medical society's monthly meeting. Today, not only physicians but also nurses, laboratory technicians, even orderlies and ambulance drivers, all must participate in an endless series of training and educational programs. In many cases, the need for continuing education becomes a serious burden; this is especially true for the physician or paramedical worker in a remote, rural area. Television, of course, can help to reduce that burden by eliminating the travel and personal expense involved in attending classes at some central site.

Even where students do congregate at one place for an educational program, video communications can be just as useful in the world of medicine as is in the world of business, and for much the same reasons: to ensure that all students are exposed to the same content, to permit individual students to study the particular material they need, to present information (such as demonstrations of technique) in a carefully prepared visual form, and to bring to all students material that otherwise might be available only to a few. Medical schools were among the first to install CCTV systems in the early 1950s and videotape recording equipment a decade later. Now, with the widespread availability of relatively inexpensive, reliable, portable VTR equipment, the use of television as a medium for medical education has exploded.

So, the next time you visit your family physician and find him sitting in his office watching TV, double check to see whether it's *The Love of Life* or *How to Perform a Coronary Bypass*.

A closely related application of television in medicine is patient education. In recent years, there has been much more emphasis than in the past on the patient as an active participant in the prevention of disease and during the course of treatment. Patients themselves have adopted a more aggressive "consumerist" attitude toward their own health care. Both trends have depended heavily on providing patients with more information, so that they can understand how to prevent disease and how to assist their physician in treating it.

At the Virginia Mason Medical Clinic in Seattle, patients routinely are taken to a Patient Information Center to watch a videotaped program about the disease they are suffering or the surgery they are about to undergo. Some of the tapes actually show the surgical procedure. Others, shown to patients after surgery or other treatment, explain how the patient should care for himself at home.

Patient education programs are not limited to hospital settings; some physicians use videotape equipment in their offices to educate patients, mostly about prevention techniques. And, of course, there are more general health education programs distributed by commercial and public television.

Another use of television in medicine is the documentation of treatment. The medical profession today is extremely sensitive to the ever-present possibility of a malpractice suit; this concern, and a growing understanding of the need to create a better record of patient treatment, has encouraged the use of video recording. A few physicians routinely videotape their surgical operations, as a record of exactly what was done and as a means of analyzing and critiqueing their own work. Videotape recording is often used in physical therapy, not only to document the work that has been done but to record and demonstrate the patient's progress over what is often a long period of time. Sometimes it is helpful to show a tape to a patient, to explain what has been accomplished and what still needs to be done. Again, the patient becomes an active participant in the treatment process—and is usually reassured about the progress of the treatment.

Similar applications have been developed in psychology and psychiatry. It is now fairly common to videotape an interview with a single patient or a group of patients, then play the tape back to stimulate the patients' insight into their own behavior. This kind of "video feedback" can become quite elaborate if the patients are engaged in role-playing and other therapeutic procedures.

Finally, television is often used as a part of the patient treatment process itself. For example, during surgery it is sometimes necessary for the surgeon to view the operating field through a microscope. Unfortunately, placing a microscope in the operating field is awkward and often interferes with the surgeon's hand movement. Squinting over a microscope eyepiece, keeping the light where it is needed, and still performing extremely delicate manipulations all at once can be nearly impossible. Instead, a television camera can be placed above the patient, out of the way; it can be equipped with a magnifying lens (and, to a certain extent, the video signal itself can be processed to increase magnification) and the picture can be displayed on a monitor alongside the operating table. The surgeon can then watch what is happening on the monitor, while hand movement and the placement of instruments are unfettered.

Other professions have not been as quick to find applications for television as has the medical profession. However, television is slowly becoming an accepted tool in yet another professional world: that of law.

Television in the World of Law

Lawyers, like physicians, have a constant need for continuing education and training, and they too have found television to be a useful medium for this purpose. However, that is only the beginning of television's applications in the legal field.

During the course of preparing for a civil suit, lawyers frequently must take depositions from the plaintiff, the defendant and various prospective witnesses. Traditionally, these depositions have been taken in the lawyer's office while a stenographer recorded the statement in shorthand; afterward, a typed transcript must be prepared and signed by the person giving the testimony. Skilled stenographers are hard to find these days, and this time-consuming process has become increasingly expensive. A deposition recorded on video-tape, on the other hand, may not need to be transcribed at all; if it must be, the work of transcribing can be performed by a secretary or clerk with only modest skills, since the tape can be stopped and replayed as often as necessary to pick up missed words. The same is true for a deposition recorded on audio tape, of course, but videotape has other important advantages: the witness's facial expression and gestures can be seen, and often these are significant clues to the witness's veracity.

A few courts have allowed videotaped depositions to be presented as evidence, in both civil and criminal trials, where it would be impossible for the witness to appear in person. In New York City, the Bronx County district attorney not only videotapes depositions, but also line-ups of criminal suspects and interrogations. A number of police departments have begun videotaping suspected drunk drivers and other offenders, to create a record of their behavior after arrest. Although some courts still resist the use of videotapes as evidence, that attitude is changing rapidly.

Some courts have gone so far as to conduct an entire trial by video. The Common Pleas Court in Sandusky, Ohio, began this practice on an experimental basis in 1971 and still uses it occasionally, especially for cases in which it would be very inconvenient to assemble all of the witnesses for a trial. Instead, the witnesses testify before a video camera, with the lawyers for both sides asking questions just as they would in a courtroom. The judge then reviews the tape to make sure that the testimony is legally acceptable; any unacceptable testimony (such as violations of the complicated rules of evidence) can be edited out of the tape at the judge's direction. Finally, the tapes can be presented in the proper sequence to a jury. The jury can review a tape repeatedly if they wish before reaching a verdict. This procedure serves much more than just the convenience of the witnesses; the jury's time is not wasted in waiting for witnesses to be rounded up, or for the lawyers and the judge to haggle over legal technicalities. Although a good deal of the lawyers' and judge's time may be spent in getting the tapes made and suitably edited, the actual time of the trial may be reduced from four or five days to half a day. Such a time savings also means a substantial reduction in cost, and, of course, allows more cases to be tried rapidly.

Outside of the courtroom, video can be used to gather evidence. The police use videotape recordings of crime sites as an investigative tool and as evidence to present in court. Civil lawyers also use video to record accident scenes and other situations that may be the basis of a lawsuit. Many lawyers now urge their wealthier clients to have either photographs or videotape recordings made of their homes and personal property as documentation for insurance or estate purposes.

One obvious use of video in law is still rare: the recording of trials by the news media. Ever since the Lindbergh kidnap and murder trial in 1935, the news media have been forbidden to bring cameras of any sort into the courtroom. However, these strictures are not based on laws in most states; they are left to the judges' discretion. In 1977 the Florida Bar Association urged the state judiciary to permit television cameras into the courtroom, under various restrictions to ensure that the dignity of the proceedings would not be violated. One major premise behind this suggestion was that televised trials would help to educate the public about the judicial process. Some—not all—Florida judges agreed to give it a try. (Ironically, one of the first televised trials was the case of a young man who was accused of murder, and whose defense attorney claimed that the boy—he was 16 years old—was innocent because he had been driven to his crime by violent TV shows. The jury found him guilty anyway.)

The Florida experiments have proven that modern television cameras are so small and unobtrusive that they do not detract from the solemnity of the proceedings. Unfortunately, the experiments also have proven that most trials are so deadly dull that they are of little interest to a home audience. Nevertheless, once the members of the legal profession realize that letting video cameras into the courtroom will not reduce the occasion to a shambles, there will no longer be any good reason to keep the news media confined to 19th century technology.

Television in the World of Education

Educators were very slow to display an interest in television. Throughout the 1940s, they were still licking their wounds from the fierce and futile battle to win dedicated AM broadcasting frequencies; they had settled for a modest allocation of FM channels, which initially seemed almost useless. Of course, the staggering costs and complexities of early television broadcasting would have been enough to daunt any but the most fearless visionary, anyway. If Federal Communications Commissioner Frieda Hennock had not bullied both her colleagues and the nation's school officials, there might not have been a reservation of television broadcasting channels for educational use, and there might not be a Public Broadcasting Service today.

Even when educators finally had been persuaded that television could be a useful tool in the classroom, the practical difficulties stood in the way for many years. The production equipment was simply too expensive and required too much in the way of skilled operators. Only a handful of the largest or the wealthiest public schools and colleges could afford modest CCTV systems.

In 1963 the FCC set aside some 30 television channels in the microwave band (2500-2690 megahertz) for an Instructional Television Fixed Service, or *ITFS*. The idea was that a school district or a large college could transmit programs on as many as four channels, using low-power transmitters—about ten watts in most cases—to reach classrooms within a five-mile radius. More distant sites could be reached either by using a narrow-beam antenna or by placing relay transmitters along the way. In essence, an ITFS system would be a private television network for a school district or college.

Still, the production equipment that would make such a system practical was not yet on the market, and the schools' interest in ITFS was agonizingly slow to develop. Helical scan videotape recording had just been developed; the economical half-inch tape size was not yet available.

Then, within just five years, the situation changed radically. Smaller, much less expensive cameras and other production gear were introduced for industrial use, and the half-inch videotape was perfected. Suddenly it was feasible for a school district to build and equip its own small studio, staffed by students and faculty members with only modest training.

Meanwhile, educational broadcast television had begun to evolve into an important resource, thanks largely to the determined efforts of the Ford Foundation, National Educational Television (NET) and a small coterie of enthusiasts. For the first time, there was a growing body of instructional program material for use in the classroom, and there was at least a rudimentary means of distributing it.

Thus three separate forms of educational television evolved concurrently, somewhat independently but with many interrelationships:

—Educational broadcasting, which consisted of instructional programs during the daytime and cultural entertainment programs during the evening, eventually becoming the Public Broadcasting System.

—Locally-originated instructional programming, using industrial-type production and distribution equipment to serve a single campus (through CCTV and videotape recording) or an entire district (through ITFS and bicycled tapes).

—Single-classroom use of instructional programs on videotape.

The uses of television in the classroom are not much different from the uses of video for education and training in industry or the professions. Actually, television has had remarkably little impact on the curriculum in the elementary and secondary grades, and even less at the college level. Even though the effectiveness of instructional television as a means of educating has been thoroughly established, there probably is not a single school—or, for that matter, a single classroom—in the United States where the television set is regarded as an indispensable teaching tool, comparable to, say, the blackboard or the textbook. It is extremely rare for students to receive more than half an hour of instruction by television on any given day. "Watching TV" is considered clearly supplementary and secondary to the "real learning" that takes place under the teacher's immediate direction.

Typically, instructional television enters the classroom in the form of a receiver tuned to the local PBS station's instructional programs. Perhaps the class watches *The Electric Company* or one of the science or art appreciation programs.

Almost immediately, teachers will complain about "The Scheduling Problem." The local PBS station does not schedule a particular program at the time when it would be most convenient for the teacher to include it in the class's activities (although most PBS stations repeat their instructional programs at various times of the day, and on different days of the week, to accommodate as many teacher preferences as possible). Furthermore, the program must be turned on at a certain time, even though the class may not have quite finished the previous activity. In short, the teacher feels constrained and controlled by the inflexibility of the broadcasting schedule.

The apparent solution is for the school to purchase a videotape recorder, usually the least expensive cassette machine available. Then someone (often a student or a clerk) could record the programs when broadcast, and each teacher could play back the programs whenever it is most convenient.

The most common application of video in business is personnel training, and few companies use video better or more thoroughly than Texas Instruments, Inc. This is a portion of TI's "Learning Center" at its Houston plant; there are comparable facilities in each TI factory or major office location. Employees are assigned to watch training tapes as part of their job, or they can "catch up" on new techniques during their lunch hour or after work. (Photo courtesy Texas Instruments, Inc.)

Of course, scheduling problems soon arise within the school, requiring the purchase of additional videotape players. It isn't long after that before someone decides that the school needs a camera. The impetus may come from a sports coach or the band director, who wants to use the camera and a VTR during practice sessions. Or an English or journalism teacher may want to teach a class in media studies, visual literacy or even television production. It is not hard to think of dozens of ways a camera *might* be used in a school (although in reality most of those hypothetical applications are never developed).

Once a school has a camera, various accessories must be added: microphones, audio mixers, lights, tripods, small monitors and so forth. A classroom or the stage at the back of the cafeteria may be set aside as a "studio." Eventually a second camera may be added and with it a switcher. A closed-circuit distribution system may be added, permitting live transmissions from the studio to any classroom or combination of classrooms.

And finally, if the school district is large and wealthy enough, or if several small but moderately wealthy districts decide to form an instructional television consortium, an ITFS system is established with a fairly well-developed central studio, two to four channels of instructional programming each day, and rather elaborate distribution systems in each school building. At last count, there were nearly 200 such systems in operation across the country, with more being planned.

The rapid growth of cable television has created an alternative to ITFS for many school districts. Most cable systems, especially those with more than a twelve-channel capacity, are willing to turn over one channel to the local school system. It is standard practice in the cable industry to provide a free cable connection, or *drop,* to each school or other public building. Thus, in effect, the school district gets a free citywide distribution system; the cable operator fills a channel at no cost and wins a few "public service" points. Some cable operators take the channel back during the evening hours, either turning it over to a public access group or using it to carry a distant broadcast signal. However, many school districts have the exclusive use of a cable channel and use it during the evening for adult education programs, public information efforts and other purposes.

What do school districts do with these capabilities—either ITFS or a cable distribution system? First and foremost, they schedule the kinds of instructional programs a PBS station would air—sometimes the very same programs. Nearly all PBS programs are produced either by a PBS station or by an independent production agency such as the Children's Television Workshop (CTW). The programs are offered, on tape or on film, to anyone who wishes to rent or buy them. Most PBS programs are offered immediately after they have completed their first run on PBS; a few programs are available to individual schools *before* they have appeared nationally. And, of course, there are thousands of programs that have been produced by either commercial or noncommercial agencies and offered to the schools on film or tape.

The relatively recent development of ITFS and cable distribution systems has infuriated the producers and distributors of 16 mm educational films, who once could count on renting the same film over and over again, since each use in a different classroom counted as a separate rental. Now there is one rental and one showing over a video system. The ready availability of videotape recorders, which can enable a district to make a copy—illegally—of every rented film, further exacerbates the problem.

There are so many programs available from these sources, and so many of them are extremely well produced, it might be hard to imagine that a local school district would feel any need to produce its own programs. However, there may be good reasons to do so.

First of all, externally produced programs are expensive. A few noncommercial producers offer programs for as little as five or ten dollars per hour; commercial producers and distributors typically charge thirty to fifty dollars per hour for one-time rental in a single classroom, and rental for use over a multi-class distribution system may run $75 to $100 per hour and more. If a program is to be used frequently, of course, it is practical to buy it outright; but typical prices are $200 to $500 per hour, and sometimes much higher. Programs on video tape are often priced much lower than filmed programs, but the cost is still prohibitive.

Secondly, even though there are thousands upon thousands of programs available to the schools, not every subject is covered, and those that are covered may be handled in a way that does not agree with the local school's curriculum. In plain words, some educational films and video programs are not well conceived and well produced. Some are obsolete in concept or content; others are simply dull or ugly or ineptly presented. For whatever reasons, the school district's program selection committee—usually composed of teachers and subject–matter specialists—often will decide that a better job could be done locally.

Finally, there is the problem of coordinating the video program with classroom instruction. Nearly all video programs are used to supplement the teacher's instruction in the classroom; obviously, it is helpful if there is close agreement in concept, content and sequence between the two. By and large, teachers are reluctant to rearrange their preferred curriculum just to fit the video programs, especially since the teacher's curriculum usually is dictated by the students' textbook. It is not helpful if, for instance, the physics class is studying levers and pulleys when today's video program launches into an explanation of atomic energy. There also may be discrepancies in approach: the literature teacher may prefer an analytical teaching method, while the video series on poetry may emphasize the *gestalt* experience.

Another, though less frequent, reason for a local school district to produce its own programs is that a local teacher or other individual is uniquely capable of presenting certain material. Really, there are fewer of these "natural-born stars" than is commonly imagined. Many exceptional classroom teachers are unable to work their magic in front of the camera; the qualities that make them outstanding depend on the interaction with living, breathing students. Conversely, it is not unusual for a competent but ordinary classroom teacher to turn into a star performer in the video studio.

For whatever reasons, it is a rare school district that does not produce some programs of its own, once it has the facilities. Most locally produced programs are pretty dreadful by the standards of prime-time commercial TV, but no matter: they serve a need, and, within reason, students are remarkably tolerant of the modest production values in local programs.

Indeed, students almost always are heavily involved in producing the programs themselves. Few school districts can afford to hire professional technicians and creative staffs. At most, a district with a sophisticated ITFS or cable distribution system may have one professional engineer and one other person who serves as producer, director, administrator and liaison with the faculty. Students aim the lights, build the sets, sew the costumes, run the cameras and perform all the other necessary chores; sometimes they also provide the on-camera talent, although that is more often the teachers' role.

Since students must be trained to perform these tasks, video production courses usually are offered for credit at the high school or even junior high school level. Thanks to these courses, there is a growing pool of young people who have at least a passing acquaintance with the basic techniques of television production. They know something about how to operate a camera and a videotape recorder; it is not some arcane mystery to them. Of course, only a tiny minority will go on to study television production in college, enter the television industry, or have any other vocational interest in the subject. But that tiny minority is growing in absolute numbers, and is joined by another growing number who may develop an avocational interest in producing television programs, either for their private amusement or for display on public access cable channels. Others will find their limited familiarity with video production useful in other fields; if they are called upon to help produce a training or orientation program for their employer, they will at least know how to begin.

In short, the coming generation of young people will not regard television merely as something to be watched passively for cheap entertainment. Many of them will have experienced the personal satisfaction of *making* a television program. They will be, in a word, video-literate.

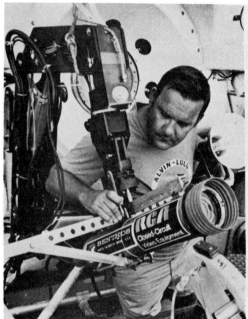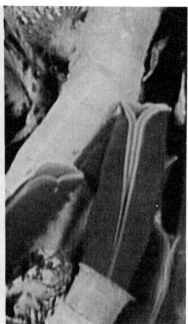

The video camera can go where human eyes otherwise could not see. Here, an experimental RCA camera, using CCD circuitry (see Chapter 1), is controlled from inside the *U.S.S. Alvin*, a research submarine. The remote-controlled camera can be lowered to depths that would be dangerous for the submarine, or it can be guided into narrow spaces that the sub couldn't enter. The photo at right shows a new form of life, tube worms, discovered by the *Alvin's* scientists using the new camera. Color photographs were made from the *Alvin's* video tapes and published in *National Geographic*. (Photo courtesy RCA Corp.)

It is hard to say whether this will mean a more demanding, more discriminating audience for commercial television in the future. That is certainly one possible implication. People who know something about making a product are better able to judge and choose a commercially produced version; this applies equally to television programs as to clothes, food or automobiles.

It could also mean that television will become increasingly a medium of two-way communication for all sorts of purposes, including those mentioned in this chapter and dozens more that have yet to be imagined. Using a TV camera may become as common as using a typewriter or telephone.

The fact that TV cameras are now readily available for home use is by no means incidental.

Chapter
10

Home Video

Once upon a time, not so very long ago, a way was found to send voices and other sounds through the air, from place to place; it was called radio. At first, this wondrous discovery was used by two sorts of people: those who had important things to say to one another, such as the owners and crews of steamships, and those who had little of importance to say but who were intrigued by the sheer possibility of saying it. This latter group of people built their own radios, piece by piece, in order to communicate with other people who also had rather little to say but an intense desire to say it.

Eventually there came to be a third kind of people interested in radio: those who had nothing at all to say, and neither the skill nor the inclination to build a transmitter, but who found it amusing to listen to other people. There were soon more of this kind of people than of the other two kinds. Large companies found it modestly profitable to build radio sets that could only be used for listening. Soon these large companies, in order to sell more of their radio sets, found it necessary to give the listeners more to listen to. Thus began broadcasting. And thus arose a world in which more than 99 percent of the people listened to what the other one percent had to say.

This arrangement seemed to please everyone. The 99 percent received all sorts of enlightenment and entertainment at virtually no cost, while the one percent grew wealthier and wealthier. After a while, the one percent found a way to add pictures to the sounds, which pleased the 99 percent even more. The 99 percent spent more and more of their time watching and listening to this new device, television; the one percent grew wealthier and wealthier and wealthier, beyond the most excessive dreams of avarice.

But now something curious and wholly unpredicted has begun to occur. The 99 percent are increasingly unsatisfied with mere watching and listening. Some of them have begun to take an interest in making their own television programs. Others, perhaps with less ambition, have merely assumed the responsibility of determining which of myriad possible programs they should be able to see, and when. In short, the 99 percent have begun to change television from a one-way medium, in which their role is merely to receive whatever the one percent choose to send, into an active, two-way or multi-way medium, in which each viewer exercises greater control over the programs to be received and, in some cases, has the option of transmitting programs as well.

This new arrangement could not take place without the introduction of certain new technology, particularly production and recording devices that are sufficiently inexpensive and easy to operate for the average person. On the other hand, the new devices would not have been introduced, and would not have been proven successful in the market, unless there were a great many people among the 99 percent who were eager to use them.

Which poses the interesting question: When, and why, did television suddenly become a participant sport?

The Videocassette Machine

The development of the helical scan videotape recorder and of half-inch recording tape opened the way to an inexpensive, easily operated device capable of recording television images. By 1970, even before a half-inch format had been standardized by the Electronic Industries Association of Japan, at a time when half-inch equipment was notoriously unreliable and able to produce a marginal picture signal at best, the industry's marketing chiefs enthusiastically envisioned a day when every home would contain not only a TV set but a videotape recorder as well.

First, however, they would have to eliminate the one aspect of operating a VTR that required a modest degree of manual skill: threading the tape through the recorder. To be sure, the procedure was considerably less difficult than, say, changing an automobile tire or even threading a movie projector. Nevertheless, there was a consensus within the industry that the average person was simply too inept to manage this. Furthermore, the industry could point to its experience with audio tape for proof: before the invention of cartridges and cassettes, audio tape recording was confined to a depressingly small band of determined aficionados. Once the tape had been neatly packaged, out of sight, and the threading procedure had been reduced to the single step of inserting the package into a slot, the market for audio tape mushroomed.

The first effort to duplicate the success of audio tape cartridges was made in the early 1970s by Cartridge Television, Inc., a subsidiary of the conglomerate, Avco. Cartrivision was introduced in 1972. The system used half-inch tape, wound on a single reel in a plastic case about twice the size of an eight-track audio cartridge. The Cartrivision system was available either in separate, "stand-alone" machines or as a built-in feature in ordinary television sets. Sears, Roebuck and Company, the world's largest retail merchants, sold Cartrivision equipment under its own brand name—or, at any rate, tried to do so. To everyone's surprise and bafflement, there were very few buyers. By 1974 Cartrivision was in big trouble; by 1975 Cartridge Television, Inc., was bankrupt; by 1976 Cartrivision had disappeared without a trace.

What went wrong? The equipment did not work terribly well, but that was also true for some of the early audio gear and that had not kept the market from developing. The Cartrivision equipment was fairly expensive, but not entirely beyond the reach of consumers; actually, one reason the manufacturer went broke so quickly was that it had cut its profit margin to the nub in order to keep its prices within the range that its market researchers considered "acceptable" to the public.

The painful truth seemed to be that no one much cared about being able to record television programs for themselves. There were virtually no pre-recorded programs available for Cartrivision because the primary sources of television program material—the Hollywood studios—had adopted a "wait-and-see" attitude toward the whole business. The Cartrivision system included a reasonably inexpensive black-and-white camera and the advertising urged consumers to make their own TV programs, the video equivalent of home movies. Of course, the recorder also could be used to record ordinary TV shows as they were being received, "off-the-air," but why would anyone want to do that? Presumably, a home videotape recorder would appeal primarily to people who were dissatisfied with the usual commercial TV fare, so why would they want to preserve it?

The failure of Cartrivision came at a time when almost every major manufacturer of television equipment was hard at work on its own home video recording system. Sony was known to be developing its own version, using three-quarter inch tape; two or three other Japanese companies were working on a half-inch cartridge similar to the Cartrivision system but somewhat less expensive (it became the ill-fated EIAJ cartridge system). CBS was almost ready to introduce its Electronic Video Record (EVR) system, which used 8 mm movie film and a laser-holography recording system rather than video tape. All of these systems were held back from the market while the manufacturers pondered the ignominious fall of Cartrivision. Sony finally brought out its three-quarter inch system, "U-matic," but strictly as an industrial-type product for CCTV and related uses; later, three-quarter inch equipment began to trickle into broadcasting stations, and by 1976 there was a full-scale stampede into the use of the U-matic system for electronic news gathering. The EIAJ half-inch cartridge also was marketed by Panasonic, Hitachi, JVC, and, very briefly, Sony; unfortunately, no one was quite sure whether it was supposed to be a home consumer product or an industrial product, and it never really found a market as either one. The EVR system was scrapped.

Then, in 1975 Sony introduced yet another packaged-tape system, Betamax, a cassette machine using half-inch tape. From the first, Betamax was marketed as a consumer product; in fact, Sony went to some pains to reassure its U-matic customers that the three-quarter inch industrial format would not be abandoned, and for several months refused to sell Betamax machines to anyone other than "individual consumers." Later, of course, "industrial-type" Betamax recorders appeared.

The introduction of Betamax was followed within a few months by no less than three competing systems: VHS (Video Home System), manufactured by Matsushita and sold by both JVC and Panasonic; GTM (Great Time Machine), also manufactured by Matsushita and sold by Quasar; and a third format, made and sold by Sanyo. (It should be noted that Panasonic and Quasar are both subsidiaries of Matsushita Electric Company of Japan, and JVC is half-owned by Matsushita.)

A Betamax video tape recorder. The Beta-format cassette is the smallest of the various types, but it also has the shortest playing time (maximum of three hours, depending on which model recorder is used). Sony's Betamax was the first videocassette system to achieve widespread popularity for home use. (Photo by the author, courtesy Austin Community Television)

American television manufacturers were befuddled by the invasion from Japan; they hardly knew how to respond. The four different formats, including Betamax, were very much alike, but of course a tape recorded on one machine could not be played on a machine of a different format. The big question was, which format would survive in the market? Soon the TV makers began choosing up sides. Zenith and Sears chose Sony's Betamax, the first of the new generation to be introduced. RCA and J. C. Penney chose Matsushita's VHS system, which had the advantage of a two-hour running time instead of the one-hour limit of the Beta format. Later, both Sony and Matsushita found ways to cut the tape speed, thus doubling and even tripling the running time; today, a VHS cassette can run for as long as six hours.

Sony, one of the shrewdest and most persistent marketing companies in the world, did what Cartrivision failed to do: promoted its product as a device for recording TV shows off-the-air. The theory was simple: with a Betamax, the viewer could watch his favorite show whenever he wanted to, instead of being forced to watch whenever the show was actually broadcast. Furthermore, according to Sony, the viewer could watch one show while another (presumably equally attractive) show was being recorded for later viewing. The Betamax put the viewer in control of the schedule. Betamax sales soared, and so did those of VHS, offering a similar appeal plus the longer running time. Within a year, about a hundred thousand Beta and VHS recorders were sold; the number reached 500,000 in two years and went past a million in three years.

Broadcasters seem to have had few qualms about home video recorders; they did not much care *when* people watched, as long as they watched (although apparently viewers who record a show and watch it later are not counted in the ratings). However, program producers went into a tizzy. After all, the home recorders not only permitted the viewer to watch a show later, but also allowed the viewer to keep a show on tape and watch it again and again. This could reduce the prospects for re-running shows in the future—and that, remember, is where the producers really make their money!

The Walt Disney Studios and Universal Studios sued Sony, demanding that the Japanese company stop selling its VTR equipment, or at least stop advertising its "time-shift" capabilities. The producers claimed that they would be irreparably harmed if every Tom, Dick and Harry could make and keep a tape recording of their TV shows and movies. Sony and the other VTR manufacturers inserted coy warnings in their ads and owner's manuals, advising consumers that they might be infringing someone's copyright interests if they copied programs off-the-air—as the ads invited the viewer to do. Finally, in October 1979 the U.S. Circuit Court in Los Angeles issued its ruling: to no one's surprise, the Disney-Universal demand for protection was denied. The principle was established long ago that a radio (or television) broadcast is not a "performance" of a copyrightable work, and therefore that no one can "own" whatever

A VHS video tape recorder. The VHS format developed by Matsushita and marketed by a number of companies, including RCA, uses a larger cassette but has a maximum playing time of up to six hours, depending on the recorder. (Photo by the author, courtesy Gray Electronics, Inc.)

is transmitted through the air. Although the Copyright Act of 1976 sought to modify that theory a little and give radio and television program producers more protection, the court felt that viewers have every right to record a program *for their own use*. At the same time, the court warned that viewers who recorded a program off-the-air could not use it for any commercial purpose such as playing the tape before a paid audience.

Disney and Universal initially threatened to appeal the Circuit Court's decision, but as of this writing the appeal has not been filed and appears to be futile at best. It is hard to imagine that even the U.S. Supreme Court would attempt to wipe out more than a million videotape recorders by decree. Furthermore, there are only minor technical differences between the home video recording equipment and the equipment used for closed circuit and broadcasting; it would be impossible to eliminate one without the other. Whatever harm may come to the Hollywood studios, it is too late to put the genie back into the bottle.

So what do people do with their home video recorders? Mostly, it seems, they record TV shows off-the-air. Few studies have been done to learn exactly what shows are preserved by the home viewer; apparently there is no particular pattern. The tape cassettes are fairly expensive, so presumably most viewers only record "special" programs: favorite movies, one-shot variety extravaganzas, and, perhaps most of all, sports. The tape manufacturers have been rather surprised to discover that people buy large quantities of raw tape, which suggests that they rarely erase the programs they have recorded; once a program is on tape, it seems to become part of an ever-growing home "library" of programs. According to some rudimentary studies, the average home video recorder consumer has a minimum of a dozen tapes; "libraries" of fifty to a hundred programs are not uncommon.

Pre-recorded tapes have not really caught the public's fancy, perhaps because the average viewer is content to take whatever comes free over-the-air rather than paying $40 to $80 for the old movies that are offered by most pre-recorded tape distributors. The most successful purveyors of pre-recorded tapes seem to be those whose catalogs feature a long list of X-rated programs (mostly dubbed onto video tape from 8 mm and 16 mm film); this is, after all, the one category of program material that is totally unavailable over-the-air. Otherwise, the producers and distributors of pre-recorded tapes have found only a limited market for their programs, regardless of their nature. However, there are still optimists who believe that the market will develop, once producers find categories of program material (besides porn) that appeal to a segment of the public who are not satisfied with the shows available over-the-air.

Home video equipment is not exactly cheap. The recorders range in price from about $800 to more than $1,400, overlapping the less expensive industrial-type equipment. Raw tape, in either Beta or VHS cassettes, costs around $20 to $30 per hour—but that cost can be reduced substantially if the cassette is used at low speed. Still, these prices limit the market considerably.

There has also been some degree of confusion over the various formats. Quasar's original Great Time Machine format was not so great after all; it was discontinued in late 1978 or early 1979, but the same trade name was used for a new series of VHS machines. Meanwhile, dealers were unloading the old GTM machines at drastic discounts. No doubt some consumers were bamboozled into thinking they were getting first-rate equipment for $400 and were unpleasantly surprised to learn, a few months later, that neither raw tapes nor spare parts were available for their video Edsels. The Sanyo format seems to have sunk without a trace.

For those who want to use their home video equipment to make home movies, a camera is indispensable—and expensive. The cheapest black-and-white cameras run about $300 and produce a picture comparable to a $50 8mm movie camera. A color video camera will cost a minimum of $800 with a fixed (non-zoom) lens and no frills; better cameras run $1,200 and up. There is little prospect of a sharp drop in these prices until something like a CCD-based camera is developed: the inherent complexity of the conventional pick-up tube, deflection coils and sync generators is just too great to permit a really cheap camera to be produced.

There are not likely to be any sudden price reductions in pre-recorded tapes, either. Videotapes must be copied essentially one at a time, or at most 10 or 12 at a time, and it ordinarily takes a full hour to copy a one-hour tape. The only practical method of copying tapes is to play the tape on one machine while recording the signal on another. The recording machines can be "ganged" so that as many as a dozen recorders are being "fed" from one player, but beyond that the simple problem of synchronizing so many recorders gets to be over-whelming. Consequently, pre-recorded tapes will continue to cost anywhere from $30 to $100 per hour, depending on the nature of the program and the producer's greed.

Fortunately, there is an alternative for people who just want to watch old movies and other pre-recorded material, who have no interest in making video "home movies" or recording off-the-air, and who do not care to spend a thousand dollars or more to get started. The alternative is the much-heralded, often-delayed TV phonograph: the video disc.

Video Discs

During the 1960s and early 1970s, while Japanese engineers were busily exploiting the videotape technology to develop first one-inch and half-inch helical scan recorders, then three-quarter inch and half-inch cassette recorders, American and European engineers were equally busy on a different quest: a video equivalent of the familiar phonograph.

A phonograph record is entirely unlike a magnetic tape recording. The latter contains information in the form of a pattern of magnetized iron particles; on a phonograph disc, the information is recorded as variations in the depth and shape of the grooves cut into the plastic surface. If a television signal somehow could be translated into a similarly tangible pattern, there could be several major advantages. First of all, phonograph records can be mass produced by impressing the groove pattern into soft plastic blanks; once the pattern is transferred and the blank hardens, it is virtually permanent (subject to physical wear or accidental damage). Mass production, of course, usually means low cost. Secondly, a signal recorded in such a tangible form is very stable. As long as the record is played back at the proper speed, reproducing the signal accurately is a good deal simpler than it is with magnetic tape. This, in turn, means that the playback apparatus can be simpler in design and, therefore, less expensive to make.

Unfortunately, the amount of information in a television signal is vastly greater than that contained in an audio signal. Recording a composite video signal (and, of course, the associated audio track) on something comparable to a phonograph record turned out to be a very tricky business. Eventually, three fundamentally different methods were found: the pressure-transduction system, the capacitance system and the reflective system.

The pressure-transduction system was developed primarily by German engineers and was more or less perfected by the Telefunken company in a joint venture with Britain's Decca company. The video signal is recorded as a series of bumps and pits on a soft vinyl disc. To play back, a stylus, much like an ordinary phonograph needle, rides in a groove over the bumps and pits. This roller-coaster ride causes the stylus to press with greater or less intensity against a contact, thus causing a varying electrical current to flow, thus producing a video signal.

The Telefunken-Decca system, marketed under the brand name TeD, works fairly well, and has been available in Western Europe since 1975. Unfortunately, the pits and bumps must be relatively large in order to produce enough pressure on the stylus to create the video signal. Because the pits and bumps are so large, the record must spin at a very high speed so that enough pits and bumps go past the needle to convey all of the information a video signal contains. (Remember how early videotape recorders had to run at tremendous speeds?) Consequently, a TeD video disc, about eight inches in diameter, only contains a 10-minute program. It takes an "album" of a dozen discs to play a two-hour movie, and there are just about as many interruptions as there are on commercial TV.

The Dutch electronics firm, Philips—originators of the standard audio cassette—experimented with both capacitance and reflective systems, and settled finally on the latter. This system, too, involves putting pits and bumps in a groove on a disc. However, there is no stylus. Instead, a beam of light—actually, a very small, low-power laser—shines on the groove. The pits and bumps reflect the light back toward a photosensitive pick-up cell; the amount of light that reaches the pick-up therefore varies according to the shapes of the pits and bumps, and thus a signal is reproduced. Because there is no physical contact with the pits and bumps, and the beam of light is extremely small (no thicker than a human hair), a great deal of information can be packed into a small space, and therefore the record does not have to spin so fast. The grooves themselves can be much narrower, too. In fact, it turned out to be possible to put about 30 minutes of program on a 12-inch diameter disc (or 60 minutes if both sides are used).

An American company, MCA, which also owns Universal Studios and several phonograph record companies, also was working on a reflective-system video disc in the early 1970s. When MCA and Philips discovered that they were developing very similar but not identical systems, they concluded that it would be pointless to come out in competition with one another. Besides, Philips was one of the world's largest electronics manufacturers but had virtually no experience in producing and marketing programs; MCA, on the other hand, was one of the world's largest and most successful producers and marketers of phonograph records, motion pictures and television shows, but had very little experience in manufacturing electronic equipment. For once, the obvious solution did *not* escape everyone's attention. In 1976 the two companies agreed to join forces to develop a single system, Discovision, to be produced by Philips and sold by its subsidiary, Magnavox, with program material to be developed and marketed by MCA.

Meanwhile, RCA was hard at work on its capacitance system. Briefly, the capacitance system involves cutting or molding a series of rectangular pits of varying depths in a groove in a metal disc. A flat stylus rides in the groove. Electric current is applied to the disc itself; the current is picked up by the stylus, but the shape of the pits causes the current to vary, and thereby a signal is reproduced. Although there is physical contact between the stylus and the disc, the pits can be extremely small and close together, so it is possible to pack enough information into a small space to permit a reasonably slow tracking speed. In fact, the RCA system has the slowest speed: it runs at about 450 rpm, compared with a speed of 1,800 rpm for the MCA/Philips system. Nevertheless, the RCA system's discs only carry about half an hour of program material on a 12-inch diameter disc—and only one side of the disc can be used.

The MCA/Philips video disc system was supposed to be put on the market in 1977, and RCA announced that its video disc system would be available before Christmas of 1978. Then the introduction of the MCA/Philips system was "temporarily delayed." In mid-1978 RCA announced that it would hold off on its video disc indefinitely. MCA/Philips said theirs would be on the market "sometime in late 1978 or early 1979," but those dates passed without a further word.

This international Alphonse-and-Gaston act frustrated a good many video freaks. What was going on? Several things, actually. First, both RCA and Philips ran into unexpected problems when they tried to put their laboratory prototypes on an assembly line. Knowing that they faced heavy competition, both companies were determined to get all the bugs out of their products before putting them on the market. The Cartrivision disaster sobered everyone in the electronics industry, and there was some doubt as to whether the public really wanted a video disc system. When Betamax and the other home video recorder systems hit the market in 1975 and 1976, the disc manufacturers decided to pull back and see what would happen; besides, they, too, were producing cassette machines, both using the VHS system.

Meanwhile, both RCA and MCA/Philips continued to show their prototype disc machines at trade fairs and conventions, always drawing enormous crowds. Hardly a trade journal in the television industry failed to contain at least one article, editorial or bit of gossip about video discs in every issue between 1974 and 1980.

Finally, in mid-1979 MCA/Philips began to sell its Magnavox Discovision system—but only in Atlanta and Seattle, as "test markets." The basic machine was priced at about $750, or slightly less than a stripped-down videocassette machine. The discs themselves—a limited catalog of old Universal movies and a few "instructional" programs (how to improve your golf swing, and the like)—were offered for prices in the $6 to $15 range, or roughly one-fifth the price of comparable pre-recorded cassettes.

The Magnavox "Magnavision" video disc machine and a selection of programs; MCA, the partner with Philips in developing the system, still calls it "Discovision." (Photo courtesy Magnavox)

If MCA and Philips seriously wondered whether anyone wanted a video disc, they need wonder no more; the success of Discovision in the test markets was immediate and total. The factory simply could not produce enough machines to supply those two cities alone, further delaying the introduction of the equipment in the rest of the country. Actually, about half of the machines sold in Seattle and Atlanta were being bought up by itinerant peddlers and dealers who bootlegged them down to San Francisco or up to New York and sold them for anywhere from $1,000 to $5,000 apiece. Consumer's Union, the product-testing organization, bought four machines in Atlanta and shipped them by air freight to the New York headquarters—but all four machines disappeared en route.

At the time of this writing, RCA's plans for its disc system are still vague; "sometime in 1980" is the current promise. So far, the only thing holding back the MCA/Philips system seems to be its production capacity. Meanwhile, Matsushita has announced that they, too, will offer a capacitance-type video disc (different from RCA's) beginning in 1981.

It is worth pointing out that a video disc purchaser must rely entirely on suppliers of pre-recorded material; a disc machine cannot be used to record off-the-air or from a camera. Consequently, the real value of the machine is dependent on the availability of pre-recorded material. MCA, with its huge reservoir of Universal movies and old TV shows, obviously has a tremendous advantage here, but RCA has already made deals for disc versions of MGM, Paramount, Columbia and other old movies (some of which also will be available on Philips discs). The curious thing is that these are basically the same kinds of program material that owners of videocassette machines generally ignore. Of course, the difference in cost is substantial, and that may account for the difference in market response. Or the two technologies may appeal to entirely different people.

In any case, purchasers of either videocassette or video disc machines have effectively declared their independence from the mass medium of television. They no longer have to watch what someone else schedules; they can watch whatever they like, whenever they choose, at least within the limits of their budget. So far, what they choose to watch does not seem to be very different from what they ordinarily would be offered by the commercial broadcasters (with the notable exception of porn). However, once there are enough cassette and disc machines in people's homes to create viable specialty markets, producers may respond with a wealth of new ideas. Something like that seems to be happening now in cable television.

The MCA/Philips video disc also offers a unique feature. The grooves in a Discovision disc are concentric; that is, each groove forms a complete circle, rather than spiralling from the outer edge to the middle the way an ordinary phonograph record's groove does. The reason for this peculiarity is that each circular groove represents one complete video frame (two interlaced fields).

A prototype of RCA's "SelectaVision" video disc system, which is supposed to be on the market in early 1981. The RCA system is electronically less sophisticated than the MCA-Philips system, but mechanically somewhat more complicated. RCA expects to be able to produce its disc player at a much lower price than the $700 or so list price for the Magnavision player. (Photo courtesy RCA Corp.)

That is also why the disc runs at 1,800 rpm, which is, of course, 30 revolutions per second. So what? Well, for ordinary video programs, the pick-up arm shifts from groove to groove. But if the arm is stopped and kept over a single groove, it will continuously repeat the same video frame: perfect freeze-framing. This would have limited usefulness for regular video programs, which are essentially electronic motion pictures. However, a full page of printed material could be recorded instead of a moving-picture frame in each groove. The viewer could then freeze-frame the image until he had finished reading that page, then shift to the next frame. Used this way, the MCA/Philips disc could hold a heck of a lot of information: about 54,000 pages worth on each disc. But that is using conventional video technology to record text: basically nothing more than aiming a video camera at a printed page. More sophisticated techniques, such as those employed in a teletext system, could pack the equivalent of perhaps 100 pages of text into each video frame, or 5,400,000 pages on a 12-inch disc.

Just don't scratch the disc or you may wipe out half your library!

Seriously, these capabilities mean that the video disc could be a great deal more than just a fancy way to sell old movies. A video disc player, with its tremendous storage capacity, combined with a videocassette recorder with equally impressive capacity plus the ability to record newly generated information, and a suitable computer, would comprise an information-handling system of almost unlimited versatility. Best of all, it would be done at a price that would be well within reach of most families. At least half the homes in America could be equipped with a computer system equal in capability to the biggest multimillion-dollar military installations of today. Not that the average family would use their computer system for the same purposes—heaven forbid! In fact, that is the real question: what will people do with this capability?

When the first transcontinental telegraph line was being built in the late 19th century, there were many people who wondered, as poet Ezra Pound did, "whether Maine and Texas would have that much to say to each other." When the first electronic computers were being built in the mid-1940s, one "expert" estimated that one hundred of those giant machines would be more than sufficient for all the computing that could be done in the whole country. Now we are faced with a similar situation: we have the capability to produce an information-handling system of unprecedented capacity. For the moment, we do not really know what to do with it. However, history suggests that we will find ways to put it to good use, perhaps much sooner than we expect.

It would be a shame if we did nothing more than watch old movies with it.

But we do not have to wait for the further development of the video disc to see what video and computers can do together. That connection has already been made.

Television and the Computer

One of the major trends in 20th century technology has been the convergence of different technologies into a single stream. When the century began, there were four main ways to transmit information over long distances, or between a single point of origination and a large number of people. Information could be sent from one point to another by *telegraph* or by *telephone;* or it could be disseminated to the public by *printing,* in the form of either books or newspapers and magazines; or handwritten or printed messages could be carried by postal messengers from one place to another. Information could be stored only as handwritten or printed matter kept in files and cabinets, or in the form of printed books stored on a shelf. *Photography,* both still and motion, was the fourth method of recording and transmitting information, either point-to-point or point-to-multipoint.

By 1925 *radio* had been established as a method of transmitting information either point-to-point (radiotelephony) or point-to-multipoint (broadcasting), in the form of voices and other sounds, and *phonograph recording* was developed as a means of storing sounds.

By 1950 two new technologies had arisen. *Television* combined radio and photography, enabling both sounds and pictures to be transmitted point-to-point or point-to-multipoint. *Computers* permitted the electronic equivalent of printed matter to be stored economically in large quantities, to be retrieved in random order, and to be processed or manipulated to generate new information from old (such as by mathematical computation). However, there was no convenient means of storing television information and no convenient means of transmitting computer information from place to place.

By 1975 these limitations had been erased. Television information could be recorded on *videotape.* Computer information could be transmitted by telephone or by radio, or the information could be transferred and stored on magnetic tape or discs.

Today verbal information can be prepared on a typewriter (a printing device) that transforms it into electronic signals, feeding it into a word processing computer that stores the information and rearranges it. The information then can be retrieved from the computer onto a video display, or it can be removed on a magnetic disc or tape and transferred to another place, or it can be transmitted by telephone line or by radio signal to another place. There it can be fed into a second computer that rearranges the information once again, forming the electronic pattern for the pages of a book. The computer can then produce pages of type that can be photographically transformed into printing plates, or the information can be transmitted by telephone or radio to yet another place where the printing plates are produced. The printing plates can be put on a press that is controlled by various small computers. The finished books can be shipped all over the country according to instructions generated by a computerized ordering system. The bookstore that sells the books may use a small computer to keep track of its inventory, and when a customer buys a copy of the book, the transaction may be recorded in the store's own computer. If a credit card or a bank check is used for the purchase, the store clerk may use a small computer terminal to send a message by telephone line to the customer's bank, to verify the customer's credit. The transaction itself might even be handled by computers, debiting the customer's bank account and crediting the store's account. Thus, from writer to reader, the information may have been processed or the processing of it may have been controlled by every one of the information-handling technologies: printing, radio, telephony, photography and computerization.

This kind of convergence has not yet taken place to a marked degree within the average person's home. For most people, the radio, the telephone, the TV set and the typewriter are all separate and distinct devices with very different purposes. Information is recorded in the form of books, periodicals (newspapers and magazines), phonograph records, still or motion pictures and individual handwritten or printed sheets of paper. Relatively few people have anything like a general-purpose computer in their homes, although most homes today contain a number of small, special-purpose computers built into various appliances.

Tomorrow's home is likely to contain a single device that combines the best attributes of all these information-handling technologies, and adds a few new features of its own. This new device will be similar to the small "hobby" or "personal" computers that have become available within the past three years, but it will also serve the functions of the present TV set—and, quite likely, the present telephone, newspaper, phonograph and bookshelf.

The kinds of small computers currently being sold for home use are essentially scaled-down versions of the giant stand-alone computers of the early 1960s, the only difference being that advances in microelectronics permit the same capabilities to be embodied in smaller, less costly machinery. A typical home computer consists of a highly sophisticated single-chip processor (the device that controls everything that happens in the computer); a keyboard, on which information is entered into the computer; a display, on which information is presented from the computer; and a storage device, which may consist of solid-state memory chips or a tape cassette (not much different from an audio tape cassette) or a magnetic disc recorder, using either 5½-inch or eight-inch diameter flexible plastic discs. An automatic typewriter may be added so that the computer's "output" can be displayed in permanent form, or the display may be merely a video screen. Such a system costs anywhere from $500 to $10,000, depending on its quality and versatility.

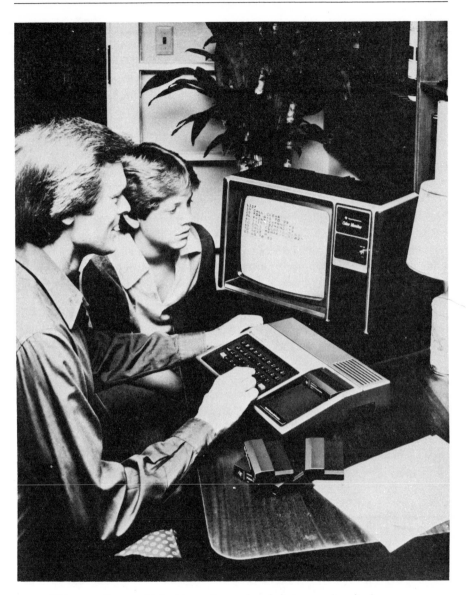

Video monitors and television sets are already being used as display devices for computer-controlled games and for minicomputers. Some home computers already are capable of exchanging information with other computers via telephone lines. As these developments continue, the familiar TV set may become the centerpiece of a sophisticated information network, as readily accessible and as commonplace in the American home as the telephone. (Photo courtesy Texas Instruments, Inc.)

Add to this basic system a telephone "modem"—a simple device that converts a computer's internal electronic signal into sounds that can be transmitted over a telephone line. Now the computer can exchange information with any other computer to which you have access (by coded telephone number); the computer can draw on another computer's memory, or transfer its data to another computer, or use another computer's central processor to manipulate its own data. Radio Shack offers a modem for its home computer system for about $200. You can also add a voice recognition device (about $170, but it does not work terribly well) and a voice synthesizer ($400). Conceivably, you could call your computer by telephone, give it verbal instructions, and have it answer you verbally.

Now replace your computer's video display—what amounts to a limited sort of television monitor, with circuits to convert the computer's signal into a video signal—with a television receiver. Connect the receiver to a cable TV system that offers a teletext "library" service comparable to the British Post Office's Viewdata service, but perhaps more elaborate in terms of interactive capabilities. You, and your computer, now have access to a theoretically unlimited source of information.

Now replace your computer's tape cassette or magnetic disc memory with a modified videocassette recorder. This would increase your computer's memory capacity at least a thousandfold. Add a video disc player; a single disc can hold a computer program of literally unimaginable complexity, or it can hold all the standard programs you would ever need (and you can have access to any non-standard programs you might need by telephone, from another computer or perhaps from the teletext library). Another disc might contain your basic reference library in "printed" form: around 18,000 volumes of information.

Everything I have just described could be done with current technology, with relatively minor adaptations of existing devices. I would guess that it might be done for something less than $10,000 altogether.

It is not hard at all to imagine how such a system could be used. For example:

—The system could operate, automatically, every sort of comfort and maintenance device in the home: the air conditioning system, lighting, burglar and fire alarms, door locks, a pressure-regulated plumbing system, and so on.

—The system could operate, under your direction, a complete food processing subsystem, automatically cooking meals, maintaining a continuous inventory of foods on hand, and such.

—The system could serve as a tutor for every member of the family, providing interactive instruction in any conceivable subject.

—The system could handle all of your family's financial transactions, paying bills, accounting for income and cash expenditures, assembling tax returns, even buying insurance and filing insurance claims automatically according to your instructions.

—The system could provide each member of the family with any sort of entertainment desired: old movies (or new programs available nowhere else) on discs, or conventional programs on any of a hundred or more cable channels, or stereophonic music of your choice, or informal instructional programs, or up-to-the-minute news and information.

—The system could serve as a communications terminal for ordinary voice communications (equivalent to the telephone), for teleconferences (probably used mostly for business purposes, or for special occasions), or for the transmission and exchange of computer data and "printed" text: a post office in your living room, and your "letters" never get lost or delayed en route.

Actually, I am a little embarrassed by this list, for two reasons. First, it so closely resembles the lists that have been offered sporadically during the past two decades by media enthusiasts who have foreseen most of these same possibilities. Their prophesies often have been ridiculed as outlandish and impractical, and it has taken much longer than they anticipated for these capabilities to be realized. Second, I am certain that the list I have just offered represents barely the beginning of the true potential of the kind of video-computer combination I have described. It is sobering to realize that when the automobile was first invented, the principal advantage claimed for it was that it did not leave smelly droppings on the ground.

It is easy enough to say that the combination of computer and video technologies will have immense, and largely unpredictable, consequences for our way of life. There are certain to be unexpected effects on our very social structure. Some of those effects might not be beneficial, at least according to our present values. No doubt some people would argue that we would be better off avoiding this new technology with its unpredictable, possibly disadvantageous, consequences. But we cannot. The technology already exists, or is on the verge of existing. Even if the vast majority of the population reject it, those few who accept and adopt it would gain all of the advantages: the ability to store, retrieve and process information in substantially greater volume at substantially greater speeds and at substantially less cost than ever before.

But still the question nags at us: What does it mean when every living room contains a machine that gives us instant access to virtually all of human knowledge?

Conclusion: The Ways It Might Be

In the Introduction, I said that television 25 years from now will scarcely resemble the medium of mass entertainment that we have known for the past 30 years or so. In the intervening chapters, I have tried to show how the medium came to its present circumstances and some of the forces that will influence its future. Now I will try to sum up.

Technologically, in the very near term, television will not change too radically. Cameras, recorders and other production equipment will continue to get smaller, less expensive and more versatile. These improvements will enable many more people to produce television programs for their own purposes, and will increase greatly the capability of local broadcasters and cable program producers to create programs of purely local interest.

There will be minor improvements in the picture quality of conventional production equipment, and major improvements as digitalization of the composite video signal proceeds from its present utilization in signal-processing gear back toward the camera itself. Unfortunately, digitalization cannot be extended downstream to the TV receiver because a digital signal would be incompatible with the millions of conventional receivers already in use, and, at least for the moment, it is hard to see how a compatible digital-analog system could be developed that would satisfy both conventional receivers and digitalized receivers.

One aspect of television technology that I have largely neglected is due for substantial improvements in the near future: television audio. Until now, the sound accompanying the picture has been treated with something like contempt by the TV industry. However, viewers (and, perhaps more to the point, advertisers) have become fairly insistent in demanding better sound. The three-quarter-inch U-matic videocassette system has the capacity for recording and playing back stereophonic sound, and that capability could be added easily to the other home videocassette systems. Stereo sound also could be added to the conventional broadcast signal, using the same techniques that are used for FM stereo broadcasting. I would expect stereo broadcasting to begin within the next five years, and TV sets with stereo capabilities will become standard within ten years.

Back in the TV studio, computerized signal-generating devices will become increasingly common. There are already occasional commercials based largely on computer-generated and computer-processed graphics. Full image synthesization—that is, computer-created images, such as animated cartoons—is no more than five years away, and could become a standard technique for commercials, program titles and similar purposes within two or three years. "Naturalistic" image synthesization is probably ten years away, and when it is introduced there may be a lot of controversy about whether the use of computer-generated "real" images is deceptive, or unfair to unionized talent, or morally reprehensible for some other reason.

Another major change in television technology will occur when the conventional cathode-ray tube is abandoned as the basis for image production in the camera (the pick-up tube) and image reproduction in the receiver (the picture tube). The charge-coupled device, or CCD, will permit much smaller cameras and a flat viewing screen. A color camera for home video recording may become available for no more than $250. Wall-sized flat screens are likely to be expensive, but very possibly less expensive than the video projectors that have become moderately popular in the past few years (and that are based on conventional technology, which will become obsolete before long). The use of CCD technology should become widespread within the next 10 years.

A truly practical system of three-dimensional television may be available in about fifteen years. Actually, there are already about five or six different ways to produce three-dimensional images and transmit them by television. All but one of the present technologies require extremely elaborate production equipment and specially modified receivers. They are used only in highly specialized situations where the illusion of depth is indispensable; for example, in certain industrial plants where hazardous materials must be handled by remote-control machinery.

There is one system of three-dimensional television that does not need special receivers. The "triangle system" is fully compatible with the existing television signal system; the three-dimensional image can be received on just about any ordinary color TV set, and to the naked eye the picture looks like an ordinary color picture. However, if the viewer puts on a pair of colored glasses (very much like the ones that were used to read 3-D comic books in the 1950s, with one red-orange lens and one blue-green lens), the picture becomes three dimensional. According to Ted Conant, a television research engineer for Shroder Technology Corporation, who helped develop the system, the three-dimensional effect is introduced by signal processing equipment *after* the image is recorded by a camera; in other words, no special camera is required, and pre-existing programs on video tape or film can be re-processed to introduce a 3-D effect. I have seen a demonstration of this system, and I must confess that I found it disappointing. The effect of depth was limited and varied from moment to moment in a jarring manner, and the colors were muddy. Conant says that different people will experience different effects, depending on the idiosyncracies of their individual optic systems. Of course, it is also possible that the demonstration tape I saw was not the best quality. In any case, the system is presently being used on a regular basis by a commercial television station in Melbourne, Australia. Presumably, if the system is successful in Australia, it will be introduced in other parts of the world. The inventors are all Americans; the basic concept was developed by Etra Technology Research Associates of Oakland, California.

Whether the "triangle system" can be sufficiently improved to be successful remains to be seen; the need for special viewing glasses is a potentially serious impediment. However, even modest success in Australia will stimulate new interest in the development of three-dimensional television, and I would not be surprised to see a successful system within the next fifteen years.

Beyond that, the most important technological changes will involve the steady convergence of video and computer technologies.

The Transformation of the TV Industry

Business Week magazine (October 29, 1979) declared, "The future is suddenly coming sooner than many television network executives thought possible." Indeed, it is. The astounding growth of cable television and of home video has caught the commercial broadcasting industry off guard.

The local broadcaster, especially the network affiliate, will feel the pinch of strong competition soonest and hardest. The independent and public television broadcasters are used to a marginal existence, and, ironically, they will be the first to benefit from the new technology—particularly the satellite-borne networks. The PBS satellite network is already in operation and, for the first time since the short-lived Public Broadcasting Laboratory (1967-69), there is a genuine national non-commercial network in the United States. Similarly, the Spanish International Network's use of satellite transmission has given its chain of independent stations a viability they could not have had otherwise. The availability of syndicated programming by satellite, from Viacom and, in time, other distributors, will strengthen all non-network commercial broadcasters. No doubt there will be, at least sporadically, "instant networks" feeding new programming by satellite to the independent stations. Eventually, local network affiliates must either adapt to the availability of satellite-borne programs, or fall by the wayside.

The present major networks have begun to enter a period of decline, and I do not believe they will ever again enjoy anything like their present dominance of the medium. Recently, the A. C. Neilsen Company reported that the average ratings for the major-network programs tend to be about four percent lower in communities that have cable television service than in other communities. A four percent loss of audience may not seem like much, but that loss is bound to grow as cable systems grow more sophisticated in finding and developing their own audiences for specialized programming—and, again, those geosync satellites will play an indispensable role. Today, about 20 percent of America's television homes are served by cable TV; within five years, it will be 35 percent, and it will be more than 50 percent within ten years. According to the FCC's elaborate studies of the television industry, cable penetration of 50 percent could produce at worst a ten percent decline in audience for local commercial broadcasters. However, this study was performed at a time when cable systems offered very little in the way of alternative programming fare. Better programs on cable inevitably must mean smaller audiences for broadcasters—and that means smaller audiences for the major networks. My guess is that the FCC study is way off, and that a cable penetration of 50 percent (which means half of all homes in the country are hooked up to a cable system) will produce at least a 25 percent decline in the major networks' audience. For ABC, CBS and NBC this is tantamount to a catastrophe, since audience size directly affects revenue.

As revenues decline, the networks must respond by cutting back on program costs, which reduces program quality, which means programs become less attractive, which means smaller audiences—and so on, down a terrible, steep spiral. The alternative is for the networks to throw away their present concept of television and begin to develop a whole new industry, as they had to do in radio during the 1960s.

I cannot see anything that can keep cable from growing at an almost frightening rate over the next twenty years. The FCC has all but abandoned its elaborate regulatory schemes that were designed, in part, to frustrate cable and protect broadcasting. The real task for cable will be to manage its own success. Cable operators must give up their cozy relationship with broadcasters—even when both broadcasting stations and cable systems are owned by the same people. In order to satisfy its subscribers and continue to grow, cable must take full advantage of its intrinsic economic advantages and of the fantastically beneficial technology of satellites. At the same time, cable system operators must be sensitive to the politicization of their industry. Municipal governments and local video enthusiasts are not unreasonable to demand an allotment of free channels for local access programming, in exchange for the cable system's access to city-owned utility rights-of-way. Although the Supreme Court threw out the FCC's public access rules, the principle of free access to a limited number of cable channels in return for the right to do business as a virtual monopoly has been so well established that the cable industry would be badly misguided to fight it.

Advances in cable technology will make ever more channels available at ever less cost. Hundred-channel cable systems are practical today; fiber optic technology will make five-hundred-channel systems possible within the next ten years. For the cable operator, the problem once again, as it was in the early 1970s, will be where to find enough programming to fill all those channels. But by the early 1990s, gigantic "space platforms" will be constructed in the geosync orbit, permitting an almost limitless number of "instant networks" to distribute programs by satellite. The only real limit will be an economic one: producing programs and transmitting them, even by the comparatively inexpensive means of satellite transmission, costs money and there must be some limit to the number of program sources that can be supported.

Nevertheless, I expect television networks—in the sense of program sources that distribute programs by satellite and cable—to be as common by the end of this century as magazine publishers are today. The original television networks will have to find their own place in that crowded environment. No doubt they will be something like the equivalent of a *Life Magazine* or a *New York Times:* leaders in the industry and financially secure, but by no means as dominant as they have been for the past thirty years.

Cable systems also will begin to offer a smorgasbord of other services, at least some of which will be based on the teletext technology that is presently being test-marketed. Services comparable to Britain's Viewdata and Oracle should be successful in the United States, especially if the visual quality of the teletext image can be improved and the cost of the receiving apparatus can be reduced. However, I expect the development of teletext to be inhibited mostly by the uncertainty about who will pay for it, and whether the public really wants it. I doubt that teletext services will be commonplace in the next 10 years, but once these basic questions are resolved, its adoption may be very rapid; by 1995, some sort ot teletext service is likely to be a standard feature of every cable system.

I am not at all optimistic about the prospects of direct satellite-to-home broadcasting. Such a system requires a very powerful satellite, which almost inevitably implies a limited channel capacity. The system also requires every subscriber to install a parabolic antenna on the roof or somewhere nearby. Even a small, one-meter-diameter antenna is a pretty cumbersome gadget. I suspect that by the time this technology is well developed, cable television will offer subscribers so much, at considerably less cost, that there will be virtually no interest in direct broadcasting. (However, direct broadcasting will have other applications, particularly in the field of teleconferencing, that can be highly successful.)

In summary, by 1990 I envision a television system in the United States in which cable systems and local broadcasters compete on a nearly equal basis; by 2000, I expect local broadcasting to all but disappear. By then, the major networks will be supplying their programs to local cable distributors, just like the present satellite-to-cable networks. It is not true, as some critics of cable insist, that cable will never be able to serve the entire population because it is uneconomical to string wires in rural areas. The electric power and telephone utilities have faced the same problem, but there is hardly a home in America that does not have electricity and a telephone. Cable actually has an advantage over the electric utilities, an advantage it shares with the telephone system: its signals can be "hopped" over moderately long distances by microwave radio.

As for public television, it will continue to struggle along in the wake of commercial television. Satellite transmission relieves the public system of a major cost burden, and simultaneously creates the opportunity to function as a genuine network (in spite of those who contend that public TV should *never* resemble the commercial networks, even to the extent of simultaneously transmitting its programs to its "affiliates"). Public TV, like most noble endeavors, tends to become suicidal from time to time, but I am optimistic that it will survive and will eventually settle into a comfortable rut, providing its specialized audience with the fare they want. At some point in the future, I think educational television—that is, the use of the medium for direct instruction—will be divorced from public TV entirely. Instructional television needs a more flexible distribution medium; cable can provide that, and so can the Instructional Television Fixed Service (ITFS) system. Schools that cannot afford either one, or that need something to supplement those means of distribution, will rely heavily on the use of videocassettes and discs.

The Transformation of the Video Society

The hardest predictions to make are those that involve large-scale social forces. It is tempting to shrug one's shoulders and say no more than, "There will be change."

The American political system has had more than fifty years in which to accommodate the electronic media, and has failed utterly. The present Federal Communications Act is itself a product of that failure, and merely reflects the sad compromises and uncertainties of the 1920s and early 1930s. The various revisions proposed by Rep. Van Deerlin in the late 1970s were very little better.

I do not suppose it is realistic to expect Congress to do any more in the next ten years. Sooner or later, the 1934 Act must be replaced; it is hopelessly obsolete. The replacement probably will confuse more issues than it clarifies. Whatever is done with respect to broadcasting will respond to the problems of the 1960s and 1970s but will ignore or overlook the reality of the 1980s and beyond.

Both cable and broadcasting probably will be "deregulated," which means in essence that they will be allowed to go their own way, responding to narrow self-interest and short-term profits without regard to the larger interests of the public. No matter; technological and social change probably would overwhelm any grand regulatory scheme Congress or the FCC might devise, as has been the case throughout the past half century.

Technological convergence probably will bring together the telephone and cable industries within the next ten years; by 1995, it may be impossible to differentiate between the two. If Congress permits AT&T to provide cable television services, Ma Bell will dominate that industry as thoroughly as she has dominated the telephone industry. On the other hand, if AT&T continues to be excluded from offering a broader menu of communication services, the telephone system could become hopelessly snarled as cable system operators and other entrepreneurs try to muscle into Bell's territory. Indeed, the relationships—technological and political—between the telephone system, cable television and data transmission may be the most difficult political issue of the 1990s.

For society as a whole, television will continue to occupy a central role. Indeed, its role will grow inexorably. It is already the most powerful, most influential and most efficient medium of communication ever devised; its power, its influence and its efficiency will increase exponentially during the next 25 years.

Ever since the first television programs wavered in America's living rooms, critics have blamed the medium for every sort of ill: eyestrain, migraine headaches, juvenile delinquency, broken chromosomes, crime in the streets, racism, functional illiteracy, malnutrition, hyperactive children and the moral degeneration of the Western World, to name a few. Many of these criticisms have been well founded, albeit exaggerated in scope and tone. Nevertheless, television offers something—whatever it may be—that the public cannot do without. In the future, television will offer a lot more of it.

Television will always have its *Mork and Mindy, Starsky and Hutch, Monday Night Football* and comparable forms of entertainment. In the future, some programs will be considerably better than the average program of today. Most programs will be no better at all, and probably will be considerably worse. But there will be far more programs from which to choose. There will hardly be a moment of the day when the most discriminating viewer cannot find something attractive on the cable; for those rare moments, there will always be the tape and disc library with its assortment of treasured favorites.

More important, television will be increasingly a system of communication in which the average person is a participant, not just a spectator. Most people will never produce a television program more sophisticated than the typical home movie. However, many people will participate, at least once in a while, in teleconferences. And many thousands of people—not the few hundred of today—will use television routinely, producing programs for their own amusement or for distribution on local cable access channels. Thousands more will be involved in the production of programs for the hundreds of commercial and quasi-commercial "networks" and local program services.

Finally, the combination of television, computers and other communications technologies will result in a home communications center that will give each individual nearly unlimited access to every kind of human knowledge, along with information-processing and manipulating capabilities that seem utterly fantastic today.

If Marshall McLuhan is right, the adoption of a new medium invariably alters the nature and structure of the society in which the medium is adopted. We can see, retrospectively, how our own society changed as the automobile, the telephone and then radio and television were adopted. During the coming quarter century, the television medium itself will be transformed, and in a sense it will engulf several other media. How society will respond, how it too will be transformed, I cannot say. All I can say is (*shrug*), "There will be change."

But it *sure* will be interesting.

A Bibliographic Note

Since I did not intend this book primarily for the academic reader, I have not bothered to litter the text with footnotes and authoritative references. However, for the reader who would like to know more about the subjects I have dealt with, let me recommend a few sources.

The essential text on the history of broadcasting is Erik Barnouw's three-volume *History of Broadcasting in the United States,* published by Oxford University Press (1966, 1968, and 1970). Unfortunately, Barnouw's history takes one only up to the mid-60s. Another indispensable source, not only for broadcasting's history but for thousands of other facts about technology and individual personalities in the medium, is Les Brown's *New York Times Encyclopedia of Television,* published by Times Books (1977, but I hope a revised and updated edition will be available soon!). Craig T. and Peter G. Norback have compiled a *TV Guide Almanac,* with the help of the editorial staff of that indispensable little magazine. The *Almanac,* published by Ballantine Books in paperback, contains a potpourri of useful and trivial information, concentrating largely on commercial broadcasting.

George H. Gibson's *Public Broadcasting: The Role of the Federal Government, 1912-1976,* published by Praeger (1977), tells not only about the political and legal development of public broadcasting, but something about its economics, social history and pioneers as well.

The history and technology of cable television, and an elaborate presentation of the implications of the FCC's 1972 Cable Television Report and Order, can be found in a series of reports, all developed by the Rand Corporation and published by Crane, Russak and Company (1974). Unfortunately, some of the content is now obsolete since the FCC has largely abandoned its cable regulatory scheme. However, the Rand series is instructive in demonstrating what people *thought* the relationship between cable and broadcasting would be.

Jonathan Price's *Video-Visions,* published by New American Library (1977, paperback), presents a media freak's perspective on private television and video production. The chapters on video as art and the development of the video synthesizer are extremely good.

Bob Shanks, who is now a high-level executive in the television industry, offers suggestions on *How To Make It in Television: The Cool Fire,* published by the Vintage Books division of Random House (1977, paperback). I have found no other text that gives the impression of telling what it is really like to be involved in the commercial television industry; Les Brown's *The Business Behind the Box* (Harcourt Brace Jovanovich, 1971) gives similar information but from a different perspective, since Brown is the television critic for the New York *Times.*

Anyone who is seriously interested in television should try to keep up with several periodicals. *Broadcasting* is generally regarded as the not-quite-official "voice of the industry." *Video Systems* and *Educational and Industrial Television* both cover private television quite well; the former tends to be somewhat more technical than the latter. *Video* is a quarterly that attempts to keep up with the fast-moving home video scene. *Cablevision* is perhaps the best nontechnical journal covering the cable industry. The only periodical, to my knowledge, that deals directly with communications satellites is *Satellite Communications;* it offers frequent articles on the use of geosync birds for television, although many of its articles are extremely technical (example: "Design and Specification Considerations of GaAs Low Noise Amplifiers").

Finally, the best all-round periodical on social change and technology is the World Future Society's journal, *The Futurist.*

INDEX

284